FIVE PLAYS

JEAN COCTEAU
FIVE PLAYS

A DRAMABOOK

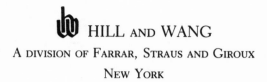 HILL AND WANG

A DIVISION OF FARRAR, STRAUS AND GIROUX

NEW YORK

CONTENTS

FIVE PLAYS

ORPHÉE

English version by Carl Wildman

NOTE

ORPHÉE *was written in 1925; first performed in Paris at the Théâtre des Arts by the Pitoëff Company on 17th June 1926; published by the Librarie Stock in 1927; and in the revival by the Pitoëff Company in 1927 Cocteau played the part of* HEURTEBISE. *It was first performed in this authorized version on 10th October 1931 at the Rudolf Steiner Hall, London, with the translator in the role of actor (*ORPHÉE*) and producer. There was a performance in a different translation at the Gate Theatre, London, in 1928.*

The outcome of seven years' intimate study of the theatre, Orphée is regarded generally as Cocteau's masterpiece. No element of the theatre is forced into an unwarranted place of prominence or of obscurity. The scenery resumes its active role. Naturalism goes by the board: "it is not a question of living on the stage, but of making the stage live. This reality of the theatre is the poetry of the theatre and is truer than truth." Orphée gives the twofold stimulus of familiar things seen in a new light: strangeness and recognition. It is the first time that darkness has been shown in broad daylight.

Orphée is like a coat of chain-mail. Each link is dependent and interdependent. But Orphée is vulnerable, if, for want of skill in the actor or want of attention in the audience, a link is missed. The English suit has been carefully modeled on the French, but the native metals have been shaped by different processes; the original was forged round an untranslatable French word.

The most celebrated heroes have a weak spot somewhere in their armor: Siegfried in the shoulder, Achilles in the heel.

Here is a play essentially of the theatre. This translation was made with only the actor in view, in the hope that to an audience the least possible might be lost, and

2

that to the reader, Orphée *might be seen on a stage in the mind's eye.*

Finally, with all its air of happy inconsequence, Orphée *is a cerebral creation, "une méditation sur la mort"* (M. Bidou).

C. W.

1932

COSTUMES

The costumes in fashion at the time of the performance should be adopted.

ORPHÉE and EURYDICE are in very inconspicuous country clothes.

HEURTEBISE wears pale blue workman's overalls with a dark muffler round his neck and white bathing shoes. He is bronzed, and hatless. He never leaves off his glazier's apparatus (windowpanes).

The COMMISSIONER OF POLICE and the SCRIVENER wear black frock coats, Panamas, goatees, and buttoned boots.

DEATH is a very beautiful young woman in a bright pink evening dress and fur cloak. Her hair, frock, cloak, shoes, gestures, and gait are in the latest fashion. She has large blue eyes painted on a domino. Her nurse's tunic should also be of great elegance.

Her assistants wear the uniform, linen masks, and rubber gloves of operating surgeons.

SCENERY

THRACE. *A room in* ORPHÉE'*s villa.* It is a strange room rather like the room of a conjurer. In spite of the April-blue sky and the clear light, one suspects that it is surrounded by mysterious forces. Even familiar objects have a suspicious air.

First of all, in a box in the form of a niche, well in the center, there lives a white horse, whose legs are very much like those of a man. On the right of the horse is another little niche in which an empty pedestal stands framed by laurel. On the extreme right a door which opens on to the garden; when the door is open the leaf hides the pedestal. On the left of the horse an earthenware wash basin. On the extreme left a French window, pushed half outwards—it looks on to the terrace which surrounds the villa.

In the foreground in the right wall is a very large mirror; in the background a bookcase. In the middle of the left wall a door opening into EURYDICE's room. A sloping ceiling closes in the room like a box.

The room is furnished with two tables and three white chairs. On the right a writing table and one of the chairs.

On the left of the stage, the second table which is covered with a cloth reaching to the floor, and thereon fruits, plates, a decanter, and glasses, like the cardboard objects of jugglers. One chair stands squarely behind this table, and one nearby on the right.

A chair cannot be added or taken away, nor the openings distributed otherwise, for this is a *practical* set, in which the smallest detail plays its part like the apparatus in an acrobatic number.

Apart from the sky blue and the pad of dark red velvet that borders the top of the little door of the box dissimulating the middle of the horse's body—there is no color.

The scenery should recall the sham airplanes and ships of certain photographers.

After all, there is that same harmony, made of harsh simplicity, between the setting, characters, and events as between model and painted canvas in the plain *camaïeu* style of card portraits.

NOTES ON PRODUCING

The mirror allows people to enter and leave the stage by an opening into the wings at the height of the frame. The opening is hidden by a glistening panel.

The bookcase should have one real pigeonhole in which a real book is slipped. At the top of the bookcase should be a slot from which a piece of paper can be taken.

The pedestal holds an actor kneeling on a cushion so that his head appears in the niche.

The horse is the front of a horse; a horse's head with very curved neck, on a man in tights. The door of the box hides the upper part of the legs and the breast.

A black curtain on a rod can close the niche.

The wash basin is a sham.

When HEURTEBISE pretends he is working, he first frees the view of the window by carrying up to the wall on the left the table, which is laid. Then, at the order "Get up on this chair" he takes the chair which was behind the table and puts it in the frame of the French window. He puts his left foot on it and his right foot on a stool hidden behind the door. He lifts his hands up to the panes. A stagehand holds him by an unseen belt from which a ring projects under his glazier's apparatus. When ORPHÉE removes the chair, he flies. This very simple arrangement, discovered by Pitoëff, is extraordinarily effective.

The glazier's apparatus of HEURTEBISE supports panes of various kinds. His head stands out against some mica. The panes behind him are of a glistening material which sends out gleams at all angles.

In the wings, near the audience, an electric machine with a deep roar. (A vacuum cleaner can be used.)

When DEATH goes into EURYDICE's room, she removes her bandage. A stagehand gives her the dove which she takes by the legs so that its wings beat. She reappears. RAPHAEL cuts the thread. She disappears behind the scenery to the right of the window, where the dove is taken from her hands; she recoils on the terrace with a gesture as if having freed the dove into the air.[1]

After the remark of HEURTEBISE: "I will bring him back, I promise you," the light lowers and becomes milky.

---

[1] It is not necessary to say that there is no symbol in the play. Nothing but simple language, *acted poetry*. This dove is a commonplace.

Once this new aquarium light is fixed, DEATH enters. Her arm appears through the mirror first, and the left arms of the assistants before the assistants themselves.

On leaving, DEATH hurries, freezes a moment, her hand extended in front of the mirror. Her assistants do the same.

When the curtain for the interval falls, wait a while to see if the spectators applaud before ringing up again, so that this card trick in the abstract does not have the appearance of a false maneuver.

The disappearance of EURYDICE. In a theater without a trap, the light is lowered on a dimmer. EURYDICE rises with a gesture of horror and slips slowly behind the table. When darkness is complete the end of some black material is passed to ORPHÉE, who stands by the door of the bedroom. He stretches the material to the table and EURYDICE escapes behind it. The material is pulled sharply into the wings and the lights are thrown on full. The whole maneuver takes place in the winking of an eye. Even in a theater furnished with a trap, EURYDICE should disappear slowly and the light be lowered with her.

Three musicians suffice for the arrival of the BAC-CHANTES. One man: drums and cymbals. Another, jazz set. A third: kettledrums. The rhythms should torture like the tom-tom of savages.

After the third *"Ladies!"* of ORPHÉE, the drums make a terrible noise. Windows are heard breaking, something heavy falls, and a chair goes over. A small lamp, hidden on the left in the footlights, comes on. It is the lighting given to the crimes in the Musée Grévin. On the ground near the cloth the head is seen against the white background of the overturned chair. The chair is knocked over and the head put into place during the blackout which blinds the spectators. The actor lies in the wings and speaks from the bedroom.

While the police are knocking on the door and the actor is picking up the head, putting it on the pedestal, and opening the door, full light is given and the actor substitutes his head for the mask. While the COMMIS-

SIONER and the SCRIVENER are going out, the actor withdraws and replaces the mask.

P.S.: According to Cocteau's latest opinion, both the nonhuman characters, DEATH and the GUARDIAN ANGEL, should wear half masks or masks in white.

DEDICATION

MY DEAR PITOËFF:

A *painter may throw himself from the fifth story, and
the art-lover would only say:* "That makes a pretty splash!"
*And you know what a dramatist flayed alive exposes him-
self to. But the public in the theater is still sometimes
surprising in its attitude; the critic seldom so. Now, your
indifference to this kind of thing is greater than mine,
and, in spite of the critics, every evening we had an audience which collaborated with us. Such audiences are
very moving to one to whom it matters above all to be
believed and least of all to be admired.*

*Your children came one Sunday. The eldest was seven.
They had come fresh from death where the great return
and were therefore on a level footing with mystery. From
that time on they ate their soup for Orphée, for Eurydice,
and for Heurtebise; Sacha imitated the horse and Lud-
milla passed through mirrors. Critics misquote my text;
children remember it, play with it, and enact it. If they
change it, they do so as dreams change our actions. In
short, they make a success of the last scene: a house
mounted to heaven. I offer my play to your children. I
hope they will never lose their childhood, or that they
will recover it thanks to the feeling and genius inherited
from your wife and you.*

JEAN

July 1, 1926

PROLOGUE

The actor who plays the part of ORPHÉE *appears before the curtain.*

Ladies and Gentlemen, this prologue is not by the author and I expect he would be surprised to hear it. The tragedy in which we are going to act develops on very delicate lines. I will ask you, therefore, if you are not satisfied with our work, to wait till the end before you express your feelings. Here is the reason for my request: we are playing at a great height, and without a safety net. The slightest untimely noise and the lives of my comrades and my own may be imperiled.

[*Exit.*

CHARACTERS

EURYDICE
ORPHÉE
HORSE
HEURTEBISE
DEATH
AZRAEL
RAPHAEL
GENTLEMAN IN AUDIENCE
POSTMAN
COMMISSIONER OF POLICE
SCRIVENER

SCENE—THRACE. A room in ORPHÉE's villa.

ORPHÉE

SCENE ONE

ORPHÉE *behind the table on the right, consulting a spiritualist alphabet.* EURYDICE *seated left, near the table, which is laid.*

EURYDICE. Can I move?

Orphée. One moment.

Eurydice. He's stopped tapping.

Orphée. Sometimes he leaves a long interval between the first letter and the others.

Eurydice. They can be guessed!

Orphée. Please, please!

Eurydice. You must admit, it's always the same word.

Orphée. H, H. . . . Carry on, horse. Go on, quick, after the letter H. . . . I'm listening to you.

Eurydice. What patience! You have no mind, but your horse has—you think.

Orphée. I'm listening. Now, horse! H, H, after H. [*The* HORSE *moves.*] You're moving, you're going to speak. Speak, horse! Dictate the letter after H. [*The* HORSE *strikes with its hoof;* ORPHÉE *counts.*] A, B, C, D, E, is it E?

The HORSE *nods its head.*

Eurydice. Of course.

Orphée [*Furious*]. Sh! [*The* HORSE *taps.*] A, B, C, D, E, F, G, H, I, J, K, L—L. A, B, C, D, E, F, G, H, I, J, K, L—L. [*To* EURYDICE.] You're not to laugh. L, L, can it be L? H, E, L, L, hell? I can't have counted right. Horse! is it really the letter L? If it is, tap once, and twice if it isn't.

The HORSE *taps once.*

Eurydice. You needn't insist.

Orphée. Look here, I ask you as a favor to keep quiet. Nothing disturbs this horse so much as incredulous people. Go to your room, or keep quiet.

Eurydice. I won't open my mouth again.

Orphée. So much the better. [*To the* HORSE.] Hell, hell . . . and after hell? H, E, L, L, hell. I'm listening. Speak. Speak to me, horse. Horse! Come along, don't be afraid. After the letter L? [*The* HORSE *taps,* ORPHÉE *counts.*] A, B, C, D, E, F, G, H, I, J, K, L, M, N, O—O. The letter O, my dear! H, E, L, L, O, hello. It was hello! Is that all? Is it just hello? [*The* HORSE *nods its head.*] Just think of that. You see, Eurydice! I might have believed you with your wrong mind, I might have been weak enough to yield and be convinced. . . . Just "hello," that's amazing!

Eurydice. Why?

Orphée. What do you mean, why?

Eurydice. Why amazing? This hello doesn't mean anything.

Orphée. What! This horse dictated to me last week one of the most moving sentences in the world. . . .

Eurydice. Oh!

Orphée. . . . dictated one of the most moving sentences in the world. I'll work it out and I shall transfigure poetry. I am immortalizing my horse, and you're surprised to hear him greet me. That "hello" is a masterpiece of tact. And I who thought . . . [*He puts his arms around the* HORSE's *neck.*]

Eurydice. Listen, Orphée, my love; don't scold me. Be just! Since that famous sentence you've obtained one word and one word only, and that word isn't really poetic.

Orphée. Do we know what is poetic and what is not poetic?

Eurydice. Aglaonice used to do table turning and her table always answered with that word.

Orphée. That's it! Drag that person into our business, as a last straw. I've told you already, I don't want to hear any more of her—a woman who nearly led you astray, a woman who drinks, takes tigers out for exercise, turns the heads of our wives, and prevents girls from marrying.

Eurydice. But that is the cult of the moon.

Orphée. Good! I can leave it to you to defend her.

Return to the Bacchantes since their customs give you pleasure.

Eurydice. I'm just teasing. You know very well that it's only you I love, and you had but to give a sign to make me leave that circle.

Orphée. What a circle too! I shall never forget the tone in which Aglaonice said to me: "Take her, since she accepts. Stupid women adore artists, but—he who laughs last, laughs longest."

Eurydice. Ugh! That made my blood run cold.

Orphée. If ever I see her again! [*He strikes the inkwell on the table.*]

Eurydice. Orphée, my poet. . . . Look how irritable you are ever since this horse business of yours. Before, you would laugh, kiss, and fondle me, you had a splendid situation, fame and fortune were yours. You would write poems which were snatched from hand to hand, and which all Thrace knew by heart. You would sing the praises of the sun, you were its high priest. But the horse has put an end to all that. Now we live in the country, you have given up your position, and you refuse to write. Your life is passed in petting the horse, in questioning the horse, in hoping that the horse will answer you. That's not being serious.

Orphée. Not serious? My life, like game, was beginning to get high, and, on the turn, was beginning to stink of success and death. The sun and the moon are all the same to me. There remains night. But not the night of others! My night. This horse plunges into my night and reappears like a diver. He brings back sentences. Don't you feel that the least of these sentences is more remarkable than all the poems? I would give my complete works for one of those little sentences in which I listen to myself as you listen to the sea in a shell. Not serious? But what can you want, my dear? I am discovering a new world, I am living again, I am stalking the unknown.

Eurydice. You are going to quote me again the famous sentence.

Orphée [*Gravely*]. Yes. [*He goes toward the* HORSE *and recites.*] Orphée hunts Eurydice's lost life.

Eurydice. That sentence doesn't mean anything.

Orphée. It is indeed a question of meaning. Listen carefully to this sentence, listen to the mystery of it. Eurydice alone might be anybody and so might Orphée, but it is a Eurydice whose lost life Orphée would hunt! "Orphée hunts—" that exciting "hunts"—"Orphée hunts Eurydice's—" mark the possessive! and the close: "Eurydice's lost life." You ought to be pleased I am speaking about you.

Eurydice. It's not you who are speaking of me. It's the horse. [*Pointing.*]

Orphée. Neither he, nor I, nor anyone else. What do we know? Who is speaking? We are knocking against each other in the dark; we are up to our necks in the supernatural. We are playing hide-and-seek with the gods. We know nothing, absolutely nothing. "Orphée hunts Eurydice's lost life"—that's not a sentence, it is a poem, a poem of vision, a flower deep-rooted in death.

Eurydice. And do you hope to convince the world? to make everyone admit that poetry consists in writing a sentence? to make a success with your horse's sentence?

Orphée. It's not a question of success, nor of the horse, nor of convincing the world. Besides, I no longer stand alone.

Eurydice. Don't talk to me about your public. Four or five heartless young hooligans, who think you're an anarchist, and a dozen fools who are trying to attract attention.

Orphée. I shall have a better following. I hope one day to charm even the beasts of the field.

Eurydice. If you despise success, why send this sentence to the Thracian competition? Why attach such importance to winning the prize?

Orphée. We must throw a bombshell and make a sensation. We must have a storm to clear the air. We are suffocating, we can no longer breathe.

Eurydice. We were so peaceful.

Orphée. Too peaceful.

Eurydice. You used to love me.

Orphée. I do love you.

Eurydice. You love the horse. I take second place.

Orphée. Don't be stupid. There's no connection. [*He kisses* EURYDICE *absent-mindedly and goes to the* HORSE.] That's so, isn't it, old boy? Isn't it, my dear old brother, eh? Does he love his friend? Piece of sugar? Then kiss me. No, better than that. There . . . there . . . isn't he just fine! There! [*He takes some sugar out of his pocket and gives it to the* HORSE.] That's right.

Eurydice. I don't count any more. If I were dead you wouldn't notice it.

Orphée. Without noticing it, we *were* dead.

Eurydice. Come near me.

Orphée. Sorry, I must be going out. I'm going into the town so as to have everything in order for the competition. Tomorrow's the last day. I haven't a minute to lose.

Eurydice [*Bursting out*]. Orphée! my Orphée! . . .

Orphée. You see this empty pedestal. Only a bust worthy of me shall be put there.

Eurydice. They will throw stones at you.

Orphée. I shall make my bust with them.

Eurydice. Beware of the Bacchantes.

Orphée. I'm not aware of their existence.

Eurydice. They do exist, and they are liked. I know their ways. Aglaonice hates you. She is going to take part in the competition.

Orphée. Oh! that woman! that woman!

Eurydice. Be just . . . she has ability.

Orphée. What?

Eurydice. Of a fearful kind, of course. But, from a certain angle and on a certain plane, she has ability. She creates fine images.

Orphée. Listen to that. "From a certain angle . . . on a certain plane." . . . Did you learn that way of speaking from the Bacchantes? Then, on a certain plane her images please you. From a certain angle you approve of my moral enemies. . . . And yet you insist that you love me. Very well then, by that angle and by that plane I declare that I have had enough of it; that I am persecuted, and this horse is the only being who understands me. [*He strikes his fist on the table.*]

Eurydice. You needn't break everything.

Orphée. Break everything! That's the limit! Madam breaks a windowpane a day, and now it's I who break everything.

Eurydice. To begin with——

Orphée [*Walking up and down*]. I know what you're going to say. You're going to say that you haven't broken a pane today.

Eurydice. But——

Orphée. Very well, go on and break, break it, break the windowpane.

Eurydice. How can you get into such a state!

Orphée. See how sly. . . . You're not breaking a windowpane because I am going out.

Eurydice [*Sharply*]. What do you mean to insinuate?

Orphée. Do you think I am blind? You break a windowpane every day so that the glazier will come up.

Eurydice. Very well then, I do, I break a windowpane so that the glazier will come up. He's a good fellow, and he listens to me. He admires you.

Orphée. Too nice.

Eurydice. And when you are questioning the horse and leave me all alone, I break a pane. You're not jealous, I suppose?

Orphée. Jealous, I? Jealous of a boy glazier? Why not of Aglaonice too! Upon my word! Look here, since you refuse to break a pane, I will break one. That'll soothe me. [*He breaks a pane.*] Glazier! Glazier! Glazier! [*Is heard.*] Hi! glazier! He's coming up. Jealous?

SCENE TWO

HEURTEBISE *appears on the balcony. The sun beats on his windowpanes. He enters, bends a knee, and crosses his hands over his heart.*

HEURTEBISE. Good day, ladies and gentlemen.

Orphée. Good day, my friend. It was I, I who broke this pane. Put it in. I'm going. [*To* EURYDICE.] My dear, you will superintend the work. [*To the* Horse.] Does he love his poet? [*He embraces him.*] Till this evening.

[*He goes out.*

SCENE THREE

Eurydice. You see. I'm not inventing anything.

Heurtebise. It's unheard of.

Eurydice. You understand me.

Heurtebise. Poor lady.

Eurydice. Since that horse followed him in the street, and he brought it home with him, since it has lived here, and they talk together——

Heurtebise. The horse has spoken to him again?

Eurydice. It said "hello" to him.

Heurtebise. It knows how to take him.

Eurydice. In short, for a month now, our life has been a torture.

Heurtebise. Surely you can't be jealous of a horse!

Eurydice. I would rather know he had a mistress.

Heurtebise. Do you mean that . . . ?

Eurydice. Without you and your friendship, I should have gone mad by now.

Heurtebise. Poor Eurydice.

Eurydice [*Looking at herself in the mirror and smiling*]. Just think, I have a faint ray of hope. He has realized I break a windowpane every day, and, instead of saying I break a piece of glass to bring me luck, I told him I break it so that you come up to see me.

Heurtebise. I should have thought——

Eurydice. But listen. He made a scene, and he broke the pane. I believe he's still jealous.

Heurtebise. How you love him——

Eurydice. The more he ill-treats me the more I love him. I already had an idea that he might be jealous of Aglaonice.

Heurtebise. Of Aglaonice?

Eurydice. He detests everything to do with my old circle. That is why I fear we may be committing a terrible indiscretion. Speak softly. I'm always afraid the horse may be listening to me.

They tiptoe up to the niche.

Heurtebise. He's asleep.

They return downstage.

Eurydice. Have you seen Aglaonice?
Heurtebise. Yes.
Eurydice. Orphée would kill you if that came to his ears.
Heurtebise. It won't.
Eurydice [*Pulling him still farther from the* Horse, *toward her room*]. Have you . . . got it?
Heurtebise. I have.
Eurydice. In what form?
Heurtebise. A piece of sugar.
Eurydice. What attitude did she take?
Heurtebise. A very simple one. She said: A bargain! Here is the poison, bring me back the letter.
Eurydice. That letter seems to cause her a lot of trouble.
Heurtebise. She even added: So that the poor dear doesn't compromise herself, here is an envelope with my address in my own handwriting. She will just have to put the letter in, stick the envelope down, and there'll be no trace of our communication.
Eurydice. Orphée is unjust. She can be very nice. Was she alone?
Heurtebise. With a lady friend. It wasn't the sort of place for you.
Eurydice. Of course not, but I don't think Aglaonice is such a bad girl.
Heurtebise. Beware of good girls and fine fellows. Here's your piece of sugar.
Eurydice. Thank you. . . . [*She takes the sugar with fear and approaches the* Horse.] I'm afraid.
Heurtebise. Do you draw back?
Eurydice. No I don't, but I'm afraid. I confess that when it comes to the point, in cold blood, my courage fails me. [*She returns in front of the writing table.*] Heurtebise?
Heurtebise. What?

Eurydice. My dear Heurtebise, I suppose you wouldn't like to . . . ?

Heurtebise. Oh! Ho! You are asking me to do something very serious.

Eurydice. You told me you would do anything to render me a service.

Heurtebise. I repeat that, but . . .

Eurydice. Oh! my dear, if it troubles you in the slightest . . . let us speak no more of it.

Heurtebise. Pass me the sugar.

Eurydice. Thank you. You're a good fellow.

Heurtebise. Only, will he take it from my hand?

Eurydice. Anyhow, try.

Heurtebise [*Near the* HORSE]. I confess I don't feel very firm on my feet.

Eurydice. Be a man!

She crosses left and stops near the door of her room.

Heurtebise. Well, here goes. [*In a weak voice.*] Horse . . . horse. . . .

Eurydice [*Looking out of the window*]. Heavens! Orphée! He's coming back. He's crossing the garden. Quick, quick, look as though you're working. [HEURTEBISE *throws the lump of sugar onto the set table and pushes it up against the wall between the window and the door of the bedroom.*] Get up on this chair.

HEURTEBISE *gets up on the chair in the framework of the French window and pretends he is taking measurements.*

EURYDICE *drops into the chair at the writing table.*

SCENE FOUR

Orphée comes in.

ORPHÉE. I've forgotten my birth certificate. Where did I put it?

Eurydice. On top of the bookcase, on the left. Shall I look for it?

Orphée. Sit still. I can find it myself. [*He passes in front*

of the HORSE *and caresses it, takes the chair on which*
HEURTEBISE *is standing, and carries it away.* HEURTEBISE
remains in the same pose, suspended in the air. EURYDICE
stifles a cry. ORPHÉE, *without noticing anything, gets up
on the chair in front of the bookcase and says:*] Here it is.
[*Takes the birth certificate, gets down from the chair,
carries it back to its place beneath the feet of* HEURTEBISE,
and goes out.

SCENE FIVE

EURYDICE. Heurtebise! Will you explain this miracle?

Heurtebise. What miracle?

Eurydice. You're not going to tell me you haven't
noticed anything, and that it is natural to remain suspended in midair instead of falling, when a chair is taken
from under you?

Heurtebise. Suspended in midair?

Eurydice. You needn't make out you are surprised, because I saw you. You stayed in midair. You stayed there
two feet above the floor, with only emptiness round you.

Heurtebise. You really do surprise me.

Eurydice. You remained a good minute between heaven
and earth.

Heurtebise. Impossible.

Eurydice. Exactly. That's why you owe me an explanation.

Heurtebise. You mean to say that I stayed without a
support between the ceiling and the floor?

Eurydice. Don't tell a lie, Heurtebise! I saw you, I saw
you with my own eyes. I had the greatest difficulty in
stifling a cry. In this madhouse, you were my last refuge,
you were the only person who didn't frighten me, in your
presence I regained my balance. It's all very well living
with a horse that talks, but a friend who floats in the air
becomes of necessity an object of suspicion. Don't come
near me. At the moment even your glistening back gives
me gooseflesh. Explain yourself, Heurtebise! I am listening.

Heurtebise. I have no need to defend myself. Either I am dreaming or you have dreamt.

Eurydice. Yes, such things do happen in dreams, but neither of us was asleep.

Heurtebise. You must have been the dupe of the mirage between my windowpanes and yours. Things do lie at times. At the fair I saw a naked woman walking along the ceiling.

Eurydice. This was nothing to do with a machine. It was beautiful and outrageous. For the space of a second I saw you as outrageous as an accident and as beautiful as a rainbow. You were the cry of a man who falls from a window, and you were the silence of the stars. You frighten me. I'm too frank not to tell you. If you do not wish to answer me, you needn't, but our relationship can never be the same. I thought you were simple, but you are complex. I thought you were of my race, but you are of the race of the horse.

Heurtebise. Eurydice, don't torture me. . . . Your voice is that of a sleepwalker. It's you who are frightening me.

Eurydice. Don't you use Orphée's method. Don't turn the tables on me. Don't try to make me believe I'm mad.

Heurtebise. Eurydice, I swear that——

Eurydice. You needn't, Heurtebise. I have lost my confidence in you.

Heurtebise. What's to be done?

Eurydice. One moment. [*She goes to the bookcase, gets up on the chair, pulls out a book, opens it, takes a letter from it, and returns the book to its place.*] Give me Aglaonice's envelope. [*He gives it.*] Thank you. [*She puts the letter in the envelope and licks the edge.*] Oh!

Heurtebise. Cut your tongue?

Eurydice. No—curious taste. Take the envelope to Aglaonice. Good-by.

Heurtebise. The windowpane hasn't been put in.

Eurydice. I'll do without it. Go along.

Heurtebise. You want me to leave you?

Eurydice. I want to be alone.

Heurtebise. You are unkind.

Eurydice. I don't like tradesmen who get suspended.

Heurtebise. That cruel play on words isn't worthy of you.

Eurydice. It isn't a play on words.

Heurtebise [*Picking up his bag*]. You'll be sorry you have hurt me. [*Silence.*] Am I discharged?

Eurydice. All mystery is my enemy. I have decided to fight it.

Heurtebise. I am going. I want to please you by my obedience. Good-by, madam.

Eurydice. Good-by. [*They cross.* EURYDICE *goes toward her room.* HEURTEBISE *opens the door and goes out. The door remains open. His back is seen gleaming immobile in the sun. Suddenly* EURYDICE *stops and her expression changes. She staggers, puts her hand to her heart, and begins to cry:*] Heurtebise! Heurtebise! quick, quick. . . .

Heurtebise [*Entering*]. What is it?

Eurydice. Help! . . .

Heurtebise. How pale you are! You're like ice.

Eurydice. I'm going paralyzed. My inside's burning and my heart's thumping.

Heurtebise. The envelope!

Eurydice. The envelope?

Heurtebise [*Shouting*]. Aglaonice's envelope. You licked it. You said it had a curious taste.

Eurydice. Ah! that wretched woman! Run quickly. Bring back Orphée. I am dying. I want to see Orphée again. Orphée! Orphée!

Heurtebise. I can't leave you alone. There must be something that can be done—take an antidote.

Eurydice. I know the poison of the Bacchantes. It paralyzes. Nothing will save me. Run quickly. Fetch Orphée. I want to see him again. I want him to forgive me. I love him, Heurtebise. I am in pain. If you delay it'll be too late. I implore you, Heurtebise, Heurtebise, you are good to me, you pity me. Ah! They are sticking knives between my ribs. Quick, quick, run, fly! Take the short cut. If he's on the way back, you'll meet him. I am going to lie down in my room and wait for you. Help me. [HEURTEBISE *helps her to her room.*] Quick, quick, quick. [*She disappears. At the moment* HEURTEBISE *is going to open the door she comes out of her room.*] Heurtebise,

listen, if you do know things . . . well . . . things like a
moment ago . . . which allow lightning movement from
one place to another. . . . You mustn't bear me ill will,
I was irritable and silly. . . . I really like you, Heurtebise
. . . try everything. Ah!   [*She goes back to her room.*

Heurtebise. I will bring him back, I promise you. [*Exit.*

*The stage remains empty a moment. The light changes.
Rolling and syncopation of drums which accompanies the
whole of the following scene—damped.*

SCENE SIX

DEATH *comes on the stage through the mirror, followed by
her two assistants,* AZRAEL *and* RAPHAEL. *She is in evening
dress and cloak. Her assistants wear surgeon's uniforms.
Their eyes are just visible. The rest of the face is covered
by a linen mask. Rubber gloves. They are carrying two very
elegant large black bags.* DEATH *walks quickly and stops
in the middle of the stage.*

DEATH. Quickly!
  Raphael. Where does madam want us to put the bags?
  Death. On the ground, anywhere. Azrael will explain.
Azrael, my cloak. [*He takes off the cloak.*]
  Raphael. It's because I'm afraid of making mistakes that
I do silly things.
  Death. You can't pick up Azrael's job in two days.
Azrael has been in my service for several centuries now. He
was like you at first. My tunic.

AZRAEL *takes the white tunic out of one of the bags and
helps* DEATH *to put it over her dress.*

  Azrael [*To* RAPHAEL]. Take the metal boxes and put
them on the table. No, first of all the cloths. Cover the
table with them.
  Death [*Going to the wash basin*]. Azrael will tell you
that I insist on having everything clean and shipshape.
  Raphael. Yes, madam. I hope madam will forgive me
. . . but my attention was distracted by this horse.

Death [*Washing her hands*]. Do you like him?

Raphael. Oh! yes, madam. Very much.

Death. What a child! I believe you'd like to have him for yourself. That's very easy. Azrael, the spirit. [*To* RAPHAEL.] You'll find a piece of sugar on the other table.

Raphael. Yes, madam, it is there.

Death. Give it to him. If he refuses, I'll give it to him ·myself. Azrael, my rubber gloves. Thank you. [*She puts on the right-hand glove*.]

Raphael. Madam, the horse won't take the sugar.

Death [*Taking the sugar*]. Eat, horse; I wish it. [*The* HORSE *eats it, withdraws, and disappears. A black curtain closes the niche*.] There you are. [*To* RAPHAEL.] He's yours.

Raphael. Madam is too kind.

Death [*Putting on the left-hand glove*]. Only a week ago you thought I was a skeleton with a winding sheet and a scythe. You imagined me as a bugbear and a scarecrow.

Raphael. Oh! madam. . . .

During these remarks AZRAEL *is hiding the mirror with a cloth.*

Death [*Going to take a chair left by* HEURTEBISE *in the French window*]. Oh! yes, you did. Everybody believes that. But, my dear child, if I were as people wish me to be, they would see me, whereas I must enter their homes unseen. [*She puts the chair near the footlights in the middle*.] Azrael, try the contact.

Azrael. It's working, madam. [*Deep noise of an electric machine*.]

Death [*Taking a handkerchief from out of her tunic*]. Good. Raphael, would you be so kind as to bind my eyes with this handkerchief? [*While* RAPHAEL *is binding her eyes* . . .] We have a wave length of seven and a range of seven to twelve. Set everything at four. If I amplify, go up to five. Don't exceed five on any account. Pull tight. Tie a double knot. Thank you. Are you at your posts? [AZRAEL *and* RAPHAEL *stand behind the table, side by side, their hands inside the metal boxes*.] I'm beginning.

*She comes near the chair. Slow movement of the hands
as of a masseuse and hypnotist around the invisible head.*

   Raphael [*Very softly*]. Azrael. . . .
   Azrael [*Very softly*]. Sh!
   Death. You may talk. It doesn't disturb me.
   Raphael. Azrael, where is Eurydice?
   Death. I was expecting that. You see, Azrael, they all ask
the same question. Explain it to him.
   Azrael. Death, to reach living things, has to pass through
an element which deforms and displaces them. Our appara-
tus allows her to reach them where she sees them, thus
saving calculations and a considerable loss of time.
   Raphael. It's like fishing with a gun.
   Death [*Laughing*]. Yes. [*Gravely.*] Azrael, prepare the
bobbin for me.
   Azrael. Yes, madam. Does madam know where Heurtebise is?
   Death. He's bringing Orphée back from town.
   Raphael. If they are hurrying shall we have time to
finish?
   Death. That is a question for Azrael. He changes our
speeds. An hour for me is only a minute for them.
   Azrael. The hand is passing five. Does madam want the
bobbin?
   Death. Disconnect it and give it to me.

AZRAEL *disappears into* EURYDICE'S *room and comes on
the stage again with the bobbin.* DEATH *counts the steps
between her chair and the room. Then she stops, facing
the door.* AZRAEL *gives her the bobbin, which is a sort of
automatic measure on which a white thread from the room
will coil.*

   Azrael. Raphael, the chronometer.
   Raphael. I've forgotten it!
   Azrael. Now we are in a fix.
   Death. Don't get alarmed. It's quite easy. [*She speaks
softly to* AZRAEL.]
   Azrael. Ladies and gentlemen, I am instructed by
Death to ask the audience if there's a spectator who would

be so kind as to lend her a watch? [*To a gentleman in the first row, who raises his hand.*] Thank you, sir. Raphael, will you take the gentleman's watch? [*Business.*]

Death. All right?

Azrael. Go! [*Rolling of drums. The wire comes from the room and enters the box held by* DEATH. AZRAEL *and* RAPHAEL, *backstage, turn their backs.* AZRAEL *counts with one hand in the air like a referee.* RAPHAEL *goes through movements like naval signals.*] Whoa!

Rolling of drums stops. RAPHAEL *freezes. The wire tightens.* DEATH *rushes into the bedroom. She comes out without the bandage over her eyes, with a dove which flaps its wings attached to the thread. The machine is no longer heard.*

Death. Phew! Quick, quick, Raphael, the scissors. [*She runs to the balcony.*] Come here; cut this. [*He cuts the thread and the dove flies away.*] Now clear things up. Azrael, show him how. It's very simple. Let him do it, he's got to learn.

AZRAEL *and* RAPHAEL *pack up the metal boxes, tunic, etc.* DEATH *leans against the table on the right. She looks into space as if worn out. She slowly passes her right arm and hand across her brow, like a sleepwalker who is reawakening, as if recalling herself from the hypnotic state.*

Azrael. Everything is in order, madam.

Death. And now, close the bags and lock them. I'm ready. My cloak. [AZRAEL *puts her cloak over her shoulders, while* RAPHAEL *is closing the bags.*] Have we forgotten anything?

Azrael. No, madam.

Death. Then, let's be going.

Gentleman in the Audience. Sss!

Azrael. Ah! Of course.

Death. What is it?

Azrael. The watch. Raphael, take the watch back to the gentleman and thank him. [*Business.*]

Death. Raphael, hurry up, hurry up.

Raphael. I'm coming, madam.

DEATH *walks quickly and comes to a standstill with out-*
stretched arms in front of the mirror. Then, she penetrates
it. Her assistants follow her. They go through the same
movements. She has forgotten her rubber gloves, which
are well in evidence on the left-hand table.

SCENE SEVEN

Directly after DEATH's *last remark,* ORPHÉE's *voice is heard*
in the garden.

ORPHÉE. You don't know her. You don't know what she's
capable of. This is one of her theatricals to get me back
home. [*The door opens and they enter.* HEURTEBISE *rushes
to the room, looks in, recoils and kneels on the threshold.*]
Where is she? Eurydice! . . . She's sulking. Here, I shall
go off my head! The horse! where's the horse? [*He opens
the niche.*] Gone!—I'm lost. Someone has opened the door
for him. Someone must have scared him; Eurydice must
have done this. She shall pay for it!

[*He makes a dash. . . .*

Heurtebise. Stop!

Orphée. Would you dare prevent me from going to my
wife?

Heurtebise. Look.

Orphée. Where?

Heurtebise. Look through my panes.

Orphée [*Looking*]. She is sitting. She's asleep.

Heurtebise. She is dead.

Orphée. What?

Heurtebise. Dead. We've got here too late.

Orphée. It can't be. [*He knocks on the panes.*] Eurydice!
my darling! Answer me!

Heurtebise. It's no good.

Orphée. You! let me go in. [*He pushes* HEURTEBISE
aside.] Where is she? [*In the wings.*] I saw her a moment
ago, sitting near the bed. The room's empty. [*He re-enters.*]
Eurydice!

Heurtebise. You only thought you saw her. Eurydice is
living in the abode of Death.

Orphée. Ah! The horse is of little consequence! I want
to see Eurydice again. I want her to forgive me for having
neglected and misunderstood her. Help me. Save me.
What can we do? We're losing precious time.

Heurtebise. Those kind words save you, Orphée. . . .

Orphée [*Weeping, collapsed on the table*]. Dead. Eurydice is dead. [*He gets up.*] Well then . . . I'll snatch her
away from Death! To seek her, I'll brave the Underworld,
if necessary.

Heurtebise. Orphée . . . listen to me. Calm yourself.
Are you going to listen to me? . . .

Orphée. Yes . . . I'll be calm. Let's consider things.
Let's find a plan. . . .

Heurtebise. I know a way.

Orphée. You!

Heurtebise. But you must obey me and not lose a
minute.

Orphée. Yes.

All ORPHÉE'S *remarks are made in a feverish docility. The
scene moves with extreme rapidity.*

Heurtebise. Death came into your house to carry off
Eurydice.

Orphée. Yes. . . .

Heurtebise. She's forgotten her rubber gloves.

*Silence. He goes to the table, hesitates, and picks up the
gloves at arm's length, as one touches a sacred object.*

Orphée [*In terror*]. Ah!

Heurtebise. You'll put them on.

Orphée. Yes.

Heurtebise. Put them on. [*He passes them to him.*
ORPHÉE *puts them on.*] You must go and see Death under
the pretense of returning them, and thanks to them you'll
be able to get to her.

Orphée. Right. . . .

Heurtebise. Death is going to look for her gloves. If
you take them to her, she'll give you a reward. She's
miserly, she prefers receiving to giving, and as she never
returns what anyone lets her take, your procedure will

astonish her not a little. I don't suppose you'll get much, but still you'll get something.

Orphée. Good.

Heurtebise [*Leading him in front of the mirror*]. That's your way.

Orphée. That mirror?

Heurtebise. I'm entrusting you with the secret of secrets. Mirrors are the doors through which Death comes and goes. Don't tell anyone. You only have to watch yourself all your life in a mirror, and you'll see Death at work like bees in a glass hive. Good-by. Good luck!

Orphée. But a mirror—that's hard.

Heurtebise [*With hand raised*]. With those gloves you'll pass through mirrors as through water.

Orphée. Where did you learn all these dreadful things

Heurtebise [*His hand drops*]. You know, mirrors are connected in a way with glazing. That's our trade.

Orphée. And once I'm past this . . . door . . .

Heurtebise. Breathe slowly and regularly. Don't be afraid; just walk straight ahead. Turn to the right, then to the left, then to the right, then go straight along. There, how can I explain it? . . . There's no more direction . . . you go round; it's a little difficult at first.

Orphée. And then?

Heurtebise. Then? No one in the world can tell you. Death begins.

Orphée. I'm not afraid of her.

Heurtebise. Farewell. I'll wait for you to come back.

Orphée. But I might be a long time.

Heurtebise. A long time . . . for you. For us you'll scarcely do more than go in and come out.

Orphée. I can't see how this mirror can be soft. Anyhow, I'll try.

Heurtebise. Yes, try. [ORPHÉE *begins to move.*] First your hands!

ORPHÉE, *with arms outstretched and the red gloves on his hands, sinks into the mirror.*

Orphée. Eurydice! . . .   [*He disappears.*

SCENE EIGHT (A)

HEURTEBISE, *alone, kneels in front of the* HORSE's *niche.*
A knock.

HEURTEBISE. What is it?
   Postman's voice. Postman. I've a letter for you.
   Heurtebise. Master's not here.
   Postman's voice. And madam?
   Heurtebise. Not here either. Slip the letter under the
door.

     A letter comes under the door.

   Postman's voice. Have they gone out?
   Heurtebise. No . . . they're asleep.

THE CURTAIN FOR THE INTERVAL
FALLS SLOWLY
AND RISES IMMEDIATELY

SCENE EIGHT (B)

HEURTEBISE *is discovered kneeling in front of the* HORSE's
niche. A knock.

HEURTEBISE. What is it?
   Postman's voice. Postman. I've a letter for you.
   Heurtebise. Master's not here.
   Postman's voice. And madam?
   Heurtebise. Not here either. Slip the letter under the
door.

     A letter comes under the door.

   Postman's voice. Have they gone out?
   Heurtebise. No . . . they're asleep.

SCENE NINE

ORPHÉE [*Comes out of the mirror*]. What, still here?
   Heurtebise. Now tell me quickly. . . .

Orphée. My dear fellow, you're an angel.

Heurtebise. Not at all.

Orphée. Oh! yes, an angel, a real angel. You have saved me.

Heurtebise. And Eurydice?

Orphée. A surprise. Just look.

Heurtebise. Where?

Orphée. At the mirror. One, two, three.

EURYDICE *comes out of the mirror.*

Heurtebise. It is she!

Eurydice. Yes, it is I. I, the happiest of wives; I, the first woman with a husband bold enough to recover her from the dead.

Orphée. "Orpheé hunts Eurydice's lost life." And to think we refused to believe this sentence had a meaning.

Eurydice. Sh! my darling. Remember your promise. We weren't going to speak of the horse any more.

Orphée. Where was my head?

Eurydice. And you know, Heurtebise, he found the way all by himself. He didn't hesitate one second. He had the ingenious idea of putting on Death's gloves.

Heurtebise. Hm! I think I shall have to take up the gloves for myself.

Orphée [*Very quickly*]. Anyway, the chief thing was to succeed. [*He makes as if to turn to* EURYDICE.]

Eurydice. Careful!

Orphée. Oh! [*He freezes.*]

Heurtebise. What's the matter?

Orphée. A detail, a mere detail. At first it appears terrifying, but with a little care it'll be all right.

Eurydice. It'll become a matter of habit.

Heurtebise. But what's it all about?

Orphée. A pact. I'm allowed to have Eurydice again, but I may not look at her. If I look at her, she'll disappear.

Heurtebise. How dreadful!

Eurydice. How clever to discourage my husband!

Orphée [*Making* HEURTEBISE *pass in front of him*]. That's all right, I'm not discouraged. What is happening to him, happened to us. Think, after we'd accepted that clause—and we had to, whatever the cost—we went through all your apprehensions. Well, I repeat, it can be done. It isn't easy by any means, but it can be done. I maintain it isn't so hard as to become blind.

Eurydice Or as to lose a leg.

Orphée. Besides . . . we had no choice.

Eurydice. There are even advantages. Orphée won't see my wrinkles.

Heurtebise. Bravo! I have nothing more to do but to wish you good luck.

Orphée. Are you going to leave us?

Heurtebise. I fear my presence may be embarrassing. You must have so many things to say to each other.

Orphée. We'll say them after lunch. The table is laid. I'm very hungry. You are too much a part of our adventure not to stay to lunch with us.

Heurtebise. I'm afraid the presence of a third may vex your wife.

Eurydice. No, Heurtebise. [*Weighing the words.*] The journey I've made transforms the face of the world. I have learned a lot. I'm ashamed of myself. From now on I shall be a new wife to Orphée, a honeymoon wife.

Orphée. Eurydice! Your promise. We weren't going to speak any more of the moon.

Eurydice. It's my turn to have no memory. Let's have lunch! Heurtebise on my right. Come and sit down. Orphée opposite me.

Heurtebise. Not opposite!

Orphée. Heavens! I did right in keeping Heurtebise. I shall sit on your left with my back turned to you. I shall eat from my lap.

EURYDICE *serves them.*

Heurtebise. I'm anxious to hear the story of your journey.

Orphée. Lord, I shall find it difficult to relate. It seems as if I'm recovering from an operation. I have a vague memory of it, like that of one of my poems which I recite to keep me awake, and of foul beasts falling asleep. Then a black hole. Then speaking with an invisible lady. She thanked me for the gloves. A sort of surgeon came to take them, and he told me to go, that Eurydice would follow me, and that I wasn't to look at her on any account. I am thirsty. [*He takes his glass and turns around.*]

Eurydice and Heurtebise [*Together.*] Careful!

Eurydice. I had a rare fright! Without turning around, my dear, feel how my heart is beating.

Orphée. How silly it is. Supposing I bound my eyes!

Heurtebise. I don't advise you to do that. You don't know the exact rules. If you cheat all is lost.

Orphée. You would hardly credit how difficult it is to do such an idiotic thing, and the mental strain it involves.

Eurydice. What do you expect, my poor dear, when you are always mooning——

Orphée. The moon again! You might as well call me a lunatic.

Eurydice. Orphée!

Orphée. I leave the moon to your late companions.

Silence.

Heurtebise. Mr. Orphée!

Orphée. I am a sun worshiper.

Eurydice. No longer, my love.

Orphée. Perhaps not. But I forbid mention of the moon in my house.

Silence.

Eurydice. If only you knew how little importance attaches to this talk of sun and moon.

Orphée. Madam is above these things.

Eurydice. If only I could speak——

Orphée. It seems to me that for a person who can't speak, you speak quite a lot! A lot too much!

Eurydice *weeps. Silence.*

Heurtebise. You're making your wife cry.

Orphée [*Threatening*]. You! [*He turns around.*]

Eurydice. Ah!

Heurtebise. Take care!

Orphée. It's her fault. She would make the dead turn.

Eurydice. It would have been better to remain dead.

Silence.

Orphée. The moon! If I were to let her talk where would we get to? I ask you. We'd go back to the reign of the horse.

Heurtebise. You're exaggerating. . . .

Orphée. I am exaggerating?

Heurtebise. Yes.

Orphée. And even if I admit that I'm exaggerating. . . . [*He turns around.*]

Eurydice. Look out!

Heurtebise [*To* EURYDICE]. Calm yourself. Don't cry. The difficulty is making you nervous. Orphée, try and make an effort yourself. You'll bring about trouble in the end.

Orphée. And even if I admit that I'm exaggerating, who began it?

Eurydice. Not me.

Orphée. Not you! Not you! [*He turns around.*]

Eurydice and Heurtebise. Hey!

Heurtebise. You're dangerous, my dear fellow.

Orphée. You're right. The best thing I can do is to leave the table, and rid you of my presence, since I'm dangerous.

He rises. EURYDICE *and* HEURTEBISE *hold him back by his coat.*

Eurydice. My dear. . . .

Heurtebise. Orphée. . . .

Orphée, No, no. Let me go.

Heurtebise. Be reasonable.

Orphée. I shall be what it pleases me to be.

Eurydice. Don't go.

She pulls him, he loses his balance, and looks at her. He utters a cry. EURYDICE, *petrified, rises. Her face expresses terror. The light lowers.* EURYDICE *sinks slowly into the mirror and disappears. The light rises again.*

Heurtebise. It was to be.

Orphée [*Pale and limp, with an expression of false grace*]. Phew! That's better.

Heurtebise. What!

Orphée [*Same expression*]. We can breathe now.

Heurtebise. He's mad.

Orphée [*Hiding his embarrassment more and more in anger*]. You have to be firm with women, and show them you don't depend on them. You mustn't let them lead you by the nose.

Heurtebise. That's going a bit strong, isn't it? Would you have me believe you looked at Eurydice on purpose?

Orphée. Am I an absent-minded man?

Heurtebise. You don't lack boldness! You looked in-advertently. You lost your balance, and you turned your head inadvertently; I saw you.

Orphée. I lost my balance on purpose. I turned my head deliberately, and I forbid anyone to contradict me.

Silence.

Heurtebise. Very well then, if you did turn your head deliberately, I don't congratulate you.

Orphée. I can do without your congratulations. I congratulate myself for having turned my head deliberately toward my wife. That's better than trying to turn the heads of other people's wives.

Heurtebise. Is that meant for me?

Orphée. If the cap fits. . . .

Heurtebise. That's very unkind. I've never allowed myself to make love to your wife. She would soon have sent me about my business. Your wife was a model wife. You had to lose her the first time to realize that, and you have just lost her a second time, lost her shamefully and tragically, and lost yourself. You have just killed a dead woman, and committed out of sheer wantonness an irreparable act. For she has died, died, died again. Never more will she come back.

Orphée. Oh! come on!

Heurtebise. What do you mean, "Oh! come on!"?

Orphée. When have you seen a woman get up from table scolding and not come back?

Heurtebise. I leave you five minutes to realize your misfortune.

ORPHÉE *throws his napkin on the floor, rises, adjusts the table, goes to look at the mirror, touches it, goes to the door, and picks up the letter. Opens the letter.*

Orphée. What's this?

Heurtebise. Some bad news?

Orphée. I can't read it; the letter is written backwards.

Heurtebise. That's a way of disguising the handwriting. Read it in the mirror.

Orphée [In front of the mirror, reads]. "Sir, Excuse my preserving my incognito. Aglaonice has discovered that the initial letters of your sentence: '*Orphée Hunts Eurydice's Lost Life,*' together form a word which is offensive to the jury of the competition." [ORPHÉE *says to himself.*] O, H, E, L, L. O Hell! [ORPHÉE *continues to read.*] "She has convinced the jury that you are a hoaxer. She has stirred up against you half of the women of the town. In short, an enormous troop of mad women under her orders is coming toward your house. The Bacchantes lead the way and demand your death. Escape and hide yourself. Do not lose a minute. From one who wishes you well."

Heurtebise. There can't be a word of truth in it.

Drums are heard approaching from a distance, beating a furious rhythm.

Orphée. Listen. . . .

Heurtebise. Drums.

Orphée. Their drums. Eurydice saw aright. Heurtebise, the horse has befooled me.

Heurtebise. A man isn't hacked to pieces for a couple of words.

Orphée. The words are a pretext which hides a deep and religious hatred. Aglaonice was biding her time. I an lost.

Heurtebise. The drums are coming nearer.

Orphée. How was it I didn't see this letter? How long ago was it slipped under the door?

Heurtebise. Orphée, I'm to blame. The letter was slipped in during your visit to the dead. Your wife's return engrossed me, and I forgot to tell you. Fly!

Orphée. Too late.

The Horse's *spell is ended.* Orphée *is transfigured.*

Heurtebise. Hide in the grove. I'll say you're traveling. . . .

Orphée. It's useless, Heurtebise. Things happen as they must.

Heurtebise. I shall save you by force!

Orphée. I refuse.

Heurtebise. This is madness!

Orphée. The mirror is hard. It read the letter for me. I know what I can still do.

Heurtebise. What are you going to do?

Orphée. Rejoin Eurydice.

Heurtebise. Not this time.

Orphée. Why not?

Heurtebise. Even if you did manage it, there'd be more scenes between you.

Orphée [*In ecstasy*]. Not there, where she beckons me to join her.

Heurtebise. Your face is drawn. You're suffering. I won't let you take your life.

Orphée. Oh! those drums, those drums! They are coming nearer, Heurtebise, they are rumbling and thundering, they'll soon be here.

Heurtebise. You have already done the impossible.

Orphée. I have held by the impossible.

Heurtebise. You have withstood other plots.

Orphée. Not at the cost of bloodshed yet.

Heurtebise. You frighten me. . . . [Heurtebise's *face expresses a supernatural joy.*]

Orphée. What are the thoughts of the marble from which a sculptor shapes a masterpiece? It thinks: I am being struck, ruined, insulted, and broken, I am lost. This marble is stupid. Life is shaping me, Heurtebise. It is making a masterpiece. I must bear its blows without understanding them. I must stand firm. I must be still and accept the inevitable. I must help and bear my part, till the work is ended.

Heurtebise. Stones!

Some stones break the window and fall into the room.

Orphée. Glass. That's good luck! Luck! I shall have the bust I wished for.

A stone breaks the mirror.

Heurtebise. The mirror!
Orphée. Not the mirror! [*He rushes on to the balcony.*]
Heurtebise. They'll hack you to pieces.

Clamoring and drums.

Orphée [*Back to audience, leans over the balcony*]. Ladies! [*Roar of drums.*] Ladies! [*Roar of drums.*] Ladies! [*Roar of drums. He rushes to the right—invisible part of the balcony. The drums drown his voice.*]

Darkness. Heurtebise *falls on his knees and hides his face. Suddenly something flies through the window and falls into the room. It is* Orphée's *head. It rolls to the right, and stops on the forestage.* Heurtebise *utters a weak cry. The drums are getting farther away.*

SCENE TEN

Orphée's Head [*Speaking in the voice of someone greatly hurt*]. Where am I? How dark it is. . . . How heavy my head is. And my body, my body hurts me so much. I must have fallen from the balcony. I must have fallen from a great height, a great height, from a great height onto my head. And my head . . . ? as a matter of fact . . . yes, I'm speaking about my head . . . where is my head? Eurydice! Heurtebise! Help me! Where are you? Light the lamp. Eurydice! I can't see my body. I can't find my head. I've lost my head, and my body; and I can't understand

now. There's an emptiness, all about me there is an emptiness. Explain it to me. Wake me. Help! Help! Eurydice!
[*Like a lament.*] Eurydice . . . Eurydice . . . Eurydice
. . . Eurydice . . . Eurydice. . . .

EURYDICE *comes through the mirror. She remains on the spot.*

Eurydice. My darling?

Orphée's head. Eurydice . . . is it you?

Eurydice. It is.

Orphée's head. Where is my body? Where did I put my body?

Eurydice. Quiet. Don't upset yourself. Give me your hand.

Orphée's head. Where is my head?

Eurydice [*Taking the invisible body by the hand*]. I have your hand in mine. Walk. Don't be afraid. Let yourself go. . . .

Orphée's head. Where is my body?

Eurydice. Near me. Against me. You can't see me now, and I may take you away.

Orphée's head. And my head, Eurydice . . . my head
. . . where did I put my head?

Eurydice. No more of that, my love, let your head be. . . .

EURYDICE *and the invisible body of* ORPHÉE *sink into the mirror.*

SCENE ELEVEN

A knock on the door. Silence. Knock. Silence.

VOICE OF THE COMMISSIONER OF POLICE. Open, in the name of the law.

Heurtebise. Who is it?

Voice of the Commissioner of Police. The police. Open or I'll break in the door.

Heurtebise. I'll open it.

HEURTEBISE *rushes to* ORPHÉE's *head, picks it up, hesitates, put it on the pedestal, and opens the door. The leaf of the door hides the pedestal. It is now that the actor who plays* ORPHÉE *substitutes his own head for that of the mask.*

Commissioner. Why didn't you reply to my first summons?

Heurtebise. Your Worship. . . .

Commissioner. Commissioner of Police.

Heurtebise. Sir, I'm a friend of the family. . . . I was still suffering from the shock, as you may well imagine——

Commissioner. Shock? What shock?

Heurtebise. I must tell you. I was alone with Orphée at the moment of the drama.

Commissioner. What drama?

Heurtebise. The murder of Orphée by the Bacchantes.

Commissioner [*Turning to the* SCRIVENER]. I was expecting this version. And . . . the wife of the victim. . . . Where is she? I should like to confront her with you.

Heurtebise. She's not here.

Commissioner. Better and better.

Heurtebise. She had even abandoned the conjugal domicile.

Commissioner. Do you hear that! [*To the* SCRIVENER.] Sit down at the table, please [*he points to the right-hand table*], and take notes.

The SCRIVENER *installs himself. Papers and pens. He turns his back to the mirror.* HEURTEBISE *is standing near the mirror. To be more at ease the* SCRIVENER *pulls the table back so that this table renders access to the door impossible.*

Heurtebise. I have——

Scrivener. Silence.

Commissioner. Let's proceed in order. Don't speak unless I question you. Where's the body?

Heurtebise. What body?

Commissioner. When there's a murder, there's a body. I am asking you—where is the body?

Heurtebise. But, sir, there isn't a body. It has been torn, decapitated, and carried away by those mad women!

Commissioner. Primo, I am not asking you to make a detrimental judgment on women who perform priestly rites. Secundo, your version is contradicted by five hundred eyewitnesses.

Heurtebise. Do you mean that I——

Commissioner. Silence!

Heurtebise. I——

Commissioner. Silence! [*Pompous delivery.*] You just listen to me, my lad. Today is the day of the eclipse. This eclipse of the sun has brought about a tremendous change of popular feeling in Orphée favor. Mourning's being worn. Triumphal celebrations are being prepared, and the authorities claim his mortal remains. Now, the Bacchantes saw Orphée appear on his balcony, covered with blood and calling for help. They were astonished, as they had come there under his window with the sole purpose of fêting him. They would have flown to his aid, if he hadn't, as they say—and five hundred mouths testify to it—if he hadn't, as I was saying, fallen dead before their eyes.

To sum up. These ladies made a long procession. They arrive with cries of "Out with Orphée!" Suddenly Orphée covered with blood rushes out and calls for help. These ladies make ready to mount the steps. Too late! Orphée falls, and the whole troop—don't forget they are women . . . women who make a brave noise, but who are frightened at the sight of blood—the whole troop, I say, turns tail. Eclipse! The town saw in this eclipse the anger of the sun, because one of its late priests had been derided. The authorities came to meet the women, and the women, through the medium of Aglaonice, retailed the strange crime of which they had just been witnesses. The whole town wanted to rush to the scene of the tragedy. Severe measures were taken to suppress the disorder and I was given charge, I, *I*, the head of the police force, I, who am conducting your examination—and I won't allow anyone to treat me like a country policeman, keep that well in mind.

Heurtebise. But, I'm not——

Scrivener. Silence. You're not being questioned.

Commissioner. Let's proceed in order. [*To the* SCRIVE-NER.] Where did I get to?

Scrivener. The bust. I beg to remind you of the bust. . . .

Commissioner. Ah! yes. [*To* HEURTEBISE.] Are you a relative?

Heurtebise. A friend of the family.

Commissioner. A bust of Orphée is required for the celebrations. Do you know of one?

HEURTEBISE *goes to the door and closes it. The head on the pedestal is discovered. The* COMMISSIONER OF POLICE *and* SCRIVENER *turn around.*

Commissioner. It isn't a likeness.

Heurtebise. It's a very fine work.

Commissioner. Who by?

Heurtebise. I don't know.

Commissioner. Is the bust not signed?

Heurtebise. No.

Commissioner [*To the* SCRIVENER]. Write down: Alleged bust of Orphée.

Heurtebise. No, no. It is Orphée, of that we're sure. There's doubt only about the authorship.

Commissioner. Then put: Head of Orphée by X. [*To* HEURTEBISE.] Your name.

Heurtebise. Pardon?

Scrivener. You were asked for your full name.

Commissioner. For, as regards your profession, I'm not to be deceived. I have eyes. [*He goes to* HEURTEBISE *and fingers the panes.*] You are a glazier, my fine fellow!

Heurtebise [*Smiling*]. Yes, I am a glazier, I confess.

Commissioner. Confess, confess, it's the only defense which carries any weight.

Scrivener. Excuse me, sir, supposing we ask him for his papers. . . .

Commissioner. Quite right. [*He sits down.*] Your papers.

Heurtebise. I . . . I haven't any.

Commissioner. What?

Scrivener. Ho! ho!

Commissioner. Going about without your papers? Where are they? Where do you live?

Heurtebise. I live . . . that is to say—er—I used to live. . . .

Commissioner. I'm not asking you where you used to live. I'm asking where you're living now.

Heurtebise. Now? . . . at the moment I am . . . without an address.

Commissioner. No papers, no fixed abode. Exactly. Vagrancy! a vagrant! Your case is clear, my friend. Your age?

Heurtebise. I am . . . [*He hesitates.*]

Commissioner [*He questions with his back turned, looking up to the ceiling, moving his feet, like an examiner*]. I suppose, at least, you have some age . . .

Orphée's head. I'm eighteen.

Scrivener [*Writing*]. Seventeen.

Orphée's head. Eighteen.

Commissioner. Born at . . .

Scrivener. Half a minute, sir. I'm erasing the figure.

EURYDICE *comes halfway through the mirror.*

Eurydice. Heurtebise . . . Heurtebise. I know who you are. Come in, we were waiting for you. You alone were missing.

HEURTEBISE *hesitates.*

Orphée's head. Hurry up, Heurtebise. Follow my wife. I'll answer for you. I'll invent something, anything.

HEURTEBISE *plunges into the mirror.*

SCENE TWELVE

SCRIVENER. Sir, at your service.

Commissioner. Born at . . .

Orphée's head. Maisons-Laffitte.

Commissioner. Maisons what?

Orphée's head. Maisons-Laffitte, two F's, two T's.

Commissioner. As you can tell me your place of birth, perhaps you'll no longer refuse to tell me your name. You're called . . .

Orphée's head. Jean.

Commissioner. Jean what?

Orphée's head. Jean Cocteau.

Commissioner. Coc . . .

Orphée's head. C, O, C, T, E, A, U. Cocteau.

Commissioner. There's a name to go to bed with. Is it true you sleep out of doors? If you don't consent now to tell us where you live . . .

Orphée's head. Rue d'Anjou. Number 10.

Commissioner. You're becoming reasonable.

Scrivener. Your signature. . . .

Commissioner. Get a pen ready. [*To* HEURTEBISE.] Come here. Come here, I won't eat you. [*Turns around.*] Great . . . !

Scrivener. What is it?

Commissioner. Great Heavens! The accused has disappeared.

Scrivener. Miraculous!

Commissioner. Miraculous. . . . Miraculous . . . it's not miraculous at all. [*He strides up and down the stage.*] I don't believe in miracles. An eclipse is an eclipse. A table's a table. An accused man's an accused man. Let's proceed in order. This door. . . .

Scrivener. Impossible, sir. To go out by this door, he would have to knock over my chair.

Commissioner. The window, then.

Scrivener. For the window, he would have to pass in front of us. Besides, the accused was answering. He answered right up to the last minute.

Commissioner. Well?

Scrivener. Well, I don't understand it at all.

Commissioner. There must be a secret exit of which the assassin—for this flight gives us proof of the crime—of which the assassin, as I was saying, knew the existence. Sound the wall.

Scrivener *taps. Investigations.*

Scrivener. The wall sounds solid. . . .

Commissioner. Right. This young dog may leave us and hide in this unmannerly fashion, but we won't give him the satisfaction of seeking him under his very nose. [*At the top of his voice.*] I have men about the house. He can't take two steps outside without being caught, and if he persists, we'll surround him till hunger drives him out. Come on.

Scrivener. What an extraordinary affair!

Commissioner. There's nothing extraordinary at all. You're always seeing something extraordinary somewhere.

They go out. While they are going out and the door hides the bust, the actor substitutes the mask for his own head. The stage remains empty.

Commissioner [*returning*]. We're forgetting the bust.
Scrivener. We mustn't return empty-handed.
Commissioner. Take it.

The Scrivener *takes the head. Exeunt.*

SCENE THIRTEEN

The scene changes to Heaven. Through the mirror come Eurydice *and* Orphée, *led by* Heurtebise. *They look at their home as if they were seeing it for the first time. They sit down at table;* Eurydice *beckons* Heurtebise *to her right. They smile and breathe calmness.*

Eurydice. You were wanting some wine, I think, my dear.

Orphée. One moment. First of all, the paper. [*He rises, also* Eurydice *and* Heurtebise. *He recites:*] O God, we thank thee for assigning us our house and home as the only paradise, and for having opened to us thy paradise. We thank thee for having sent Heurtebise to us, and we are guilty of not recognizing him as our Guardian Angel. We thank thee for having saved Eurydice, because, through love, she killed the devil in the shape of a horse, and in so doing she died. We thank thee for having saved me because I adored poetry, and thou art poetry. Amen.

They sit again.

Heurtebise. May I serve you?
Orphée [*Respectfully*]. Let Eurydice. . . .

EURYDICE *pours out for him to drink.*

Heurtebise. Perhaps we can have lunch at last.

CURTAIN

ANTIGONE

Adapted from the Greek by Jean Cocteau.
English version by Carl Wildman. Revised by E.B.

CHARACTERS

ANTIGONE } *daughters of* OEDIPUS
ISMENE

EURYDICE, *Queen of Thebes*
CREON, *King of Thebes*
HAEMON, *their son*
TIRESIAS, *a sage and priest*
A GUARD
A MESSENGER
A CHORUS

ANTIGONE

Scene—Thebes. Before the palace.

Sophocles' Antigone was first performed in Athens in 441 b.c. This shortened version was first produced in Paris at the Atelier Theater in 1922 with scenery by Picasso, music by Honegger, and costumes by Chanel.

The extreme rapidity of the action does not prevent the actors from speaking very distinctly and moving very little. The Chorus and its leader are concentrated into a single voice which speaks very loudly and quickly as if reading a newspaper article. This voice issues from a hole in the center of the scenery.

For a revival in 1927, five monumental plaster heads of young men framed the chorus. The actors wore transparent masks after the fashion of fencing baskets; beneath the masks one could make out the actors' faces, and ethereal features were sewn onto the masks in white millinery wire. The costumes were worn over black bathing suits, and arms and legs were covered. The general effect was suggestive of a sordid carnival of kings, a family of insects.

When the curtain rises, Antigone and Ismene are standing near each other, motionless, looking straight into the auditorium.

[J. C.]

Antigone. Ismene, my sister, do you know of a single scourge in the heritage of Oedipus that Jupiter[1] has spared us? I think I can tell you of another. One more shame that our enemies have in store for us. Guess what it is.

Ismene. No, Antigone. Our two brothers have died at each other's hands. The Argive horde has disappeared. And today I do not see what could make me feel more wretched—or less unhappy.

---

[1] My substitution of *Jupiter* for *Zeus* is supported by La Fontaine and Maurras. *Jupiter* sounds better in our language. [J.C.] The same is true of the English language. [C.W.]

49

Antigone. Listen. I wanted you to come out here so that no living soul should hear us.

Ismene. What is wrong? Your look terrifies me.

Antigone. You ask what is wrong? Is not Creon allowing funeral rites to one brother and denying them to the other? Eteocles will have the burial he deserves; Polynices may be neither buried nor mourned. He is to be left to the crows. Those are the orders of the noble Creon for you and me. Yes, for me too. He will come in person to this very spot and read his decree. He attaches the utmost importance to the carrying out of his orders. To infringe them is to be stoned to death by the people. I hope you will show what you are made of.

Ismene. What can I do?

Antigone. Decide if you will help me.

Ismene. Do what?

Antigone. Raise up the body.

Ismene. You mean to bury it in defiance of the king?

Antigone. I do. He is our brother. My brother—and yours. I shall bury him. No one shall say I have left him to the beasts.

Ismene [*Horrified*]. Unhappy girl! Despite Creon's ban?

Antigone. Has he the right to cut me off from my family?

Ismene. Antigone! Antigone! Our poor father put out his eyes to expiate his crimes. He died in the mud. Our mother, who was *his* mother, hanged herself. Our brothers slew each other. Just think: we two are quite alone! What a sinister end will be ours if we defy our masters! Antigone, we are just women. Women unskilled in the art of subduing men. Those in command are stronger. May Polynices forgive me, but I shall acquiesce. I shall obey the powers that be. To attempt what is beyond one's strength is folly.

Antigone. I do not wish to force you. If you were to help me, your heart would not be in it. Do as you think best. I am for the burying. After that, I shall be glad to die. One sweet crime and two friends will rest side by side. For, Ismene, the time I shall have to spend pleasing the dead is far longer than the time I must spend pleasing the living. Your conduct is your affair. Despise the gods, if you must.

Ismene. I don't despise them. I merely feel unable to fight a whole town.

Antigone. Seek out excuses! I shall raise him a sort of grave.

Ismene. This is madness! I tremble for you.

Antigone. Let me alone. Think of yourself.

Ismene. At any rate, tell no one what you intend. Keep it dark—as I shall.

Antigone. Keep nothing dark. You are free to speak. I should begrudge you your silence more than your tittle-tattle.

Ismene. Cool down. You are far too excited.

Antigone. Never! I know that I please where I should.

Ismene. Yes, if all goes well. But you are attempting the impossible.

Antigone. I shall stop. When my strength fails.

Ismene. Why try and catch the wind?

Antigone. Go on like this, and I shall detest you. You will excite the hatred of the dead. Leave me alone with my plan. It it fails, I die a glorious death.

Ismene [*Mounting the steps on the left*]. Very well then. Go your rash way. Your heart is your undoing. [*Exit.*

ANTIGONE *remains alone, braces herself for the day ahead, and disappears in the left-hand wings.*

Chorus. Under your frantic eye, O sun, the Argive troops have fled. As fast as their legs would run. They had come on the heels of Polynices and his dreams of power. Jupiter detests boasting. He has struck the plumes and armor of pride with his thunderbolt. The seven chiefs who marched against our seven gates have laid down their arms. Only two brothers of opposite camps stayed their ground.

Now victory is established in Thebes. And the people sing. But here is Creon, our new sovereign.

Creon [*At the right-hand gate*]. Citizens, the gods have saved this town from ruin. I have called you together knowing your respect for the house of Laius and your loyalty to Oedipus and to his sons. The sons have slain each other. All power passes into my hands.

Before a man has shown his worth, it is hard to know him. Personally, I condemn the man who rules without consulting those about him. Still more, the head of a state who would sacrifice the masses to the interests of a single individual. I will flatter no adversary. A just prince will not lack friends. Such are my principles.

And so I have dictated the decree concerning the sons of Oedipus. Eteocles is a soldier: let him be buried with full honors. Polynices returned from exile as an incendiary seeking to flout us and reduce us to slavery. No honors shall be paid to him. I command that his body be left to the dogs and crows. I shall never confuse virtue with crime. I have spoken.

Chorus. Well said, Creon. You have a free hand. You can dispose of the dead. And of us.

Creon. Carry out my order.

Chorus. Ask the young men.

Creon. Guards keep watch over the body.

Chorus. What must we do then?

Creon. If laws are broken, be inflexible.

Chorus. No man is so mad as to seek death.

Creon. Death would be his reward. But the hope of a purse often makes men mad.

Guard [*Enters, kneels, coughs nervously, and speaks*]. Prince, I can't exactly say I have flown here to you. Oh, no. I stopped many times on the way. I kept saying to myself: "Don't go to him, don't go. But, on the other hand, if Creon learns about it from somewhere else, you might be in for much worse. It's not far to go." But it was. . . . So you see. . . . You see. . . . I've nothing good to tell you.

Creon. What is it that's scared you out of your wits?

Guard. Well, I'll tell you about number one first of all. It wasn't me. It wasn't my fault. And I don't know who it was. It wouldn't be fair of you to punish me.

Creon. You're beating about the bush. It looks to me as though you're trying to break some bad news gently.

Guard. Danger kind of paralyzes you.

Creon. Speak. Then you can go.

Guard. Right, I'll speak. The body has been buried.

Creon. What? Who has dared . . . ?

Guard. Not the slightest idea. There's no sign of spades or picks. No footprints. No cart tracks. Nothing to give the criminal away. By the early morning the body had disappeared under a layer of dust. Just enough to prevent sacrilege. Of course, everyone was accusing everyone else and getting worked up. We were going to fight it out. The whole guard was under suspicion because there was no proof against anyone in particular. We swore we would walk on live embers without flinching and grasp red-hot irons. That's how to tell the guilty and their accomplices. In the end, we decided to make a clean breast of it. To you. We drew lots and I was the unlucky one.

Chorus. Prince, I wonder if this isn't a plot hatched by the gods.

Creon. Enough nonsense from you, old man. The gods don't inter iconoclasts, incendiaries, pillagers of temples. Have you ever known the gods to favor evil? No; I should say not. But this act is an eye-opener. I knew there were traitors in this town, murmuring against my yoke. I knew of subversive activities. The culprits are in the traitors' service.

Men have invented money. Money, vile money. Money has wrought the ruin of towns, the corruption of honest men, a general demoralization. But those who have interred Polynices, bribed by a purse, have dug their own tomb. If you do not bring them to me I shall hang you. Then someone will denounce them.

Guard. In any case, it wasn't me.

Creon. I wonder. You seem to me precisely the kind of fellow who would sell himself, and cheap at that!

Guard. It's sad that a fair-minded prince can't see straight.

Creon. He's passing judgment on me, I do declare.

Guard. I sincerely hope the guilty parties are found. I'm off.   [*Exit* GUARD, *then* CREON.

Chorus. Man is amazing. Man navigates, man plows,

man hunts, man fishes. He tames horses. He thinks. He speaks. He invents codes, he warms himself, and roofs in his house. He recovers from sickness. Death is the only sickness which he cannot cure. He does good and he does evil. When he listens to the laws of heaven and earth, he is a good fellow; when he does not heed them, he ceases to be so. May a criminal never by my guest. Heavens, what strange portent is this? O gods! Incredible, but true! Is it not Antigone? Antigone! Antigone, can you have disobeyed? Can you have been mad enough to cause your own undoing?

From the left-hand wings appears ANTIGONE. *The hands of the* GUARD *who is pushing her forward are visible on her shoulders. Then the* GUARD *himself becomes visible.*

Guard. Caught red-handed. Where's Creon?

Chorus. There he is, coming out.

Creon. What is happening?

Guard. Prince, chance brings me back where I had hoped not to set foot again. Question this girl. She is the guilty one.

Creon. Where and how did you take her?

Guard. She was burying the body. I caught her in the act.

Creon. You swear it?

Guard. Yes, I swear it. She was burying the man.

Creon. Give me some details.

Guard. We were scared by your threats and got the sand off the corpse and left it naked on the earth. Then we sat down on a mound where there was a breeze—because of the stink. Then we fooled around so as not to fall asleep. Suddenly, at midday, a dust storm arose and broke the branches and blinded us. When it had passed, we saw this young woman standing near the body. Screaming her head off. She covered the body with dust, brought out a vessel from under her dress, and began libations. Psst! We pounced on her, and arrested her in half a second. We questioned her and she confessed without offering resistance. I'm sorry I had to trade one life for another, but guilt is guilt, and, when all's said and done, it's only natural I should try and save my own skin.

Creon. And you. You with the unassuming eyes, what do you say to this? Is it true?

Antigone. I did it. I avow it.

Creon [*To the* GUARD]. Get out. Get yourself hanged somewhere else. You're free. [*To* ANTIGONE.] You knew of my ban?

Antigone. Yes. It was public.

Creon. And you had the audacity not to observe it.

Antigone. Jupiter did not issue that decree. Nor does justice impose such laws. I was not aware that your decree could make the caprice of a man prevail over the rule of the immortals, over Unwritten Laws which nothing can efface. Such laws do not date from today or yesterday. They are for all time. No one knows when they were made. Ought I, then, for fear of a man's opinion, to disobey my gods? I knew death would follow my act. I shall die young; so much the better. The real misfortune was to have left my brother without a tomb. The rest is all the same to me.

After this you may call me mad yet in reality be yourself the madman.

Chorus. By her unyielding nature we recognize the daughter of Oedipus. In the face of adversity she stands her ground.

Creon. Remember: the hardest spirits are the most easily broken. The hardest iron is the first to snap. A little curb calms an unruly horse. What pride she has, for a slave . . . a slave to duty. She deliberately insults me. She sets me at defiance and boasts about it. If I let her, she would be the man. Though I am brother to Jocasta, neither Antigone nor her sister shall escape their fate. For Ismene must be her accomplice: Let her be brought before me. A moment ago I caught sight of her in the palace, panic-stricken as a bat. The spirits of night betray themselves quickly. What I hate beyond all else is a criminal who, when caught in the act, tries to glorify his crime.

Antigone. You demand more than my death?

Creon. No.

ANTIGONE *and* CREON *stand close together as they speak to each other. Their foreheads touch.*

Antigone. Then why drag things out? I do not like you. You do not like me. All these people would applaud me if it were not for the fear which paralyzes their tongues. Despotism adds to its thousand privileges the right to say and hear what it likes.

Creon. You alone in Thebes are discontented.

Antigone. They are all discontented but in your presence —silent.

Creon. Are you not ashamed?

Antigone. Ashamed of honoring a brother?

Creon. And your brother Eteocles? Was he not also your brother? Eteocles, who died at our side?

Antigone. We had the same father and mother.

Creon. Why insult him, then, by unpatriotic homage?

Antigone. That is not how the dead man testifies at my trial.

Creon. What? You serve a traitor?

Antigone. Dead, he is not Eteocles' enemy but his brother.

Creon. He came to attack his country. Eteocles was defending it.

Antigone. Death demands a single law for all.

Creon. But invaded and invader should not be treated alike.

Antigone. Who knows if your frontiers have meaning in the land of the dead?

Creon. An enemy dead never became a friend.

Antigone. I was born to share love, not hatred.

Creon. Descend to the dead and love whom you please. But while I live, no woman will make the laws.

Chorus. Here is poor Ismene in tears. Grief disfigures her and waters her cheeks.

Creon. Ah! there you are, viper. Come along, speak: did you or did you not know of the high treason that has been committed?

Ismene. If my sister confesses, I confess, and wish to take the consequences.

Antigone. The court forbids you to do so. You did not want to follow me. I acted alone.

Ismene. You are unhappy. I want to follow you now. You are in trouble.

Antigone. Too late, Ismene, too late. The underworld and those who live there have seen me act alone. I set little store by a sister who loves me in words.

Ismene. Antigone, do not take from me the honor of dying with you, the honor of having buried our brother.

Antigone. Do not die with me and do not boast, my dear. It is enough that *I* should die.

Ismene. Without you, how can I enjoy life?

Antigone. Ask Creon. Aren't you his puppet?

Ismene. Why do you like to hurt me?

Antigone. I laugh at you. A hollow laugh. And my mockery hurts me.

Ismene. What can I do to help?

Antigone. Spare your days. I don't envy you that good fortune.

Ismene. Let me share your destiny.

Antigone. You have chosen to live, I to die.

Ismene. You can't say I didn't tell you often enough!

Antigone. Your advice was good; I found my project better.

Ismene. Your fault is ours.

Antigone. Don't worry. You will live. My heart has been dead a long time already. It can only be of use to the dead.

Creon. These two girls are raving mad.

Ismene. We have suffered enough to make us lose our reason.

Creon. That's what happens if you insist on sharing the criminal's punishment.

Ismene. How do you expect me to live without Antigone?

Creon. No more of her. She is dead.

Ismene. You will kill your son's betrothed?

Creon. He will find other wombs.

Ismene. This is the only marriage he desires.

Creon. I will not have a bad daughter-in-law.

Antigone. O, my dear Haemon, how your father speaks of you!

Creon. I begin to weary of you and your wedding.

Chorus. Can you deprive your son of the one he loves?

Creon. Death shall break off their engagement.

Ismene. Is her death certain?

Creon. Certain. Enough time wasted! Guards, arrest these women! The bravest flee when death approaches.

[*They go out.*

Chorus. Happy are the innocent. Fatality has settled on this family. I see new misfortunes heaping up on the old for the house of Labdacus.² A god pursues them. Relentlessly. Jupiter, you never sleep: you dwell on Olympus, eternally young. But the race of man cannot enjoy unbroken peace. It runs into every disaster. For, when a god leads us to destruction, he alters the positions of good and evil. But here is Haemon. Is he coming to make complaint?

Creon. My son, you know the crime and the sentence. Do you come to us as a rebel? Or are we still as dear to you?

Haemon. I bow to your will. After your wise counsel, there can be no question of marriage.

Creon. Well said. A son should obey. Of what good are sons if not to love our friends and inflict on our enemies the damage they deserve? In the embrace of an unworthy spouse, you would freeze. So let this young woman marry someone in the underworld. She talks of laws of Jupiter, laws of kinship! So far, so good. But if I suffer my next of kin to rebel, what can I expect from the Thebans? Severity for all or none. I will not sing the praises of anyone who opposes my rule. Anarchy is the greatest evil. It ruins towns, breaks up families, infects the army—and a woman anarchist is the end of everything; better yield to a man. It shall not be said that a woman led *me* by the nose.

Chorus. If age has not entirely disturbed my brain, it seems to me, O King, that you express yourself with exquisite wisdom.

² Founder of the Oedipus family. Laius, son of Labdacus, was the father of Oedipus and Creon.

Haemon. You are wise, Father, but others can be wise too. I am so placed that I hear what everyone thinks of you. You terrorize the people. They whisper the words you prevent them from speaking out loud. I can hear them. I wander about. I stumble upon secret meetings. I know how Thebes judges this noble and glorious girl whom you condemn. "What? Is she to be killed for burying her brother? Why, she ought to be honored for it!" Such is the public rumor.

As for me, I respect your rule beyond everything else. But, Father, do not persist in thinking you are always right, and you alone. The man who thinks that he alone has wisdom, eloquence, and power is exposing himself to ridicule. Intelligence allows one to contradict oneself. If a captain blindly kept his canvas stretched, he would soon capsize his ship. Lower your sail. Be calm. Believe me. I am very young, but I know I am pleading a just cause.

Chorus. O King, if he is right, listen to him. If he is wrong, may he listen to you. On either side the trial is in excellent hands.

Creon. What, what? Are we to learn justice from a schoolboy?

Haemon. Again unjust! Age does not count. Do not consider my age; consider my acts.

Creon. Is it acting well to praise anarchists?

Haemon. I could not praise the wicked.

Creon. And is this woman not wicked? Is she not eaten up with wickedness?

Haemon. That is not the opinion of the street.

Craen. Splendid! Now *the street* is to show me my way!

Haemon. Now *you* have spoken like a young man, and you know it.

Creon. Am I to guide the city in one direction and my life in another?

Haemon. No city was ever made for one man.

Creon. The city is the legitimate spouse of her lord.

Haemon. Live in an empty city if you want to rule alone.

Creon. He seems to side with a girl!

Haemon. That makes *you* a girl, for you are my chief concern.

Creon. Brat! You are insulting your father!

Haemon. Because I see my father being unjust.

Creon. Is it unjust for me to uphold my prerogatives?

Haemon. Your prerogatives! You are trampling on the will of the gods!

Creon. Soft heart! You let a woman get around you!

Haemon. Maybe. At any rate, false proceedings will never get around me.

Creon. You are just pleading for her.

Haemon. And for you and for me and for the infernal gods.

Creon. You shall never marry her alive!

Haemon. Then I'll marry her dead. In the underworld!

Creon. You threaten me with suicide!

Haemon. I threaten nothing. I am trying to combat your injustice.

Creon. You will repent, Mr. Reasoner!

Haemon. If I were not your son, I would say you were evading the issue.

Creon. Slave to women, beware! Do not drive me crazy with your tongue-wagging!

Haemon. You talk all the time and listen to no one.

Creon. Ha! Is that how things are? Soldiers, bring in the madwoman, bring in the madwoman! Quick! Quick! That she may die before the eyes of her betrothed.

Haemon. You are mistaken. She will not die in my presence. This is the last time I speak to you. Farewell. Exercise your rage before your courtiers; they will put up with it.

Chorus. O King, he is leaving. He is running. He is beside himself. At his age, despair can be dangerous.

Creon. Let him try his utmost. He will not save them.

Chorus. What! Are you condemning Ismene as well as Antigone?

Creon. No. Not her who has not touched the corpse. Your remark is just.

Chorus. And what kind of death have you in store for the other?

Creon. I shall wall her up alive in a desert cavern. I shall leave her some food, just enough for her expiation. She will have plenty of time to pray to Pluto. She will see if the infernal gods will protect her.[3]

Chorus. Love that seizes all and sundry. Love that makes the rich poor and the poor rich, love that fires the maiden's cheek, love that crosses the sea and penetrates the cattle stalls—none can escape you, among the immortal gods or among short-lived men. When she unleashes desire, Venus is invincible. At this very moment, I myself, unfaithful to my prince, weep to see Antigone walking toward her tomb.

ANTIGONE *appears on the left between two* GUARDS. *She stops.*

Antigone. Citizens of my country, behold me. I start out on my last journey. I look for the last time at the light of the sun. The god of Hades will take me alive. I shall not have known marriage. No wedding song will have echoed my name. Death will espouse me.

Chorus. Then you will die without sickness, without a wound. You will go to Pluto free, virgin, living, renowned, alone among mortals.

Antigone. I have heard how the daughter of Tantalus died. Suddenly, at the top of Sipylus, she felt the rock take her and grow around her like strong ivy. And now the snow cloaks her and its icy tears run down her body. Such will be my bed, and such the caresses that await me. [*Advances.*

Chorus. Ah yes, but we are just poor human beings and she was a goddess and daughter of a god. After all, for a simple mortal like you, it is a great consolation to have the fate of a divinity.

Antigone. Mock me! It is the right moment. Mock me! They do not even wait for me to disappear! My city! Thebes, the town of the fine carriages! See how they laugh as they push me toward a nameless hole. [*Stops.*

[3] Creon has no intention of *murdering* Antigone. Being walled up is a formal ordeal: the infernal gods may save her if they approve her conduct. (Pluto, the infernal gods, and the underworld [Hades] did not have associations like those of Satan, the minor devils, and hell.) [E.B.]

Nameless! For I am going to a dwelling place not of men, nor of shades, nor of the living, nor of the dead.

Chorus. It is your own fault. You have done violence to justice. You are still paying for Oedipus.

Antigone. I am a daughter of incest. That is why I die.

Chorus. The cult of the dead is a fine thing. But it is not a fine thing to disobey our masters. It is pride that has undone you.

Antigone. Nothing. Nothing. Nothing and no one. I go to my execution quite alone, with no one to pity me, no husband, no friend, no encouragement. Never again shall I see the light. Never see day's golden eye. Never see the sun! [*Advances.*

Creon. You have said this already. If we all made such a song and dance about dying, there'd be no end to it. Quick now! Take her away! Imprison her and leave her!

As ANTIGONE *springs forward, the left-hand* GUARD *drops his lance in front of her. The right-hand* GUARD *grasps the end.* ANTIGONE *seizes the lance. She looks like a woman in a prisoner's dock between two policemen.*

Antigone. Farewell. Let them steal my share of life. I go to see my father and mother again, and Eteocles. When you died I washed you and closed your eyes. I closed your eyes, too, Polynices—and—I—did—right! I should never have made that fateful effort for children or for a husband. A husband—he can be replaced. A son—another can be conceived. But, our parents being dead, I could not hope for more brothers. It was for this reason that I acted, that I am being struck down, and that Creon is denying me marriage and maternity.

What, then, have I done to the gods? They abandon me. If they approve my executioners, I shall know it tomorrow and regret my act. But, if the gods *dis*approve—let them inflict on my executioners my tortures! [*Advances.*

Chorus. Her spirit does not relax.

Creon. It will cost her escort dear if they insist on dawdling.

Antigone. My death will not last long.

Creon. Do not imagine that the torture consists simply in frightening you.

ANTIGONE, *escorted by the* GUARDS, *comes to the lower forestage. One of the* GUARDS *enters the trap, the other follows, pulling* ANTIGONE *lightly by the cloak. She disappears in her turn.*

ANTIGONE [*Waist-deep in the trap*]. My Thebes! it is finished. They bear me away. Chiefs! Theban chiefs! Your last princess is suffering outrage. See what I suffer. See what men punish me for my love.   [ANTIGONE *disappears.*

Chorus. Danaë also was buried alive and sleeps in bronze; and yet, my child, she was of high descent and bore the golden seed of Jupiter. Bacchus turned the son of Dryas into stone. That young man much regrets having jostled the Maenads, having put out their torches and laughed at the Muses.[4]

TIRESIAS *enters left, guided by a young boy.*

Tiresias. Theban chiefs, we are here, one in two. For I am blind and can only walk with a guide.

Creon. What news, Tiresias?

Tiresias. You shall hear. But obey.

Creon. I have always believed you.

Tiresias. And so you have governed in a straight line— but you now turn from it.

Creon. You frighten me.

Tiresias. This child leads me and I lead others. He has seen our altars covered with the rotting remains of Polynices. Dogs and vultures brought them. Since then, the gods reject our sacrifices and beasts, gorged with carrion, are howling everywhere.[5] Believe me, my son. That a man may make a mistake we can well admit, but that he should persist is a proof of stupidity. Cease striking a dead man. It is my love for you that speaks.

Creon. So! I am now an archer's target. And you all attack me in your fury. All right! Get rich! Trade away! Win

[4] Because they took a terrible revenge. [E.B.]
[5] Bad omens.

all the gold of Sardis and India. Polynices shall never be buried. Were eagles to bear his carcass to Jupiter's throne, I should still refuse. A mortal cannot defile the gods. You are paid money, Tiresias: that is the sign of your downfall.

Tiresias. Oh for a man! A man who knows! Who would understand!

Creon. The oracle clique[6] is greedy for money.

Tiresias. And that of the kings is greedy for taxes.

Creon. You realize I am your king?

Tiresias. I realize it all the more since you owe your throne and the welfare of Thebes to me.

Creon. You like paradoxes.

Tiresias. You force me to say that which I wished to dissimulate.

Creon. Speak, but do no service to whoever it is that pays you.

Tiresias. Do I appear so rich?

Creon. And know that I shall not change my mind.

Tiresias. Know in your turn that the death of your son will pay for the crime of burying a woman alive and contending with Pluto for a corpse. Your palace will be filled with lamentations. Anger is rousing the towns against you. For men see the beasts dragging gory hunks of flesh. Lead me, little one. May this man learn in future to moderate his language and respect my age and yours.

[*Exit.*

Chorus. Creon, his oracles are never wrong.

Creon. Alas! My mind is disturbed . . . let me see . . . it is terrible to yield . . . on the other hand it is terrible to bring on misfortune by persisting. What do you advise?

Chorus. Save the girl.

Creon. That! And you want me to give way?

Chorus. But you must hurry. The vengeance of the gods comes full speed.

Creon. Well, if I must. . . . [*He groans.*] . . . it is hard . . . very hard.

Chorus Go. Go. Go. Do it yourself.

Creon. I fly. Follow with axes, picks, and crowbars. I fear

---

[6] The group of priests who guard the oracle. [E.B.]

it is impossible to keep to the old laws always.   [*Exit.*

Chorus. O you who are crowned with a thousand names: Bacchus! dweller in Thebes, metropolis of Bacchantes, you make the stars dance and the night sing. Tread the mountain with your great feet as if it were grapes. Run! Fly! Help us! Leap this way with your drunken horde!

Empty stage and music.[7]

Messenger. Fellow citizens of Cadmus,[8] fortune is fickle. I used to envy Creon. Now his luck is failing him. Riches and a throne: what are they without joy?

Chorus. Speak.

Messenger. Haemon has committed suicide.

Chorus. O Tiresias! Here is Queen Eurydice. She must have heard something.

Eurydice [*Appearing at the top of the steps, left. She speaks with difficulty*]. That is . . . at least . . . I have . . . overheard a little. I was opening the door of the temple of Minerva—I nearly fainted. What has happened? I must listen. I can bear to listen to you. Go on. I am strong. I have some experience of misfortune.

Messenger. O my dear mistress, listen to a witness' tale. Having, with the help of the king, buried the remains of Polynices and prayed to the goddess of the cross-roads,[9] we were running to Antigone's cavern, when Creon thought he heard his son shouting inside. We broke in with pickaxes and saw a pitiful sight: Antigone hanging from a rope made up of her veils. Haemon was pressing the unhappy girl to his breast. At the sight of Creon, Haemon lost his head, drew his sword, and spat at his father. Creon saw the rage and disgust in his eyes, saw the danger too, and fled. Then Haemon plunged the blade into his own body. His heart bespattered Antigone. They are married in death and blood.

[7] In the 1927 revival, a masked prologue, a sort of living statue which preceded the play, crossed the stage during this musical interlude. [J.C.]

[8] Cadmus was the founder of Thebes. [E.B.]

[9] Hecate. As a goddess of the underworld she was offended by the denial of the funeral rites. [E.B.]

Having received the full force of this blow,
EURYDICE *recoils and disappears.*

Chorus. Not a word from the queen. What must we think?

Long pause.

Messenger. She does not wish to make a show of herself.

Long pause.

Chorus. Silence is more frightening than cries.

Long pause.

Messenger. Yes. I am going to investigate.

The MESSENGER *enters the palace.*

Chorus. The king! Bearing his son.
Creon [*Dragging the body on his back. He makes it roll on to the ground, kneels and caresses its hair*]. My son! My son! Haemon! Oh, my son! I am a murderer. I killed you.
Chorus. This is very late.
Creon. A god held me by the throat, a god pushed me in the back. The whole house of happiness collapses upon me.
Messenger. Yes, prince. One tragedy upon another.
Creon. Another tragedy! What? [*He points to his son stretched out.*] What more could happen?
Messenger. Your wife is dead.
Creon. My wife is dead? It is not true! Ah, Pluto, you devour all. My wife after my son. You are lying. Where is she?
Messenger. Look! The door is open.

CREON *mounts the steps on the left.*

Creon. Eurydice!
Messenger. She committed suicide at the foot of the altar, calling you murderer.
Creon. I am afraid. Kill me! Kill me quickly! I am falling into a bottomless hole!

Messenger. She accused you of the murder of Haemon and of Antigone.

Creon [*Stupefied*]. What was it? You were saying? . . . She has killed herself? My wife has killed herself?

Messenger. I say it again.

Creon. Help! Take me away! Take me away from here! I am less than nothing, less than nothing. I do not know where to look. I do not know where to put my hands, my feet. Everything is going, slipping from under me. A thunderbolt is falling on my head.

Chorus. One should beware of insulting the gods. Too late, Creon, too late.

CURTAIN

INTIMATE RELATIONS

(*Les parents terribles*)

English version by Charles Frank

CHARACTERS

YVONNE. *Yvonne confesses somewhere in the play that she is forty-five years old. She is not very tall and has the kind of face that makes her look eighteen one day and a hundred the next. She can be full of charm or full of poison, and she never mixes the two. It would be hard to say whether Yvonne has been or still is beautiful. It depends entirely on whatever impression she wishes to make on the person she happens to be dealing with at the time.*

LÉONIE. *Léonie (or Léo, as everybody calls her) is Yvonne's elder sister. She is supposed to be forty-seven. However, the two ladies do not look like sisters at all. Léo is tall, exceedingly well groomed, and highly attractive. Everything about her is shiny and resplendent. She is the representative of "order" as against Yvonne's, Michael's, and George's preference for "disorder."*

MADELEINE. *Madeleine is twenty-five. Her hair is a natural golden blonde. She is not perhaps of a classical beauty, but she is extremely attractive. In fact, she is irresistible. She is not tall, and she is very simply but delightfully dressed.*

GEORGE. *George is a well-preserved middle-aged man. He may be a little older than his wife, Yvonne, but not much. He is of medium height, not terribly tall, and he has never had the looks of the proverbial film star, but he has a good face and a kind face and is altogether a most likable fellow.*

MICHAEL. *Michael, Yvonne's and George's son, is twenty-two. He is a little taller than his father, very good-looking, very charming, and in many ways young for his age. He is, however, not quite as young anymore as his mother likes to think.*

The time is today.
The place is PARIS.

NOTE: Both sets must be built solidly enough to allow for the doors to be slammed ad lib.

Yvonne's room represents the world of disorder, Madeleine's the world of order.

INTIMATE RELATIONS

ACT ONE

SCENE—YVONNE's *bedroom. The door to* LÉO's *room is on the left in the wings. Downstage left, there is an arm-chair and a dressing table. Upstage left, there is a door leading to the rest of the flat. Upstage right, another door leading to the bathroom, which appears to be white and brightly lit. The door to the hall is in the wings on the right. Upstage right, with the foot toward the center, a very big and very untidy bed. Dressing gowns, scarves, towels, etc., are scattered over it. By the end of the bed, a chair. Upstage center, a large cupboard, large double doors below, small double doors above. One wing of the upper double doors has the awkward habit of open-ing slowly at the most unexpected moments, and fre-quently, during the action,* LÉO *automatically tries to shut it, only for it to open a few seconds later. Near the bed, a small table with a lamp. The chandelier in the center of the room is not alight. More dressing gowns lie about un-tidily. The windows are felt to be at the side of the audi-torium. An unpleasant half light comes from them, that of the block of flats opposite. The lighting in the room is dim.*

As the curtain rises, GEORGE, *dressed in an ordinary flannel suit, runs from the bathroom to* LÉO's *door and, knocking on it frantically, calls:*

GEORGE. Léo! Léo! Quick—where are you?

Léo's voice. What is it? Michael?

George. No! Never mind Michael! Hurry up!

Léo [*Fastening a very smart dressing gown*]. What's the matter?

George. It's Yvonne. She's poisoned herself.

Léo [*Flabbergasted*]. Poisoned herself?

George. With her insulin. She must have taken much too much.

71

Léo. Where is she?

George. There—in the bathroom.

YVONNE *opens the bathroom door already ajar and enters. She is wearing a somewhat dilapidated bathrobe. She is deadly pale and can hardly stand on her feet.*

Léo. Yvonne—what have you done? [*Crosses over to her and supports her.*] Yvonne! [YVONNE *shakes her head.*] Tell me, what have you done?

Yvonne [*Almost inaudibly*]. Sugar . . .

George. I'll get the doctor. It's Sunday. He'll be out!

Léo. Don't lose your head. Fetch the sugar. [*She helps* YVONNE *to lie down on her bed.*] Don't you know yet if you don't eat after taking insulin, you must take sugar?

George. Good Heavens, of course! [*He rushes into the bathroom and comes back stirring the sugar in a glass of water.*]

Léo [*Taking it and making* YVONNE *drink it*]. Drink it up . . . come on, try . . . make an effort . . . surely you don't want to die before you've seen Michael again!

YVONNE *braces herself up and drinks.*

George. I'm stupid! If you hadn't been here, Léo, I should just have let her die. . . .

Léo [*To* YVONNE]. How do you feel?

Yvonne [*Very faintly*]. It's working. I'm better. Please forgive me.

George. I can still hear the doctor say: "No ordinary household sugar; get some cane sugar." Why didn't I think of it? The glass is always prepared in the bathroom.

Yvonne [*Her voice is a little clearer*]. It was my fault.

Léo. One never knows where one is with a crazy creature like you.

Yvonne [*Sitting up and smiling*]. I was a touch crazier than usual.

George. Exactly! That's what muddled me up.

Yvonne. Léo, at any rate, is not crazy. Still, I had no intention of springing this pleasant little surprise on Michael.

George. I wish he was as considerate.

LÉO *arranges the pillows behind her back.*

Yvonne. Well, this is what happened. It was five o'clock, time for my injection. Just when I'd finished and should have taken the sugar, I thought I heard the lift stop at our floor. I ran to the hall to see if it was Michael. On the way back to the bathroom, I almost fainted. George turned up by a miracle.

George. It *was* a miracle.

Léo. Nonsense, you were working up in the clouds as usual and you heard five o'clock strike down here on earth, and walked along here automatically to see if Yvonne had remembered her injection. It wasn't a miracle at all.

Yvonne [*To* GEORGE]. Never mind her. Without you . . .

George. And without Léo . . .

Yvonne. If you two hadn't been here, both of you, I would have caused you a lot of unnecessary suffering and only because I'm feeling a bit hurt myself.

George. You *have* been caused a lot of unnecessary suffering! Michael did not come home last night! Damn it all, he knows you! He can guess the state you must be in. Your nerves are all to pieces or you wouldn't have forgotten your sugar. It's outrageous.

Yvonne. If only nothing has happened to him. Do you think it has, and they daren't ring us up?

George. If something had happened, we'd have heard. No, no! It's in-cred*d*ible! [1]

Yvonne. But where can he be? Where is he?

Léo. Don't excite yourself after this shock. Don't excite her, George. Why don't you go back to your work? We'll call you if we need you.

Yvonne. Yes, you go back and try to work.

George [*Mumbling as he goes*]. I can't seem to get my figures right. I put them down and I add them up, but they're always wrong and I keep starting all over again. . . .

[1] This word is to be pronounced in a special fashion and is for reasons of this particular pronunciation spelled with double "dd" except when pronounced in the ordinary way.

LÉO *listens at the door to make sure* GEORGE *has gone.*

Yvonne. Léo, where did that child spend the night? He must know I'm going mad here with worry! Why doesn't he ring me up? Surely he could phone. . . .

Léo. That depends. Certain . . . honest . . . slightly awkward boys . . . like Michael, are not much good at lying on the telephone.

Yvonne. Why should Mick lie to me?

Léo. Well, it must be one of two things. Either he daren't come home or else he feels so happy wherever he is that he's forgotten. At any rate, he is hiding something.

Yvonne. You can't teach me anything about Mick. "Forgotten to come home"—it's ridiculous. Perhaps he's in some terrible danger; perhaps he *can't* phone!

Léo. One can always telephone. Michael can but won't. [*She picks up a stray silk stocking and puts it away.*]

Yvonne. You're so calm and composed. You must know something.

Léo. Yes, but there's no point in my telling you, you wouldn't believe it, you'd only say "It's in-cre*dd*ible!" And it *is* incredible the way you've all started to use that word lately.

Yvonne. Nonsense, it's one of Michael's expressions.

Léo [*Softly*]. Maybe. It's rather funny how a word sometimes sneaks into a family and gets itself adopted. Where does it come from, I wonder? I'd very much like to know.

Yvonne [*Laughing*]. Well, and why shouldn't a bunch of lunatics and gypsies like us, a family that lives in a caravan——

Léo [*Interrupting*]. You're trying to be funny because I once said this flat was like a gypsy caravan. Well, so it is, and I repeat it. And I also repeat that you're a bunch of lunatics.

Yvonne. The house is a caravan. Agreed. We're all lunatics. Agreed. And whose fault is it?

Léo [*Exasperated*]. That's it: dig up grandfather again!

Yvonne [*Unperturbed*]. Grandfather who collected semicolons. He counted the semicolons in Victor Hugo. He

said: "I make it 37,000 semicolons in *Les Misérables*."
And then he started all over again in case he'd made a
mistake. Only in those days they wouldn't call him crazy,
they would say, "He had a mania." Nowadays with a bit
of good will, you can call anybody crazy.

Léo. So you admit you're lunatics. I see.

Yvonne. And you're a lunatic, too, in your own way.

Léo. Possibly. I certainly have a mania for order and
you for disorder. You know very well why uncle left his
money to me. He knew I should have to keep you all.

Yvonne. Léonie . . . !

Léo. Don't get excited. I'm not complaining. Nobody
admired George more than I. And I am only too glad that,
thanks to this legacy, he can carry on with his research.

Yvonne. Well, that you of all people should take this
research business seriously—it beats me! Now George, now
there's a typical lunatic for you! Perfecting the underwater
rifle! Between you and me, it's ridiculous, and at his age,
too.

Léo. George is a child. He likes pottering about but he *is*
an inventor. You're being unfair.

Yvonne. The electronic underwater submachine gun!
The one thing that was missing in our caravan! We've
already got the fortuneteller, that's me telling the cards
in my old dressing gown. Then there's you, the lion tamer;
you'd be terrific as a lion tamer. And Mick . . . Mick . . .

Léo. The Eighth Wonder of the World!

Yvonne. Don't be nasty. . . .

Léo. I am not being nasty, but I've been watching you,
Yvonne, since yesterday. There are two kinds of people
in this world: the children and the grownups. I, alas, belong to the grownups; you, George, Mick . . . you belong
to the children, who never stop being children, who would
commit crimes——

Yvonne [*Stopping her*]. Sh! . . . Listen! [*Silence.*] No,
I thought I heard a taxi. You were talking of crimes, I
think you were calling us criminals just now——

Léo. Why can't you listen to me properly. . . . I am
talking of crimes that people commit simply because they
don't know what they're doing. There's no such thing as

simple souls. Any country priest will tell you that. Even in the tiniest village there exist instincts of murder, incest, and theft such as you won't find in the big cities. No, I wasn't calling you criminals. On the contrary! The background of real criminals is sometimes preferable to the twilight which you enjoy so much and which I detest!

Yvonne. Mick must have had too much to drink. He is not used to it. He has stayed with a friend. Perhaps he's asleep. Perhaps he's ashamed. It's unforgivable of him to make me go through that awful night and this endless day, but I must say I can't call it criminal.

Léo [*Approaching* YVONNE's *bed*]. Tell me, Yvonne, are you pulling my leg?

Yvonne. I beg your pardon. . . .

Léo [*Taking her by the chin*]. No, you're not. I thought you were putting on an act, I was wrong. You're just blind.

Yvonne [*Brushing* LÉO's *hand away*]. Explain yourself, will you!

Léo [*Taking a step back*]. Michael has spent the night with a woman.

Yvonne. Michael?

Léo. Yes, Michael.

Yvonne. You must be out of your mind. Mick is a child. You said so yourself just now. . . .

Léo. Oh, Heavens, he's no longer a child the way you're thinking. He is a man. [YVONNE *looks at her amazed.*] Well, he's twenty-two!

Yvonne. Well . . .

Léo. You're fantastic . . . you're reaping what you've been sowing, but you don't see it.

Yvonne. What have I been "sowing"? And what am I "reaping"?

Léo. You've been sowing dirty washing, cigarette ends, and the Lord knows what, and you're reaping this: Michael is suffocating in your Caravan and he has gone to get some fresh air.

Yvonne. And you're suggesting that he's gone to get this fresh air in the company of women, of prostitutes?

Léo. Ah, now we're back at the old clichés! D'you want

to know why Michael did not telephone? So as not to hear at the other end: "Come home at once, your father wishes to speak to you," or some such middle-class rubbish. Now I ask you, what does it mean: a family of the upper middle class? It means a well-to-do family with everything in perfect order and with domestic servants. Here, there's no money, no order, and no servants. No maid stays longer than four days, I've had to make do with a daily who doesn't come on Sundays. But the old principles and the old slogans are still going strong!

Yvonne. What's the matter with you, Leo . . . ? You're getting so excited. . . .

Léo. I'm not getting excited, but there are moments when you go too far! D'you know why there's a mountain of dirty washing piling up right in the middle of Michael's room? D'you know why the dust on George's desk is so thick that he could write his figures in it with his finger? Why the bath has been stopped up for a week and hasn't been seen to yet?

Yvonne [Surprised]. Is the bath stopped up?

Léo [Exasperated]. Oh! Because sometimes it gives me a kind of morbid satisfaction watching you sink and sink and drown, till my mania for order gets the better of me and I have to come to your rescue.

Yvonne. Hm. And according to you, our Caravan has driven Michael to find himself a better home . . . with some woman or other.

Léo. He isn't the only one.

Yvonne. You mean George. . . .

Léo. I mean George.

Yvonne. Are you accusing George of being unfaithful to me?

Léo. I'm not accusing anyone. I don't indulge in gossip.

Yvonne. Have you found out that George is deceiving me?

Léo. Well, you're deceiving him, aren't you?

Yvonne. I . . . deceiving George . . . with whom?

Léo. Ever since Michael was born you've been unfaithful to George. You stopped looking after George, and

you only cared for Michael. You adored him . . . you
were crazy about him. And the more he grew up, the
crazier you got about him. . . . And George was left
alone. And you are surprised that he should have looked
elsewhere for a little affection.

Yvonne. All right . . . suppose all this nonsense is
true, that George who is only interested in his so-called
invention is having an affair, and that Michael who tells
me everything and who calls me his best friend . . . has
spent the night with a woman—why didn't you tell me
before?

Léo. I couldn't believe you were blind. I thought: it's
impossible. Yvonne is making the best of it. She is shutting
her eyes to it . . .

Yvonne [*Very strained*]. George . . . in a way . . .
I could understand. . . . After twenty years of married
life one's love changes. . . . There is a kind of relationship which would make certain things . . . very embarrassing . . . almost indecent . . . in fact, quite impossible.

Léo. You are a strange woman, Yvonne. . . .

Yvonne. Not at all . . . but I must appear strange to
you, there's such a world between us. Just think: you've
always been beautiful, elegant, well-groomed and well-
permanented—and I came into the world with chronic
hay fever, my hair in a constant mess, and my dressing
gowns riddled with cigarette holes. And if I use powder
and rouge I look like a tart.

Léo. You are forty-five and I am forty-seven.

Yvonne. You look much younger than I do.

Léo. All the same, George chose you. He was engaged
to me. Suddenly he decided you were the one he wanted,
you were the one he was going to marry.

Yvonne. You couldn't have wanted him very much.
You almost threw us together.

Léo. That's my business. I was afraid that with me
everything came from here [*She taps her head.*]—with
you it was all there—[*She taps her heart.*]—or thereabouts.
I didn't know you wanted a son so desperately—and of
course spoiled children like you always get what they want

—and I didn't think that you'd be so crazy about him that you'd drop George altogether.

Yvonne [*Sarcastically*]. George could always have gone to you for comfort.

Léo. So you would have liked me to sleep with George to get him out of your way. . . . No, thank you, I prefer to remain an old maid.

Yvonne [*Wearily*]. Oh, really. . . .

Léo [*Equally ironically.*] Besides, he wouldn't have wanted me anyway, it's youth he's after!

Yvonne. Well, well, well!

Léo. You needn't believe it, but it doesn't alter the fact, Yvonne. There are certain things even an old maid notices. There's a phantom, a female phantom, a very young one, flitting about the house.

Yvonne. It's in-cred*d*ible!

Léo. There's that word again! George brought it here. Michael caught it and then you . . . like measles.

Yvonne. Is that so! And I suppose Michael, too, is unfaithful to me, I mean is lying to me——

Léo. You were right the first time; there's no need to take it back: he's *been* unfaithful to you, he is *being* unfaithful to you.

Yvonne. I can't imagine it. It's impossible. I don't want to, I cannot imagine it.

Léo. You don't seem to mind the idea of George deceiving you. But Michael, that's another story. . . .

Yvonne. It's a lie! Michael and I have always been friends, he can tell me everything.

Léo. No mother is a friend to her son. Soon enough he finds out that the "friend" is a bit of a spy and the spy nothing but a jealous woman.

Yvonne. Mick doesn't see me as a woman.

Léo. That's where you're so wrong. You just refuse to see Michael as a man! To you he is still the little Michael you used to carry to bed and who was allowed to play in your bedroom while you were dressing. In Michael's eyes you have become a woman. And you're very silly not to try and be a little more glamorous. He has watched you and judged you, and he's left the Caravan.

Yvonne. And where would the poor boy find the time to devote himself to this mysterious woman?

Léo. Time is elastic. With a little ingenuity one can be in one place and pretend to be in another.

Yvonne. What are you talking about? I've seen the drawings he brings back from Art School.

Léo. D'you find Mick very gifted at drawing?

Yvonne. He is gifted at all sorts of things.

Léo. Exactly! He knows a bit of everything and nothing properly. Maybe if he really went to the Art School, his drawings would look a little different.

Yvonne. I stopped him from going to life classes.

Léo. How could you make yourself so ridiculous!

Yvonne. He was only eighteen. . . .

Léo. You have the most peculiar ideas about age and sex.

Yvonne. Michael *is* working hard.

Léo. Not a bit of it. Besides, you don't want him to. You're not a bit keen that he should work.

Yvonne. Well, that's a new one!

Léo. Yvonne, you've always prevented Michael from taking a job!

Yvonne. If you can call them that.

Léo. He was offered a number of jobs, and he could have earned his living.

Yvonne. I made inquiries every time. They were such stupid jobs. He would have had to mix with a lot of film people and car people—awful people! George always found him the most ridiculous jobs!

Léo. One of them was very good. But he would have had to go abroad. You wouldn't even let him go to the interview.

Yvonne. It was Michael who didn't want to go.

Léo. Have you ever encouraged him? Did you ever let him meet boys and girls of his own age? Ever thought of him getting married?

Yvonne [*Horrified*]. Mick . . . getting married?

Léo. Why not? Lots of young men get married at twenty-three or twenty-four . . .

Yvonne. But Mick is a baby!

Léo. And if he weren't a baby any longer?

Yvonne. I should be the first to find him a wife.

Léo. Yes . . . some stupid, ugly girl who would let you go on playing first fiddle and dominating your son.

Yvonne. You're quite wrong. Michael is completely free. That is, as far as is good for such an unsophisticated boy . . . who's so much sought after.

Léo. Well, I warn you, don't try to lock him up. If he finds out . . . he may not like it.

Yvonne. I didn't know you were such a psychologist. [*Without a break.*] Oh, dear, someone's ringing at the door! [*The doorbell rings.*] Oh, you go, Léo, go quickly! I haven't the strength.

Léo *exits by the door on the right. She is barely gone when* YVONNE *snatches the handbag that* Léo *has left on the bed. She opens it, looks at herself in the mirror, powders her nose, puts on lipstick, and tidies her hair. The door opens. She has just time to throw back the bag where it was. Enter* Léo *and* GEORGE. GEORGE *puts on the light.*

Yvonne [*Turning away*]. Who put the light on?

George. I did. I'll turn it off. I thought . . . it's so dark in your room.

Yvonne. I like it dark. . . . Who was it?

George. Someone for the doctor upstairs. I told him the doctor was out. He always goes shooting on Sundays. [*Silence.*] Any news?

Yvonne. No.

George. The specialist's gone shooting, too. If you're ill on a Sunday, you can just die. [*Silence.*]

Yvonne. How silly of me . . . of course, Michael's got the keys.

George. It is absolutely intolerable that the keys of the flat should be dragged about all over the place!

Yvonne. He might easily have lost them.

George [*Very angrily and full of authority*]. And one day one wakes up and finds oneself murdered. He's got to return them at once.

Léo. It's a great pity one can't make a gramophone record of your conversation.

They are all grouped in the foreground. While they are talking, MICHAEL *enters through the door on the right without being heard. He looks very cheerful, like a boy who has just made a wonderful joke.*

Yvonne. What time is it?

Michael. Six o'clock. [*They all jump, even* YVONNE, *who stands near her bed.*] It's all right, it isn't my ghost, it's me.

George. Michael—how could you have frightened your mother like this! Look at her! How did you get here?

Michael [*While* LÉO *helps* YVONNE *back to bed*]. Through the door. I ran up four at a time . . . let me get my breath back . . . Sophie! What's the matter with you?

George. First of all, I find it impossible that at your age you should persist in calling your mother "Sophie."

Yvonne. That's been an old joke between us ever since I read him the forty-nine installments of *Sophie, The Problem Child.*

George. Your mother is not at all well, Michael!

Michael [*Tenderly*]. Sophie—did *I* get you into such a state? [*He approaches to kiss his mother.*]

Yvonne [*Pushing him away*]. Don't. . . .

Michael. Cheer up, all of you; I didn't commit a crime.

George. You very nearly did, my boy. Your mother almost died of anxiety. She lost her head over her injection. Luckily your aunt and I didn't lose ours!

Michael. I was so looking forward to seeing you all . . . to being back in the Caravan. . . . I wanted to kiss Mummy . . . I am terribly sorry. . . .

George. And so you should be! Where have you been?

Michael. Give me a chance. I've got an awful lot to tell you.

Léo [*To* GEORGE]. You see . . .

Michael. Aunt Léo's the only one who hasn't lost her head. As usual.

Léo. We had every reason for losing our heads, Michael.

I'm not joking. Today I sympathize entirely with your mother's attitude.

Michael. What have I done?

George. You didn't come home last night! You've spent the night out! And you didn't let us know when to expect you back!

Michael. I am twenty-two, Dad. . . . I've never done it before. I mean, really . . .

Yvonne. Where've you been? Your father's been asking you where you've been.

Michael. Listen, children . . . oh, sorry . . . listen, Dad, listen, Aunt Léo, don't spoil it all. . . . I wanted to——

Yvonne. You wanted to . . . you wanted to . . . your father gives the orders here. Besides, he wishes to speak to you. Follow him into his study.

Léo [*Copying them*]. In-creddible!

Michael. No, Sophie. First of all, Dad hasn't got a study; he's got a very untidy room. And then I'd like to speak to you alone, first.

George. My dear boy, I don't know if you visualize——

Michael. I can't visualize a thing, it's pitch dark in here. [*He switches on the table lamp.*]

Yvonne. Since Michael finds it easier to talk to me first . . . would you mind . . . ?

Léo [*Ironically*]. Of course—!

Yvonne. If Mick has something on his mind, it's only natural he should confide in his mother. George, go back to your work. Léo, take him with you.

Michael [*To* GEORGE *and* LÉO]. Don't be angry with me, I'll tell you everything. I can hardly wait.

Yvonne. It's nothing serious; is it, Mick?

Michael. N . . . o, yes and no.

Yvonne. George, you embarrass him.

Michael. That's right, Dad embarrasses me. And you, Aunt Léo, you're too clever.

Yvonne. And I'm his best friend. You see, Léo, I told you so.

Léo. Well, good luck. Come along, George. Let's get out of the confessional. [*She turns back toward* YVONNE.]

Don't you want the light switched off? You scolded George for turning it on.

Yvonne. That was the chandelier; the lamp doesn't worry me.

George [Before leaving]. I still want to talk to you, my boy; I haven't finished with you yet.   [*They exit.*

Michael. All right, Dad.

He shuts the door. Turning toward YVONNE, MICHAEL *puts his finger to his lips. He then winks at her and tiptoes back to the door, jerking it open.* LÉO, *who had had her ear against it, tumbles into the room.*

Léo [Shrugging]. Very funny. . . .   [*Dignified exit.*

Michael [Leaping across the room like a small boy and onto his mother's bed]. Sophie, my darling Sophie, you're not angry with me, are you. . . . [*He grabs her and kisses her forcibly while she struggles to free herself.*]

Yvonne. Can't you ever give me a kiss without knocking me about. . . . Stop pulling my hair. . . . [MICHAEL *continues.*] Not in the ear, Michael! I hate that. . . . Michael. . . .

Michael. I didn't do it on purpose.

Yvonne. I should hope not . . .

Michael [Leaning back and in a tone of phony surprise]. Oh, I say!

Yvonne. What—?

Michael. Oh, but Sophie, you've got lipstick on!

Yvonne. What, me?

Michael. Yes, you! *And* make-up. Nice goings-on! Is it for anyone in particular? It's in-creddible! Make-up . . . real make-up. . .

Yvonne. I was as white as a sheet, I didn't want to frighten your father.

Michael. Don't wipe it off, it looks nice on you. . . .

Yvonne. As if you ever noticed me. . . .

Michael. Sophie! You're actually making a scene! As if I didn't know you by heart. . . .

Yvonne. You may know me by heart but you never so much as look at me; you ignore me.

Michael. Far from it, madam. I am looking at you out of the corner of my eye, and I was even thinking that you were rather neglecting yourself lately.

Yvonne. Really—!

Michael. Yes. Now, if you'd only let me do your hair for you and make you up . . .

Yvonne [*Dryly*]. That would be charming.

Michael. Stop sulking, Sophie; you're still angry with me.

Yvonne. I never sulk. No, Mick, I'm not angry with you. I'd just like to know what's going on.

Michael. Patience—and you shall know everything.

Yvonne. I'm listening.

Michael. Don't look so solemn, darling, please don't look so solemn!

Yvonne. Michael!

Michael. Promise me not to put on the family act, the Caravan act! Promise me not to scream and that you'll let me explain to the end. Promise?

Yvonne. I don't promise anything.

Michael. You see—!

Yvonne. Other people are making much too much fuss over you. But when I tell you things as they are——

Michael. Sophie—I am going in to Dad. I'll tell him to take off his goggles and listen to me——

Yvonne [*Interrupting*]. Don't you make fun of your father's work.

Michael. You've always making fun of the electronic underwater submachine gun. . . .

Yvonne. That's different. It's bad enough that I let you call me Sophie . . . except in public. . . .

Michael. We're never *in* public.

Yvonne. Very well, then, you may call me Sophie, but you've been having things much too much your own way, and I haven't been able to put a stop to your untidiness. Your room is a pigsty . . . don't interrupt me . . . a pigsty, that's what it is! Nothing but dirty washing.

Michael. Aunt Léo looks after the laundry . . . besides, you've told me hundreds of times you liked my things lying about, that you hated cupboards and moth-balls and——

Yvonne. I never said anything of the sort!

Michael. I beg your pardon! Oh, darling——

Yvonne. Years and years ago I said I liked to find little children's things lying about. It was perfectly natural. But one day I noticed that these little things were men's socks, men's shirts, men's pants. I then asked you to keep your things out of my room.

Michael. Mummy——

Yvonne. You remember now, don't you! It upset me enough at the time.

Michael. You wouldn't tuck me in any more . . . we had a fight.

Yvonne. Mick! I carried you to bed till you were eleven. After that you got much too heavy. You were hanging round my neck. Then you put your little bare feet on my slippers, you held on to my shoulders and we marched together to your bed. One evening you made fun of me because I was tucking you in, and I told you to go to bed on your own in the future.

Michael. Sophie! Let me come up on your bed.

Yvonne. No, Michael!

Michael. I'm taking off my shoes. [*He throws his shoes off, snuggles up against* YVONNE, *and puts his head against her shoulder.*] Now listen: I don't want you to look at me . . . this is lovely, stay like that, don't move . . . we'll look straight ahead at the window opposite . . . all right?

Yvonne. I don't like these preparations.

Michael. You promised you'd be very, very nice.

Yvonne. I promised nothing at all.

Michael. You're awful.

Yvonne. Don't try to get round me. If you have some-thing to tell me, tell me now. The longer you put it off, the harder it'll be. Are you in debt?

Michael. Don't be ridiculous.

Yvonne. Michael!

Michael. Please——!

Yvonne. All right, Mick. Go on. I'm listening.

MICHAEL *begins, rather quickly. He is a little embarrassed; while he talks, without looking at his mother,* YVONNE's *face becomes distorted with pain and anger to the point of almost becoming frightening.*

Michael. Sophie . . . I am so wonderfully happy . . . I wanted to make quite sure everything was all right before letting you know. Because I couldn't be happy if you weren't happy with me. You understand that, don't you? [YVONNE *nods briefly.*] Well, here it is: at the school, I met a girl——

Yvonne [*Trying to control herself and to speak casually*]. It isn't a mixed school——

Michael [*Putting his hand over* YVONNE's *mouth*]. Will you listen to me, please? I'm not talking of the drawing classes, I'm talking of the shorthand-typing class. Dad told me that he had a secretary's job in mind for me and that shorthand was essential. I tried it, but when you talked me out of the job I gave up the course. I only went there three times. And the last time I went she was there, too. It was a miracle. She is a young girl, or rather a young lady; she is three years older than I. There is an old chap of fifty who is interested in her. She's like a daughter to him. He's a widower and he lost a daughter who apparently looked just like her. Anyway, she told me her whole story. It was awfully sad. We met again. I cut the drawing classes. I prepared my sketches in advance . . . jugs and tulips and things . . . I shouldn't have dreamed of going on with it if she hadn't made up her mind to drop the old bloke and to start from scratch. I'm so in love with her, and she loves me, and you'll love her, too, and now she is free, and our Caravan has got the right spirit, and tomorrow please let me take you to her, you and Dad and Léo. Tonight she'll explain it all to the old boy. He thought she had a sister from the country staying with her, and he didn't come to see her any more. They hardly ever met any longer. There is no point in being jealous at all. It would have been far worse if she'd been a married woman, because I should hate anything that wasn't . . . well, you know . . . above board.

Yvonne [*Making a superhuman effort to talk*]. And this person . . . helped you . . . I mean, you've never got a penny. She must have been helping you. . . .

Michael. One can't keep a thing from you; she did help me a bit for meals, cigarettes, taxis. . . . [*Silence.*] Oh, I'm happy, I'm so happy. . . . Are you happy, Mummy?

YVONNE *swings around at him. He is horrified by her expression.*

Yvonne. Happy? [MICHAEL *recoils.*] So that's my reward! That's why I brought you into the world, that's why I've been looking after you night and day, making a fool of myself for you all these years . . . that's why I neglected my poor George, so that an old woman should take you away, should steal you from us and get you involved in her revolting machinations.

Michael. Mother!

Yvonne. Revolting, I say; and you take money from her! I suppose you know what that's called!

Michael. What are you talking about? Madeleine is young, and——

Yvonne. So that's her name!

Michael. I never meant to keep it dark. . . .

Yvonne. And you thought all you had to do was to put your arms around me and to flatter me. It's no use flattering *me*, my boy! To think that my son is being kept by the lover of a peroxided old woman.

Michael. Madeleine is blonde—you're right there—but not peroxided, and I tell you again she is twenty-five. Will you please listen to me! And there's no other man but me!

Yvonne [*Pointing her finger at him*]. Ah, now you admit it!

Michael. What do you mean I admit it? For an hour I've been telling you everything in detail!

Yvonne [*Jumping up and putting her hands in front of her face*]. I'm going mad!

Michael. Don't excite yourself, go back to bed.

Yvonne [*Marching up and down*]. Back to bed! Ever since last night I've been lying on that bed like a corpse.

I should *not* have taken the sugar. It would all be over by now. I needn't be dying of shame.

Michael. You talk of suicide because I'm in love with a girl?

Yvonne. To die of shame is worse than suicide. Don't try to be clever with me. If you were in love with a young girl . . . if you had come to me with a nice decent romance worthy of you and of us, I should probably have listened to you without getting angry. Instead of which you daren't look me in the face and you come out with a disgusting story.

Michael. I forbid you——

Yvonne. What?

Michael [*On an adoring impulse*]. Kiss me, darling——

Yvonne [*Pushing him away*]. You've got lipstick all over your face.

Michael. It's your own!

Yvonne. I'm afraid I couldn't bring myself to kiss you . . . now.

Michael. Sophie, that's not true! [*He starts to balance himself on a stool.*]

Yvonne. Your father and I will take the necessary steps to have you locked up, to prevent you from seeing that woman, to protect you against yourself. Stop it, Michael, you won't be satisfied until you've broken that stool!

Michael. You're a mother all right, Sophie, a real mother. I thought you were my friend. How often did you tell me——

Yvonne [*Interrupting*]. I am your mother. Your best friend would do exactly as I do. [*Pause.*] How long has this been going on?

Michael. Three months.

Yvonne. Three months of lies . . . of shameful lies. . . .

Michael. I didn't lie to you, Mother, I just said nothing.

Yvonne. Three months of lies, of plots, of false affections!

Michael. I didn't want to upset you.

Yvonne. Thanks very much. Don't worry about me. I can look after myself. It's you who are in trouble.

Michael. Me?

Yvonne. Yes, you . . . you poor little fool, fallen into the clutches of a woman older than yourself, a woman who's bound to lie about her age. . . .

Michael. You only have to look at Madeleine . . .

Yvonne. God forbid. Your Aunt Léonie makes out she is thirty. You don't know women.

Michael. I'm beginning to get an idea.

Yvonne. Don't be impertinent!

Michael. Really, Sophie, why should I want to go elsewhere for what I've got at home, and better than anyone else? Why should I try and find a woman of your age?

Yvonne [*Jumping up*]. Now you're insulting me!

Michael [*Stupefied*]. What?

Yvonne. I may look like an old woman, but I only look it! You'll do as I say!

Michael. I think we've said enough. We'll only hurt each other more.

Yvonne [*Furious*]. Oh, no, oh, no! That would be too easy! I'll say what I like! It's my turn now! As long as I live, you'll never marry that bitch!

Michael [*As if hit in the face*]. Take that back. . . .

He gets hold of her arms, she makes an effort to free herself, but she slips and falls to her knees.

Michael [*Terrified*]. Get up, Mother! Mummy!

He tries to lift her up, but she neither lets go of him nor does she attempt to get up.

Yvonne [*More furious than ever*]. I'll show you. . . . I'll tell everyone what you're doing to me. . . .

Muffled knocks are heard from below.

Michael. There! The neighbors have heard us! They're knocking on the wall!

He tears her hands from his jacket, which she is clutching.

Yvonne [*Giving a little sound of pain*]. You've hurt me, you beast! You've twisted my arm! You want to kill me! Look at your eyes!

Michael. And you, look at yours!

Yvonne [*Pulling herself up until she stands on her feet, but without letting go of him*]. You want to kill me . . . that's what it is . . . you want to kill me. . . .

Michael. You're raving mad—!

Yvonne. Just you wait. . . . I'll stop you from going out. . . . I'll have you locked up. . . . I'll call the police. . . . [*Suddenly she lets go of him and tries to rush toward the window, i.e., the public.*] I'll open the window. . . . I'll call out the whole street. . . .

Michael [*Putting his hand over her mouth and trying to stop her*]. Aunt Léo . . . Aunt Léo . . . Dad . . . quickly . . .

Léo [*Rushing in and putting her arms around* YVONNE]. Yvonne, control yourself.

Yvonne. Go to hell!

GEORGE *appears in the door;* MICHAEL *stands aside, stupefied.*

Léo. George, get a glass of water. . . . Lie down on your bed, Yvonne.

Yvonne. Leave me alone. . . .

Léo. The neighbors are knocking. . . .

Yvonne. The neighbors be damned, who cares?

George [*Reappearing with a glass of water, which he holds awkwardly in his hand*]. Well, I do. I've had just about enough trouble with our neighbors because of the noise we're making. We'll probably be given notice. . . .

Yvonne. Notice . . . or no notice . . . what does it matter now! Your son is a scoundrel! He has insulted me, he has hit me!

Michael. That's not true, Dad——

George [*Drinking up the glass of water, which* YVONNE *has pushed away*]. Come to my room.

Michael [*To* YVONNE]. I shall talk to Dad. Certain things should only be discussed among men! [*He picks up his shoes and exits behind his father and bangs the door.*

Yvonne [*Choking*]. Léo, Léo . . . listen to him. . . .

Léo. Yes, banging the doors again for a change.

Yvonne. Léo . . . you were listening at the door . . . you must have heard him. . . .

Léo. I couldn't help hearing, but I didn't get everything.

Yvonne. You were right, Léo. He is in love. With a typist or something like that. He would leave us all for her. He looked at me in the most horrible way. He doesn't love me any more.

Léo. That doesn't follow at all.

Yvonne. Yes, it does, Léo. What you give to one you take from another. You can't help it.

Léo. A boy of Michael's age must live his own life, and you mothers had better shut your eyes to certain things. It may not be easy for a boy to get a woman out of his system.

Yvonne [*Interrupting*]. And what about us mothers? Didn't we carry them in our system? But those are things you can't possibly imagine.

Léo [*Coldly*]. Possibly not. But sometimes you just have to make a special effort to control yourself.

Yvonne. You can talk. Could you do it if you had to?

Léo. I've had to.

Yvonne. It all depends on the circumstances.

Léo. The circumstances were bad enough. You all live in the clouds, of course, but your selfishness, yours, Yvonne, in particular, surpasses everything.

Yvonne. My selfishness?

Léo. What exactly do you think I've been doing in this house for twenty-three years? I've been going through hell. I loved George and I still do and I shall probably love him till I die. [*She silences* YVONNE *with a gesture.*] When he broke off our engagement without the slightest reason, out of the blue, and decided it was you he wanted to marry, *and* went as far as to ask *me* for my advice, I pretended to take the blow lightly. To try and talk him out of it would have made me unhappy. To send you away would have meant losing him. And like the fool I was I sacrificed myself. Yes, it may seem unbelievable to you, but I was young, in love, an idealist and a fool.

I thought you two had more in common, that you'd be a better wife, a better mother. That was twenty-three years ago. What have I been in this house since? I ask you! A maid!

Yvonne. Léo, you hate me. . . .

Léo. No . . . I did hate you, though . . . not when he broke it off . . . the idea of my sacrifice thrilled me and kept me going. I began to hate you after Michael was born. I hated you because you loved Michael too much and you neglected George. At times, I've been unfair to Michael, because I blamed him for it all. It's odd . . . I might have hated you if your marriage had been a success. No, I can't analyze my feelings toward you. You're not really bad, Yvonne; one just can't hold you responsible. You do people harm without realizing it. You don't notice a thing. Not a single thing.

Yvonne. I see.

Léo. No, you don't. You trail around from room to room, from mess to mess, with your eyes shut. Long ago I noticed that George was up to something. And I was furious with you for not seeing it and trying to stop him. I felt all along he was getting involved and I felt it was getting him nowhere. And now that Michael's been trying to do the same thing, I felt I had to talk to you and warn you.

Yvonne [*Scathingly*]. Not to save the family, I bet. You were glad! For me to lose Michael made up for your loss of George!

Léo [*Furious*]. That's typical of you, Yvonne!

Yvonne. I don't know what you mean.

Léo [*Exploding*]. Yes, I'm glad if Michael takes money from that woman! Maybe that'll teach you not to let a man go out without enough money to buy himself a lollipop. I'm glad if Michael marries a tart! If your bloody Caravan turns over in the ditch it can stay there and rot! I shan't lift a finger to get out of it. Poor George . . . twenty-three years . . . and life is long, my girl, long . . . long . . . [*She feels that* GEORGE *is entering behind her back and without transition, she carries on in a very feminine voice.*] . . . and the jacket is short, and if you take it off, you're in evening dress and you can go anywhere in it.

YVONNE, *at first bewildered, sees* GEORGE.

George. You can talk about clothes. You're lucky.

Yvonne. What's the matter with you? You look ill. . . .

George. I've been listening to Michael. . . .

Yvonne. Well—?

George. Well . . . he's sorry if he's hurt your arm . . . he's sorry if he's upset you . . . he'd like to see you. . . .

Yvonne. Is that all he's sorry about?

George. Yvonne . . . the boy's unhappy . . . don't ask him to apologize or some such nonsense. . . . It's rather serious. . . . I shall stay with Léo. . . . I'd like you to stay with Michael for a bit.

Yvonne [*Stubbornly*]. No.

George. Please, Yvonne . . . you'd help him and you'd help me. I can't do any more.

Yvonne. I hope he didn't manage to twiddle you around his little finger. . . .

George. Listen, Yvonne, I tell you again: this is serious! The boy is in love, very much in love . . . there's no getting away from that. . . . Don't bother him, don't question him . . . he's sitting on a pile of dirty washing; just sit down beside him and hold his hand.

Léo. George is right.

Yvonne [*Going over to the door*]. I'll go, on one condition. . . .

George [*Smiling sadly*]. Go . . . unconditionally . . .

He kisses her and pushes her out through the door at the back on the left.

Léo. George, something's happened . . . what is it?

George. I'll tell you quickly, Léo; they may be back any minute.

Léo. You frighten me. . . .

George. Wait till I tell you. I've just been hit over the head with a sledge hammer.

Léo. Is it about Michael?

George. It's Michael all right. I tell you there hasn't been a better farce in years.

Léo. Go on, George. . . . [*Silence.*] George! [*She shakes him.*] George!

George [*Coming to*]. Oh, yes. I'd forgotten where I was. I'm sorry. Léo, I've been a fool and I'm paying dearly for it. Six months ago I needed a shorthand-typist. I was given an address and I found a young woman of twenty-five, unhappy, good-looking, simple, perfect. I was feeling very lonely at home. You're always running about. Yvonne thinks of nothing but Michael. Michael thinks of nothing but . . . anyway . . . I took on a false name, I said I was a widower, that I had a daughter who died, who looked just like her. . . .

Léo. My poor George . . . who can blame you . . . you wanted some air . . . here—one can't breathe.

George. And so I went on inventing; I invented so much I didn't even tell her about my inventions. She told me she loved me . . . that young men bored her, and so on and so forth. After three months her attitude changed. A sister from the country came up to stay with her. Some married sister, very severe, very narrow-minded. I borrowed quite a nice sum of money from you——

Léo. Just as I thought. . . .

George. You're the only person I can talk to. Anyway —with the money that was supposed to help me with my work, I took some horrible basement flat. But she hardly ever came. Every time there was another excuse, and I was getting into a terrible state. You can guess the rest. The "sister" was a young man she'd fallen in love with. And the young man was Michael. He just told me so himself.

Léo. Does he suspect anything?

George. Not a thing. He's in seventh heaven. He thought I was shocked for the same reason as his mother.

Léo. What did he want?

George. He's just informed me that Madeleine—we might as well call her by her name—that Madeleine was making arrangements to see me tonight. The idea was . . . how shall I put it . . . ?

Léo. To give you your notice. . . .

George. Yes, and to confess everything, it seems. Confess everything to Mr. X, so that they can be free and proper and worthy of each other. It'll kill me, Léo; I am crazy about her.

Léo. I don't know if this is a tragedy or a farce; but it certainly is a masterpiece.

George [*Grimly*]. It's a rotten masterpiece. How can such a coincidence happen in an enormous city like Paris . . . ?

Léo. I thought you didn't believe in coincidence. You people who are always so fond of "miracles," here's a good one for you. How did you feel facing Michael?

George. Terrible—terrible. I'm not angry with him. It's not his fault.

Léo. What're you going to do?

George. I wish you'd tell me. I shan't go and see her tonight, of course.

Léo. Now I know why there was such a false sense of order about the Caravan lately. When one of you was in, the other was out. My poor George. . . .

George. What I've had to swallow! Michael kept referring to "the old bloke." He admitted that Madeleine used to help him out.

Léo. With your money. . . .

George. No, with yours.

Léo. Now that is rather funny. It's just as well that our money should finally land in your son's pocket. And in all fairness that'll teach you not to let a boy of his age run around without a penny.

George [*Rather hurt*]. I know I'm ridiculous . . . but I'm very unhappy.

Léo [*Taking his hand*]. George, darling . . . I'm going to help you.

George. How, Léo?

Léo. You must hit and you must hit hard and you must make this marriage impossible. Michael wants the whole Caravan to visit this woman tomorrow. All right, we shall go.

George. Are you mad?

Léo. On the contrary.

George. Yvonne will never agree.

Léo. She will.

George. Can you imagine the scene . . . *I* walk in . . .

Léo. The girl will bite off her tongue rather than give herself away.

George. But when she sees me, she might faint or scream or something. . . .

Léo. Leave that to me. You go and let her have it.

George. She has asked for it, Léo.

Léo. Break with her first, and then, if she refuses to give up Michael, threaten her. Threaten her that you'll tell *Michael everything!*

George [*Taken aback*]. You're a devil. . . .

Léo. I am very fond of you, George. I want to protect your home.

George. Yes, but Yvonne. . . . She will never, never in her life will she . . .

Léo. Sh! She's coming——

George. What big ears you have, grandmother. . . .

Léo. The better to keep you from being eaten, my child!

The door at the back opens. YVONNE *appears.*

George. Well—?

Yvonne. We didn't say a word. After a while he looked as if he wanted to be left alone. So I came out. I'm finished. I don't know what I'm doing. I'd like to sleep, but I don't think I could. What's going to happen? You can see Michael isn't himself. He is under a bad influence.

Léo. Well, we'd better get to know this bad influence.

George. I know it only too well.

Léo [*Giving* GEORGE *a warning glance*]. I mean, we must be very careful. We musn't get Michael's back up.

Yvonne. No, no—we must make a clean break.

Léo. D'you think you can stop these children from seeing each other?

Yvonne. What children?

Léo. Good Heavens, Yvonne—Michael and his girl.

Yvonne. But Léo, how can you talk of a "girl"? There's a woman who goes to bed with anybody . . . a woman

Heaven knows how old she is . . . a little hypocrite who
Mick believes is a saint.

Léo. All the more reason to make him see her as she
really is.

Yvonne. I am counting on George to show some character for once and strike while the iron is hot.

George. That's a good old cliché.

Yvonne. Besides, even if that woman really does want
to leave her . . . protector . . . even suppose she *were*
set on marrying Mick, it would be your duty to stop him
taking such an absurd responsibility. Mick can't just make
her drop this old man and then leave her in the lurch.

Léo. Now at last you've talking sense.

Yvonne. And how did he expect to keep her?

George. He told me he was fed up doing nothing: he's
made up his mind to get a job.

Yvonne. And to live on our money, or rather his aunt's.

Léo. You know what little money I have is yours.

Yvonne. Yes, but not that woman's. I'm not dreaming
now, I see it all quite clearly: George must go and settle
it. Léo . . . tell him, it's up to him.

George. That's easily said. . . .

Yvonne. All you've got to do is to be firm and to
forbid her——. . . . .

Léo. D'you think it's any good giving orders to people
in love?

Yvonne. Mick doesn't love this girl. He thinks he does.
It's his first romance. He imagines he's found the ideal
love, the love that lives forever.

Léo. Even if he only imagines it, it's just as real to
him.

Yvonne. Nonsense! He'll start writing poems, he'll
paint pictures, he'll go for endless walks, he'll get over it
that way. I know my Mick.

Léo. Shall we say: you used to. . . .

Yvonne. You really *are* in-creddible, both of you! I've
been watching this boy for twenty-two years. And you
say that any Miss What-you-may-call-her can just come
and change him through and through in three months.

George. Not in three months, Yvonne, in three minutes. That is love.

Yvonne. My goodness . . . if I were a man, if I had to talk to her, I'd know what to say.

Léo. Well, that's just what Michael wants you to do. . . .

Yvonne. Perhaps he expects me to obey his orders!

George. Who's talking of orders? Why do you dramatize everything? Yvonne—!

Yvonne. Just a minute. . . . If I'm not mistaken . . . you're presuming you and George——

George. I'm not presuming anything. . . .

Yvonne. All right, all right! You consider it feasible that I should accompany George to see this . . . this woman, with Léo bringing up the rear?

George. It's a reconnaissance, a simple reconnaisance . . . in enemy territory.

Yvonne. The Caravan in full marching order paying their respects on New Year's Eve. . . .

Léo [*Loudly*]. I'm afraid you don't understand at all, Yvonne. Can you face the prospect of living with a Michael who doesn't tell you anything any more, who tries to avoid you or who tells you lies from morning till night? Can you bear the thought of having to live without Michael . . . of Michael leaving the house altogether?

Yvonne. Please, don't. . . .

Léo. You silly little idiot. . . . Do you know what would happen? You'd go and humiliate yourself again and again . . . you'd run after him, you'd go down on your knees to him . . . you'd go and beg that woman to——

Yvonne. Don't . . . don't . . . please, Léo, don't!

Léo. Darling, now wouldn't it be so much simpler to use a little cunning to win Michael back? One day he'll thank you for it.

Yvonne. I couldn't deceive Mick like that. It would only make matters worse afterwards.

Léo. You'd be deceiving him for his own good! Of course, you can always agree to this marriage if you find the girl is—all right.

George. Believe me, Yvonne, at first this idea gives you a shock. It gave *me* a shock. But eventually you realize that Léo's suggestion isn't as mad as it sounds.

Yvonne [*Pacing up and down*]. No, I won't! I'm always giving way, I'm sick of it, and I won't go near that woman! I won't!

Léo [*Walking up toward* YVONNE *and making her stop*]. And another thing, Yvonne, the most important point of all: if someone had left me who was very dear to me, I just couldn't bear not knowing where he'd gone. Don't you want to know what that creature is like? What her place is like? The place where they both hurt you so much! When something that belongs to you has been stolen, don't you try and imagine where you may find it again?

Yvonne [*Between her teeth*]. In the hands of that thief. . . .

Léo [*At her most formidable*]. Then go to that thief, Yvonne. Go and get back what is yours. Go with George. And I . . . I shan't let you go alone.

YVONNE *sits down on the edge of her bed, her hand in front of her eyes. Only by this gesture, by her silence, does she at last accept.*

George. I admire you, Yvonne. You are always stronger than one would expect.

Yvonne. Or weaker.

Léo. It takes courage, for you to leave your dark room and go out into the sun.

Yvonne. If that's what you call the sun, give me the night any day.

Léo. Be very, very careful how you break the news to Michael, he may smell a rat.

George. Léo, you go and fetch him . . . tell him you've got a surprise, you've got good news for him.

Léo. Leave it to me. . . . [*She exits by the door at the back.*

Yvonne. What a nightmare. . . .

George. You're telling me. . . .

Yvonne. If I go to see this person . . . I'll hide myself somewhere with Léonie while you talk to her.

George [*Grimly*]. I promise you I'll talk to her alone.

Yvonne. Don't make me talk to her, George, I'd lose my temper. . . . I'm not used to this type of woman.

George. Neither am I. . . . At my age it's not easy to get used to things. . . .

The door at the back opens. LÉO *pushes* MICHAEL *into the room. His clothes and his hair are in disorder. He appears to be on the defensive.*

Léo. Go on. . . .

George. Come in, Michael.

Michael. What is it?

George. Your mother will tell you.

MICHAEL *advances into the room.* LÉO *shuts the door.* YVONNE *begins to speak with an effort, looking down.*

Yvonne. Mick, I'm afraid I've been unkind and I didn't appreciate your frankness. I am sorry. Your father is very kind. We talked it over. Mick, darling, we wouldn't want to hurt you for the world, you know that . . . on the contrary . . . I only want what is best for you and I hate being unfair. What you asked us to do is almost impossible——

Michael. But——

George. Let your mother finish.

Yvonne. Anyway . . . this almost impossible step you asked us to take . . . we have decided to . . . to . . . we shall go and see your friend.

Michael [*Jumping toward his mother*]. Mummy, Dad . . . is that true?

George. Yes, Michael. You may announce our visit for tomorrow.

Michael. I can't believe it. . . . How can I ever thank you. . . . Mummy . . . [*He tries to kiss* YVONNE.]

Yvonne [*Turning her face away*]. Don't thank us, thank your aunt.

Michael. You, Aunt Léo! [*He runs toward* LÉO, *picks her up and swings her around and around.*]

Léo [*Screaming*]. You're choking me. . . . Stop it . . . Mick . . . stop it. . . . I had nothing to do with it.

. . . Mick . . . stop it . . . please . . . don't thank me, thank the Caravan!

ACT TWO

SCENE—MADELEINE's *apartment. A large well-lit room. Downstage left, a spiral staircase leading to the attic above. Upstage left, the entrance door. Downstage right, the door to the bathroom. Downstage center, a large divan and a small table. On all walls, especially in the back wall, but wherever possible, bookshelves full of books. The room is kept scrupulously tidy.*

MADELEINE *sits on the divan while* MICHAEL *is heard singing rather loudly in the adjoining bathroom. Suddenly there is the noise of a glass falling and breaking. The singing stops and* MICHAEL *appears holding the pieces of the glass, in shirt and trousers but without socks and shoes.*

MADELEINE. Oh, darling . . . it's in-cred*d*ible!

Michael. D'you know that everybody at home says "it's incred*d*ible"? I sometimes think we said it before I met you and that you got it from me. Mother'd be mad if she knew she's copying you.

Madeleine. I don't see what's so peculiar about my way of pronouncing this word. I say it like everyone else.

Michael [*Tenderly*]. You say it like no one else and without rhyme or reason. It's a habit that you've passed on to me and I've passed on to all the others, to Mother and Father and to Aunt Léo. Now they all say: "it's incred*d*ible!"

Madeleine. Michael. . . .

Michael. Yes. . . .

Madeleine. Did you remember to pull the plug out?

Michael. No. . . . [*He runs into the bathroom.*]

Madeleine. Well, hurry up. Your mother would never believe that you had to have your bath *here*, because yours is stopped up.

Michael. It's all Aunt Léo's fault. The bath is her department. Usually she's order personified. You two'll get on like a house on fire.

Madeleine [*Proudly*]. *My* bath works.

Michael. We wash in the basin, when Léo decides to let us down. But she's much too fond of her comfort; she can't keep it up.

Madeleine. May I dry your hair?

Michael. It would never have occurred to me that my having a bath here would annoy Mother; and it would, you know! You're like Aunt Léo, you're a great diplomatist.

Madeleine. You seem to have studied your aunt pretty closely.

Michael. Only because we all live on top of each other. Usually I'm not very observant.

Madeleine. What I like about you is that you're so clean.

Michael. That's a good one.

Madeleine. You're not really dirty. You're dirty like a child. Children's knees aren't really dirty.

Michael. Childish and ignorant, that's me.

Madeleine. And what about me?

Michael. Oh, you . . . you're my learned friend: you read the classics!

Madeleine. I don't read them, I only bind them.

Michael. You're too clever for me. One of these days you'll make a living out of this bookbinding of yours. You'll have to keep me.

Madeleine. You're going to work, my darling. You might even help me, and one day we'll open a shop.

Michael. And we'll make a fortune. And then—when we've got our own house . . .

Madeleine. A "flat," Michael. Why do you always say "a house"? It's so frightfully grand!

Michael. At home, we always say "house"; this house, our house, my house. . . .

Madeleine [*Laughing*]. It's in-cred*di*ble!

Michael. But that's how it is. Now listen: when we've got our own house, if you won't let me be untidy, I'll drag

you over to the Caravan, and lock you up and force you
to share my room with me and my dirty washing and my
ties in the flowerpot.

Madeleine [*Vastly superior*]. Within five minutes, my
dear, your room would be in perfect order.

Michael. You're the devil. If this was our house, your
whole bookbinding studio would be down here in the
sitting room; or the sitting room would be all over your
studio. Things keep following me like cats. How *do* you
do it?

Madeleine. I have a feeling for order. You either have it
or you don't.

Michael [*Finding his socks underneath* MADELEINE].
Look where I find my socks. I'm sure I took 'em off in the
bathroom.

Madeleine. You took them off in the sitting room.

Michael [*Putting on his socks*]. There's no such thing as
a sitting room at our place. Every drama takes place in
Mother's bedroom, the scene of the crime. . . . When the
rows get too noisy, the neighbors knock on the wall, and
the truce, the peace treaties, and the stormy silences take
place in a kind of phantom dining room, a waiting room,
an empty hole with a big, ugly, awkward table which
keeps on falling to pieces, and which the charwoman keeps
screwing together again.

Madeleine. And does your father put up with . . . ?

Michael. Oh, Dad. . . . Dad thinks he's a great inventor . . . [*Smiling.*] Actually, he's about ten years
younger than I am. . . .

Madeleine. And your mother?

Michael. When I was little, I wanted to marry Mummy.
And when Dad told me "You're too young," I said: "Then
I'll wait till I'm ten years older than Mummy."

Madeleine [*Very moved*]. Oh, my darling. . . . [*She
kisses him.*]

Michael. I am sorry to keep on about my family. You
see, I didn't want to talk too much about them until I'd
told *them* everything. . . . I'm not very clever, you know
. . . so I just shut up about them altogether. I'm making
up for it now.

Madeleine. It was very sweet of you, and I do understand.

Michael. When I told them . . . Sophie was wonderful, and Dad and Aunt Léo, too. But it started with a scene all right.

Madeleine [*Frightened*]. A scene. . . .

Michael. Mother wanted to call the police, to have me arrested.

Madeleine [*Stupefied*]. The police? Whatever for?

Michael. Oh, that's Mother's style . . . it goes with her room.

Madeleine. It's——

Michael ⎫
Madeleine ⎬ —in-creddible!
⎭

Madeleine [*Laughing*]. And whose fault was the scene, Michael?

Michael. It was my fault. No, it was your fault. I just couldn't resist spending a night with you. And in the morning . . . in the morning I . . .

Madeleine [*Imitating him and taking his foot off some piece of furniture*]. And in the morning you had the jitters.

Michael. Quite.

Madeleine. I told you a hundred times to go and ring up.

Michael. Don't put your foot in it, my love—although I grant you: it's an adorable foot—don't tell Sophie that you told me to telephone.

Madeleine. Look who's talking! You can't walk a step without putting your foot in it.

Michael. Quite.

Madeleine. And that's another thing I love about you, my stupid darling: you're incapable of telling lies.

Michael. It's just too complicated, that's all.

Madeleine. I hate lies. I realize you have to shut up sometimes or rearrange things a bit not to hurt people's feelings. But lying . . . just for the sake of lying . . . I am not a particularly moral person myself . . . but I always feel that telling a lie is apt to set off some mechanism or other outside our control which upsets and ruins everything in the end.

During this MICHAEL *has finished lacing up his left shoe;
he now commences to search for the other one.*

Michael. Hm. Where's my other shoe?
Madeleine. Look for it.
Michael. This *is* incredible; I saw it a minute ago. . . .
Madeleine. Keep looking.
Michael [*On all fours*]. You know where it is, don't you?
Madeleine. I can just see it from here. It's staring you
in the face.
Michael [*Walking away from the table on which the
shoe lies*]. Getting hot?
Madeleine. You're freezing.
Michael. And then you tell me to hurry up.
Madeleine. Diplomatist! Here you are!

*She picks up the shoe on one lace and lets it swing in front
of* MICHAEL's *eyes.*

Michael. That's the end. Mother would have fished it
out of my bed.
Madeleine. What an adorable woman your mother must
be. And what a pity I'm scared to death.
Michael [*Putting on the other shoe*]. Mummy thinks
she's ugly, but she's much more beautiful than if she
were beautiful, if you know what I mean. She'll be done
up in all her war paint. I bet you Aunt Léo insists on
Mummy making up and getting the mothballs out of the
furs.
Madeleine. I'm scared . . . I'm scared. . . .
Michael. It's they who're scared! Aunt Léo will break
the ice, she is very strong!
Madeleine. Do you always go everywhere in a gang?
Michael. Mother never goes out at all. Dad goes out,
pottering. Aunt Léo goes out shopping. And I go out because I love you.
Madeleine [*Taking his hands*]. Do you, Michael?
Michael. Have a look. [*He turns around and around on
the spot.*] I'm all set, nice and clean and ready to ask your
hand in marriage. Oh!

Madeleine [*Alarmed*]. What's the matter?

Michael. I wanted to have my hair cut.

Madeleine. You can't. It's Monday. They're shut on Mondays.

Michael. How do you manage to know everything?

Madeleine. Everyone knows they're shut on Mondays!

Michael. No. . . . [*He kisses her.*] How do you know it's Monday? I only know when it's Sunday because our cleaning women doesn't come on Sunday and I have to help in the kitchen.

Madeleine. You can tell it's Sunday by other things. People are freer. There's disorder in the air . . . a sad kind of disorder.

Michael. You with your order and your disorder!

Madeleine. What are your people expecting to find here?

Michael. They're expecting the worst. They expect to find a peroxided old woman.

Madeleine. I *am* an old woman. I am three years older than you.

Michael. I have a presentiment that their old woman will give them the surprise of their lives!

Madeleine. Knock on wood. . . .

Michael [*Taking her in his arms*]. Madeleine, darling, you would conquer anybody. No, there's only one thing that worries me a little.

Madeleine. What's that?

Michael. I so much wanted this other business to be over and done with.

Madeleine. He's put it off till tomorrow. Tomorrow everything will be in order.

Michael. You seem to be glad he put it off.

Madeleine. In a way, yes. When George rang up I didn't insist, I didn't have the courage.

Michael. Dad's name is George.

Madeleine. You can imagine what my talk with the first George is going to be like. But it doesn't worry me half as much as meeting your George.

Michael. Anyway, you don't love the man.

Madeleine. I do, Michael.

Michael. You love him?

Madeleine. It isn't as simple as all that, Michael. I only love you. But I love George, in a way.

Michael. Well, I'll be——

Madeleine [*Interrupting*]. If I did not love him . . . in a way . . . I shouldn't love you. Because I should never have known you. I should be dead. I told you what I was going to do just before I met him.

Michael [*A little snootily*]. You're certainly grateful to him, anyway. . . .

Madeleine [*Quite seriously*]. No, Michael, it's more than that.

Michael. Now I don't understand anything any more. . . .

Madeleine. But you must, my darling. A number of men offered me what George offered me. I refused. If I nearly accepted his offer, it was because I loved him . . . in a way.

Michael. Oh, well, you didn't know *me* then.

Madeleine. You horrible little egoist! [*She kisses him.*] No, I didn't love him all that much; I was waiting for something different. And when I met you, I'd found it. Still, I was sufficiently in love with him to hide it, to delay things, even to accept his help. In fact I love him enough to be ill at the thought of having to fire this news at him point-blank.

Michael. It's in-cred*d*ible!

Madeleine. Listen, Michael, be fair! Try and put yourself in his place. He's a widower. He's lost his daughter. I look just like her, it seems. You're asking me to sign his death warrant. He's convinced I would never lie to him. I'm everything to him!

Michael [*Exasperated*]. But take him, take him after all, there's still time! I'll cancel the family! No problem at all. . . .

Madeleine. Don't be absurd. Did I say I wouldn't do it? When you are in love . . . as I am with you . . . you can do anything . . . however difficult . . . and I mean that. So that is all settled.

Michael [*After a moment's pause*]. I'm sorry, we shouldn't have talked about it.

Madeleine. I never mentioned you to him. He knows nothing about you. I thought it was better that way.

Michael. Look . . . if Mother . . . if I had to choose . . . I wouldn't hesitate a moment . . .

Madeleine. Yes, you would. And you'd be right. And that's one of the reasons why I love you. But it isn't a fair comparison, Michael. Your mother has your father and your aunt.

Michael. No. She has only me.

Madeleine. Then—she must hate me very much.

Michael. No one could hate you! Mother will love you as soon as she understands that you and I are one and the same person.

Madeleine. You shouldn't have told her about the other man.

Michael. I don't have to hide anything from Sophie. She's my friend.

Madeleine. Then why didn't you tell her about us at once?

Michael. Because I was embarrassed about the other chap. Our family is full of prejudices . . . of conventional nonsense . . . and there are always scenes. I wanted them to see you free with nothing to hide between us at all. When I did tell them, I told them our whole story from A to Z.

Madeleine. You were right. Absolutely. Once you begin you must tell everything.

Michael. I'm glad you agree. If you think that it'll help you tomorrow.

Madeleine. Let's not talk about it any more. Just think that I was as fond of George as I shall be of your father.

Michael. But——

Madeleine. Sh—! [*She stops him with a gentle kiss.*]

Michael. Are you angry with me?

Madeleine. I'd be angry if you weren't jealous.

Michael. They're awfully sweet, really they are. I mean this visit proves it, doesn't it?

Madeleine. This visit terrifies me. It's all too simple. You told me your mother wouldn't hear of it. Next minute she has changed her mind completely. It terrifies me.

Michael. First they get mad and shout and bang the doors, then Aunt Léo calms them down. Sophie is like that. Impulsive. She says: "No, young man, never!" Then she locks herself in and I sulk. Then she comes back, gives me a kiss and says: "All right, Mick." And I give *her* a kiss and that's that.

Madeleine. I can't understand it.

Michael. I'm telling you: Aunt Léo is the guardian angel of the Caravan. She is very beautiful, very elegant, and very outspoken. She criticizes our disorder all the time, but if it came to the point, she couldn't do without it.

The doorbell rings. They both jump.

Madeleine. They're here! I'm off! I'm going upstairs!

Michael. Don't leave me!

Madeleine. You come and fetch me!

Michael. Madeleine, please!

Madeleine. Yes, yes—it's much better like that.

She climbs up the little staircase rapidly, while MICHAEL *leaves the stage to open the door.*

Michael [*Offstage*]. Oh, it's you, Aunt Léo . . . you're alone?!

LÉO *enters through the back stage door, followed by* MICHAEL.

Michael. Has anything been changed? Are they coming?

Léo. Don't worry. They're coming. I arranged to get here well ahead of the others.

Michael. That's very good of you.

Léo [*Looking around*]. I say: what order!

Michael. That's me. You can see that. That's me all over.

Léo. I wonder. Oh, what a gorgeous view—that's what your mother ought to have, spending all day in her room, instead of that ugly building opposite.

Michael. Don't run down the Caravan. I look out on the courtyard—I like it.

Léo. Where's your friend?

Michael. Upstairs. She's got a bookbinding studio upstairs. [*He begins to climb up.*]

Léo. Can't you call her?

Michael. No, you can't hear a thing up there.

Léo. That's a bit of luck.

Michael. Why?

Léo. Your father is in a very good mood. He must talk to your friend alone. It would be no good your mother being here and interfering all the time. I'll take her up there; and when we come down, everything will be over.

Michael. Angel! [*He gives her a kiss.*] I'll bring her to you.

He runs upstairs four at a time. He bangs the studio door behind him. Léo goes to the bathroom, opens the door, looks, grunts surprised approval of what she sees, and shuts the door again. She now proceeds upstage and begins to look at the titles of the books.

MADELEINE, *pushed forward by* MICHAEL, *appears at the top of the staircase. She comes down slowly with* MICHAEL *holding her by the shoulders.*

Michael [*To* MADELEINE]. I tell you she's alone. You're not going to be afraid of Aunt Léo . . . she's the advance guard.

MADELEINE *smiles timidly at* LÉO; *LÉo stretches out her hand;* MADELEINE *takes it gladly; they shake hands.*

Léo. How do you do?

Madeleine. How do you do? [*It is almost a whisper.*]

Léo. You are very beautiful, my dear.

Madeleine. Oh . . . thank you. . . . Michael was right. . . .

Michael. I told her that you were cross-eyed, hunch-backed, and lame.

Madeleine. He always talks about how beautiful, how elegant, you are. Won't you sit down?

Léo [*Sitting on the divan*]. He didn't mention my "order" by any chance? I can see I'm not the only one to appreciate it.

Madeleine. I'm afraid disorder terrifies me.

Léo. I shall congratulate you if you can do anything in that line with Michael.

Madeleine. He's making progress.

Michael. Yes. I now leave my shoes on the sitting-room table instead of Mother's bed. I was sure you'd be impressed by her order. Tell me, are you?

Léo [*Smiling*]. Very . . . !

Michael. You see, Madeleine, Aunt Léo is very impressed. What's the matter with Mother and Dad? Where are they?

Léo. I said I was going to meet them here. Your mother didn't like it, but I hate arriving anywhere in a gang. I said I had some shopping to do. I don't mind telling you I wanted to get here first and prepare the ground.

Michael. Aunt Léo thinks of everything.

Madeleine. I can certainly see that.

Léo. Well, now we're partners in crime. [*Pointing at the staircase.*] Your studio is just what we need. I was afraid you'd only have one room.

Madeleine. It's an old attic, in fact the whole thing is just two attics converted.

Léo. And you're sure one can't hear from the attic what goes on down here?

Madeleine. Quite sure.

Léo. That's most important. They won't be here for a few minutes. So let's make quite sure: upstairs, you two, lock yourself in, I'll shout something down here.

Michael. What?

Léo. Oh—anything!

MADELEINE *and* MICHAEL *run upstairs giggling like schoolchildren,* MICHAEL *bangs the door to the attic.* LÉO *picks out a book from the library; it is Alfred de Musset's Lorenzaccio, opens it at random and begins to yell. While she recites,* MICHAEL *and* MADELEINE *reopen the attic door and, creeping forward on their hands and knees, listen to* LÉO *in extreme silence.*

Léo. Help! Help! They're killing me! They're cutting my throat! Oh death, death, death! Stamp your foot . . . this way, archers . . . Lorenzo, the Devil! Thou art a wretch, a cur! I'll bleed you, swine! His heart . . . go for his heart! There, my men! Tear his guts! Now wilt thou cry, now stamp thy foot, now try and kill me if thou canst! Let's cut him into pieces, friends, and throw them to the winds. . . ."

Michael. Bravo!

Léo. Michael! You weren't in the attic!

Michael. I was, but I couldn't hear a thing, and I wanted to hear you scream.

Léo. You ought to be used to that at home.

Michael. Ah, but I wanted to listen to you *here* . . . you were terrific, Aunt Léo, you'd make a wonderful actress!

Madeleine. You were grand!

Léo. Your mother can be quite a good actress, too, when she wants to be. Between ourselves, I believe our grandmother was a singer, and she had to give it up when she married grandpapa. But of course, these things are never mentioned in the family. [*The doorbell rings.*] Here they are. [*To* MADELEINE.] Upstairs, quickly! Remember: I haven't seen you. I don't know you. I've only just come. [*To* MICHAEL, *while* MADELEINE *goes upstairs.*] And you, Michael, you refused to show me your friend. Go on . . . remember . . . your mother first. . . .

The doorbell rings again. MICHAEL *runs to open the door. The voices of* GEORGE, YVONNE, *and* MICHAEL *are heard in the hall.*

George's voice. I thought we'd come to the wrong door.

Yvonne's voice. No maid?

Michael's voice. No, same as at home. [*He enters ahead of* GEORGE *and* YVONNE.] Aunt Léo, did *you* hear them ring?

GEORGE *and* YVONNE *enter.*

Yvonne [*Suspiciously*]. Is Léo here?

Léo. I just got here. I rang three times. We nearly met at the door.

Yvonne. Have you been here long?

Léo. I tell you I just got here. Didn't I, Michael?

Michael. Aunt Léo thought she was late and would find you here.

Yvonne. You're . . . alone?

Michael. Madeleine's upstairs. She's got a bookbinding studio upstairs.

Léo [*To* GEORGE]. Michael wouldn't dream of showing her to me before showing her to Yvonne . . . [*Quickly turning to* YVONNE.] . . . and to George. . . .

Michael. Upstairs you don't hear the bell, you don't hear a thing. She's been hiding up there for half an hour.

Yvonne [*Raising her eyebrows*]. Hiding?

Michael. Well . . . she's afraid of the family.

Yvonne [*Coldly*]. We're not monsters.

Michael. It's only natural that Madeleine should be a bit nervous.

Léo. I see her point.

Yvonne [*Looking around*]. What luxury!

Michael [*Modestly*]. It's quite neat . . .

Yvonne. That never used to be your strong point.

Michael. Give me a chance. I don't come here very often. If I lived here or came more often, it wouldn't stay like that for long.

Léo. I wonder.

Yvonne [*Almost snapping at* LÉO]. Why do you say that?

George [*Cutting in quickly*]. Michael—don't you think you should announce our arrival?

Michael. Yes, of course. . . . Oh Dad, don't be so stiff, and you, Sophie, sit down . . . sit down both of you . . . try to look natural. Aunt Léo, make them comfortable, do the honors. Poor Madeleine is very nervous. If you aren't going to help her, she'll stand there like a poker and you'll think she's putting it on.

George. I wonder, my boy, if you realize the seriousness of this visit? It wouldn't appear so.

Léo. He's only trying to break the ice.

Michael [*Meaning it*]. I'm going to cry in a minute.

Yvonne. Now please, Léo, George is rather concerned about all this. It's at times like these that we become fathers, mothers, and sons; one can't treat these things lightly.

Léo [*Dryly*]. In that case, try not to become conventional fathers and mothers, just because the situation is somewhat unconventional. I think Michael is very brave and very sweet. Go and fetch the child.

Yvonne [*Between her teeth*]. If you can call her that.

Michael [*At the foot of the staircase*]. Now listen: this means my whole life to me. For the last time, I ask you to help Madeleine and not to cold-shoulder her.

Yvonne. We didn't come here with that intention.

Michael. Mother, darling, Dad, Léo—don't be angry with me . . . I'm in a bit of a state. . . .

Léo. We're not angry with you. We're all putting on an act because we all feel frightfully self-conscious. We'll get over it. Go on!

Michael [*Running upstairs*]. All right!

Yvonne [*To* GEORGE]. You look even worse than I do. . . .

George. Sit down, Yvonne, I'll just stand over here behind Léo.

They form a group. LEO *sits on the left nearest to the staircase,* YVONNE *by her side.* GEORGE *stands behind the sofa, i.e., behind* YVONNE.

Michael [*Walking down backwards, talking over his shoulder*]. Smile, please!

MADELEINE *comes downstairs without looking.* YVONNE *rises and advances toward* MADELEINE. GEORGE *stays where he is, still covered by* LÉO.

Michael. This is my mother.

Madeleine. How do you do?

Yvonne. You're charming, my dear. You look very young. May I ask how old you are?

Madeleine. I am twenty-five. I am so glad to . . . [*At this instant she discovers* GEORGE. *Her voice fails her. She takes a few steps in his direction.*] Oh God. . . . What are you doing here? [*She turns toward the ladies, her face quite drawn.*] Excuse me, this gentleman . . .

Michael [*Coming forward laughingly*]. This gentleman is my father. Dad, this is Madeleine.

Madeleine [*Trying not to draw back, but she cannot help herself altogether*]. Your father . . . !

Michael. Nobody ever believes Dad is old enough to be my father. If we went out together they'd think we were brothers.

Léo. Introduce me.

Michael. I don't know what I'm doing. . . . Madeleine . . . [*He takes her by the hand.*] Darling, how cold you are! Feel her hand, Léo!

LÉO *takes* MADELEINE's *hand. She makes a superhuman effort not to faint.*

Léo. Her hands are like ice. [LÉO *smiles at* MADELEINE.] Are we as bad as that?

Michael. Shake hands with Aunt Léo!

Madeleine [*Has no voice left*]. How do you do. . . .

Léo. I'm Michael's aunt, and now that you've met us, I trust there is nothing to frighten you any longer.

Michael. Well, that's the lot. You've met the family. You see, there was nothing to it.

MADELEINE *drops onto the divan but she gets hold of herself at once and manages to sit up.*

Michael. Darling . . . are you all right?

Madeleine. Yes, Michael . . . I'm all right.

Yvonne. I believe Michael wants to show us how nicely the attic has been arranged. No, please don't bother to get up. [MADELEINE *tries to get up.*] No, really, Miss . . . my sister will come up, too. Come on, Michael. . . .

Michael. But——

Yvonne. Lead the way. Léo and I will follow you.

George [*Making a move*]. I could perhaps . . .

Yvonne. No, I think you'd better stay.

Michael. We've got the tea ready upstairs . . . and three cups. And sugar. And some evaporated milk. We know how to entertain!

YVONNE *walks over to the staircase and is about to climb up.* LÉO *follows her.* MICHAEL *kisses* MADELEINE *quickly on the shoulder and moves to follow* LÉO.

Madeleine [*Quickly rising to her feet*]. Are you leaving me alone?

Michael. Not alone . . . with Dad!

Madeleine. No . . . please . . . don't leave me . . . listen, Michael . . .

Yvonne. Michael!

Madeleine. Please, ladies . . . let me show you the way . . . I must pour the tea . . .

Yvonne. We'll manage. Michael will help us. I shall be curious to see if there are still three cups left when we've finished.

Michael. As a matter of fact, there were six, I've only broken three.

MADELEINE *makes a move to follow* MICHAEL *toward the staircase.*

George [Speaking to MADELEINE *without moving from where he stands].* Please stay. I promised Michael to have a talk with you, and, since my wife is much more nervous than I am, to speak to you alone. It is nice of Michael to say that I look so young; but don't be afraid. I'm an old man really, compared with you two.

Yvonne [From the top of the stairs]. Hurry up, and let us know when you've finished.

Madeleine. No, please! Couldn't your sister please stay with us? A woman would——

Yvonne [Interrupting]. My dear child . . . would you mind if we had our tea now? I am against women getting mixed up with certain problems. You've heard yourself what Michael said about his father. You will be talking to a friend of Michael's, a very good friend, easy to get on with, much more easy than I should be.

Michael. They don't wish us any harm, Madeleine, on the contrary. . . . Use your charm, make Dad fall for you in a big way . . . but don't run off together, you two. . . . Would you like me to bring you down a cup of tea?

Léo. She'll have her tea afterwards. [Léo *pushes* YVONNE *through the attic door and exits herself, followed by* MICHAEL.

Michael [Popping his head out again]. Make her smile, Dad! Be good! [*He blows* MADELEINE *a kiss and bangs the door.*

George. Well, this is it.

Madeleine [*Burying her face in her hands*]. This is monstrous. . . .

George. Exactly. It's monstrous. It's unbelievable, but it's true. It's a masterpiece. [*He walks up to the bookshelves and taps the backs of books.*] All these gentlemen here who have written masterpieces, have written them around little monstrosities such as this. That's why they're so interesting and so popular! There is, however, one little difference: I'm not the hero of a tragedy. I'm the hero of a comedy. A blind man makes them weep, a deaf man makes them laugh. My part makes them laugh. Just think of it: a man deceived by a woman, that's funny already. A man of my age deceived in favor of a young man, that's funnier still. But if that young man is the old boy's son, that is the farce to end all farces. We're classical figures, you and I! Aren't you proud of yourself? I should be if I were you.

Madeleine. George . . .

George. I hope they can't hear us from the studio.

Madeleine. You know they can't.

George. You're right. That was a stupid question. The first couple of times your "sister" came, I was locked in up there. I imagine that was Michael? [*She nods.*] Admirable. But you didn't mind my taking a furnished flat. Only you hardly ever came. Why did you bother to continue with me? And why did you lie to me? I suppose you had to live. Did you help Michael out?

Madeleine. Michael was even poorer than I was. I paid for his cigarettes, or for a meal once in a while.

George. So after all it was quite respectable, as it was I who paid for my own son.

Madeleine. I'm making enough with my bookbinding to look after myself.

George. I prefer to think that it was I who paid. I thought the slightest lie makes you ill. So why did you lie to me?

Madeleine. It's no use, you wouldn't believe me.

George. You . . . of all people . . . a liar!

Madeleine. And you, why did you lie to me? What confidence you had in me! You were very careful, weren't you?

George. I was very unhappy. My home wasn't a home at all. I was all alone. I made up my mind to give myself another chance. I invented a story. And when I was with you, I was happy. I forgot everything, even my inventions, even Michael. Not once did I allow my other life to interfere with ours—so you can imagine what I felt when Michael told me the truth yesterday.

Madeleine. You should have told me your real name.

George. You would have met Michael just the same.

Madeleine. I would have avoided him.

George. Oh, nonsense! The only difference would have been, you would have broken it off with me three months ago. But why didn't you tell me? I suppose you liked the arrangement: an old man, a young man. . . .

Madeleine. George, I beg you . . . don't say such filthy things! I lied to you because I loved you, because I love you still. . . .

George. You're in-cre*d*dible!

Madeleine. Yes, George, I am very, very fond of you.

George. Oh, sure, sure. . . .

Madeleine. Please, let me finish. I am sorry if I couldn't give you all you wanted from me. You told me that you had lost a daughter. You were kind. You weren't like all the others. I was in an awful state when you met me. I was pretty well through with everything. I met you and I clung to you with all my heart. . . .

George. All I want to know is: did you love me? Because I did. I was crazy about you. I asked you a thousand times, "Do you love me?" and you always said: "Yes, George, I love you." That's true, isn't it?

Madeleine. George, there are certain reservations which one can guess even if you don't put them into so many words. I often told you: "I love you a lot," but every time you'd lose your temper and then you'd beg me and worry me and insist on an answer; so in the end I gave in and said: "Yes, George, I love you."

George. You shouldn't have said it!

Madeleine. These last months . . . what a nightmare! I did everything to open your eyes. You didn't want to see anything.

George. It was too late! If you had told me in time,

"I don't love you, but I shall try, you must wait. . . ."
But you let me sink in up to the neck, you let me love you
more and more, until I was caught for good. And you let
it drag on and you kept putting me off till what *you* call
love dropped on you from the sky. And then, since I was
in the way . . .

Madeleine. You're quite wrong. I couldn't bring myself
to hurt you. That was the reason. The idea of breaking
with you was torture to me. I said so to Michael.

George [*Face to face with* MADELEINE]. Do you love
Michael?

Madeleine. Are you asking for yourself or for him?

George. I am asking as his father.

Madeleine. He is my whole life. I can't imagine myself
without him. Unhappiness makes one very humble. I had
given up hope for love. I mean, greater love than yours
and mine. It had to be Michael to make me realize that
love is something very different. . . .

George. And does Michael love you?

Madeleine. I think . . . today . . . proves it. But if
he knew, if he ever found out the truth . . .

George. There is no question of him finding out.

Madeleine [*Immensely relieved*]. You really will put
Michael's happiness before anything else? Oh, George,
all my life I shall be grateful to you.

George. So you imagine that I am going to give you
Michael, do you?

Madeleine. . . . D'you want to take Michael away
from me?

George. At once.

Madeleine. No—! [*It is hardly more than a sound.*]

George. What did you expect? That I would give in,
that I would throw Michael into your arms and watch
you together for the rest of my life?

Madeleine. You're mad! He is your son! You are talking
of your son's happiness, of Michael's happiness!

George. What sort of happiness would that be, do you
think, with an unfaithful woman? Since you have deceived
me, how do I know that you're not going to deceive him?
How do I know that you haven't even done so already?

Madeleine [*Rushing at him, taking him by the shoulders*]. George . . . George! You don't mean that! Tell me you don't mean that!

George. No, I don't. To tell you the truth, I don't.

Madeleine [*Smiling through her agony*]. I knew it. [*She tries to take his hand.*]

George [*Turning away from her*]. But, my dear Madeleine . . . since this third person does not exist . . . and we know that he doesn't . . . we'll have to invent him.

Madeleine. Invent him . . . ?

George. We must invent a young man of your age. A bit older than Michael, a man who fascinates you completely . . . a man you can never give up. On the other hand, you're ashamed of him, and you are only going to marry Michael to ensure your social position and so make the best of both worlds.

Madeleine. You're not serious, George. . . .

George. I've never been more serious in my life.

Madeleine. What you're suggesting is horrifying, it's ghastly.

George. It's got to be done, Madeleine, or I'll tell Michael the truth.

Madeleine. You wouldn't tell your son, your wife. . . .

George. Don't—don't concern yourself about my wife. I have decided to tell her everything, whatever happens. I owe it to her.

Madeleine. She'll—she'll tell Michael!

George. She will if you force her to, if you don't leave Michael alone.

Madeleine. So this is what I've dragged him into. How right I was to be afraid. He was so innocent, so trusting. Suppose I lie to him . . . suppose I tell him this appalling story, he'll never believe me! Michael knows me.

George. Didn't you tell him again and again how much you hated lying? You can never lie—to him. "Michael knows you."

Madeleine. If you can bring yourself to do this, don't think I'll ever see you again.

George. See you again . . . ? No. I'm cured. And I intend to cure Michael.

Madeleine. Of loving me?

George [*Icily*]. I shall cure him of a project of marriage which circumstances render inadmissible.

Michael [*Opening the attic door and speaking from the top of the staircase*]. Have you finished? Can we come down?

George. Not yet. We're talking like old friends.

Michael. Well done! . . . Madeleine, I've broken a cup. Get us out of here soon! [*He exits, banging the attic door.*

Madeleine. Sometimes . . . when people you love are away, you don't realize they're still alive. A minute ago, when I was talking to you it was nothing but words. I have just heard Michael's voice. He is alive. . . . I'm not going to "leave him alone," as you said. I'll keep him.

George. I've thought it over, too, Madeleine. You're free. And I'll tell him the truth. Michael will know who the other man was. I shall lose him, but we'll lose him together.

Madeleine. That's blackmail . . . it's wicked. . . .

George. You leave me no alternative. [*He turns away from her toward the staircase.*]

Madeleine [*Running after him*]. George . . . George . . . listen to me, believe me. . . .

George. D'you really think I am so naive . . . ?

Madeleine. Yes, naive and kind. You're everything I used to love. Everything I worship in Michael. Haven't I been punished enough by your coming here today? I might have given everything away.

George. I knew that you'd control yourself, if you really loved Michael.

Madeleine. Ah, you see . . . you know I love him.

George. This marriage is absurd. I want quite another sort of life for Michael. For one thing, he must marry in his own class.

Madeleine. I am the daughter and the granddaughter of a workman. I'll change Michael. He'll work. He's changing already. If you make him unhappy now, you'll regret it for the rest of your life.

George. He won't be unhappy for long.

Madeleine. That's where you're wrong! Michael is a child. Children remember pain! And you, George, you're a child, too. Someone has broken your toy. Because that's all I was . . . I'm not important to you, George. But to Michael, I mean a lot. Michael needs me. How can you compare our adventure, built on entirely false foundations, a false name and address, even, how can you compare that with the adventure of a boy who gives himself body and soul?

George. His mother would never agree.

Madeleine. So you're both against me! But his Aunt Léonie, perhaps she——

George [Interrupting]. She loved me when she was a girl. She's still got some affection for me. Perhaps she's still in love with me, I don't know. She'd hate you if I were to be made to look ridiculous because of you.

Madeleine. She'll see me love Michael and Michael love me, and if we have children——

George. Children! Bring children into the world out of a sordid mess like this—!

Madeleine. Please, George, don't take it like that, be fair!

George. We want Michael back. We must invent this third person. Make up your mind to tell this lie or else I shall tell them the truth.

Madeleine. You're mad!

George. I am a father who is saving his son from falling into a trap he fell into himself.

Madeleine. You're lying! You're not a father! You're a man who's been turned down and who is trying to get his own back!

George. I forbid you——

Madeleine [Going for him]. Yes, you liar, you liar! [*He pushes her back.*] I don't mind you knocking me about, I prefer it even, but don't tell me it's because of your son! You don't give a damn whether he's happy or unhappy, you're jealous!

George. For the last time! Which story is it to be?

Madeleine. The truth!

George. All right. I hope you realize the implications of the truth?

Madeleine. No . . . no . . . don't . . . don't tell him . . . I was mad. . . . If he doesn't know . . . there is still hope . . . even if he leaves me . . . there must be a chance . . . but if he knows, I've lost everything.

George. You see, I was right.

Madeleine. I shall never have the strength.

George. I'll help you.

Madeleine [*Her eyes shut, in a whisper*]. This is increddible. . . .

George. Don't you think it was "in-creddible" for me yesterday, when Michael told me that he loved you, that you were his mistress, referring to me as "the old bloke"?

Madeleine [*In tears for the first time*]. He was so proud of you, of your youth. . . .

George [*Through his teeth*]. *You* were my youth. . . .

Madeleine. Be generous, George! It's his turn to live!

George [*Icily*]. May I repeat, this is not a personal question. All I am trying to do is to save my son's future and to guide it in the right direction.

Madeleine. You're lying . . . you're lying . . . you're cold and hard and inhuman, all of you . . . only Michael is human . . . and you're going to destroy him . . .

George. Have you made up your mind? [*Silence.*] Do I tell them the truth?

Madeleine [*With an outcry*]. No!

George. You'll do as you're told?

Madeleine. Yes.

George. You swear it?

Madeleine. Yes.

George. Swear it on Michael.

Madeleine. Yes.

George. "I swear it . . ."

Madeleine. I swear it . . . on Michael. I once tried to kill myself. I've no need to try it again. I'll just die.

George. Thank you for not blackmailing me with suicide. You'll live. You'll work. And you'll forget Michael.

Madeleine [*Very quietly*]. Never.

George. I see. [*He begins to climb up the staircase. He opens the attic door and calls.*] All right.

Without waiting for them, he climbs down and moves over to the far side of the divan where MADELEINE *first saw him.* YVONNE *appears first, followed by* LÉO *and* MICHAEL.

Michael. Is it animal, vegetable, or mineral?

George. Michael—I'm afraid you're going to be hurt.

Michael. Hurt? [*He turns toward* MADELEINE *and sees the state she is in.*] Madeleine! What's the matter, darling?

George. I've had a long and very interesting talk with your friend.

Michael. Madeleine can't have told you anything I haven't told you already.

George. She couldn't bear to hurt you, but talking to me she summoned up her courage. Apparently there is somebody else.

Michael. No one is more sorry than Madeleine about that. Tomorrow everything will be in order; isn't that so, Madeleine?

George. Forgive me if I do the talking; I promised her I'd do that. She is quite prepared to sacrifice the man you're thinking of. . . . That leaves the other one.

Michael. Which other one?

George. As far as you knew, there were two of you. There are three.

Michael. Three . . . ? What are you talking about?

George. Look here, Michael, you are young, very young. You don't know women and you don't know much about life. This young woman is in love——

Michael. With me!

George. She may be in love with you. I don't wish to dispute that. I don't wish to discuss it either. But she is utterly dependent, she's a slave if you like, of another man —a man of her own age, a man she never let you meet because she's ashamed of him. She only wants to marry you to insure her social position.

Michael. That's a lie, an invention; I know Madeleine! Madeleine! Tell them it isn't true! [*Silence.*] I know Madeleine's life from A to Z. You're lying!

Yvonne. Michael!

Michael. Madeleine! Help me! Tell them they're lying!
Tell them to go to hell!

George. I realize this is a great blow to you, but . . .
has it ever occurred to you that you saw very little of this
young woman, you only saw her in the day, her nights
were free. . . .

Michael. But who, who?

George. She says you don't know him. She was hoping
for a miracle. She's tried everything. That fellow has a
hold over her. It's an old story.

Michael. If that's true! [*He rushes at* MADELEINE.] Tell
me, you——

Yvonne. Michael! You're losing your head! You can't
hit a woman . . .

Michael. Can't I!!! [*He raises his hand but, face to face
with* MADELEINE, *he falls on his knees and buries his face
against her.* MADELEINE *is clinging helplessly to a book-
shelf, her body shaking with sobs.*] Madeleine, forgive
me. . . . I know they're lying . . . I know they only
want to know if I love you . . . tell me you forgive me
. . . I beg you . . . I was forgetting last night . . . as
if you could deceive me! As if our marriage could be a
plot!

George. I didn't say that. I said she couldn't give up
this other man.

Michael. But I don't understand . . . everything was
wonderful, and I didn't know . . . I swallowed it all.
. . . Who is he? Tell me? Who is he?

George. She says you don't know him . . . you can't
possibly know him.

Michael [*Rushing over to his mother*]. You were right
in everything you said. And I wouldn't believe you!

Yvonne. My love, mothers always know. They seem
foolish, unbearable spoilsports—but they know. Come!
You've still got your old mother. There . . . there . . .

Michael [*Freeing himself and turning back to* MAD-
ELEINE]. Once more, Madeleine, answer me! It's a lie,
isn't it, it's a nightmare, wake me up, shake me . . .
Madeleine!

Yvonne. Michael—try to keep calm!

Michael. Calm! I kept saying to myself: Daddy is discovering how wonderful Madeleine is, he'll help to convince Mother. Aunt Léo is already on our side. And I find a woman who confesses her past, a hypocrite, an abomination——

Madeleine [*Without a voice*]. Michael . . .

Michael. And she dares open her mouth! She dares to speak to me!

Yvonne. Michael, don't! This lady could have gone on with the game if she'd wanted to, she could have bamboozled your father, entered our home under false pretenses. Instead, she has been decent enough to warn us in time. [*To* MADELEINE.] May I thank you on our behalf. If at any time——

Madeleine. Enough!! I can't stand any more! I can't stand it! [*She turns to the staircase, stumbles up the stairs and into the attic, banging the door behind her.*

Michael. Madeleine!

George. Michael!

Yvonne. Michael, my boy——

Michael. Take me away, I want to go home . . . no! I'll stay here. [*He sits down on the divan.*] I want to know it all!

George. What for?

Michael. You're right. I don't want to know anything. I want to go home. I want my room. . . .

Yvonne. No one will disturb you. *I'll* look after you.

Michael. I should never have left the Caravan.

Yvonne. You needed this experience.

Michael. I could have done without it, thank you. How wise you are, never to go out. People are vile.

Yvonne. Not all of them, Michael——

Michael. All of them! [*He looks around.*] What order, eh, Léo! Not a chance of getting the visits mixed up, no forgotten umbrellas or shirts or hats or cigarette ends . . . but every modern convenience.

MADELEINE *appears on the top step. She can hardly stand on her feet.*

Madeleine [*Imploring*]. Will you please go. . . .

Michael. Number three is getting impatient. Don't go. I'm taking my time now. And this woman has dared to tell me she was in love with me. She loves us all! A mighty big heart. There's room in it for everybody. Bitch!

MADELEINE *trips upon one of the steps. For a moment it looks as if she has fainted.* LÉO *rushes over to her, as she comes to, guides her gently toward the divan, which* MICHAEL *vacates contemptuously.*

Yvonne. Mick, my boy. . . .

Michael. Never mind, Léo. Leave her alone. Let her faint. It's an act.

Yvonne. Don't be hard. She needn't have told us anything.

GEORGE *slips out into the hall.*

Michael. If Dad hadn't found her out, she'd have taken me in completely. Deeper and deeper into the muck. It's good to know there are some people left who care for you, who don't know anything about plots and frame-ups. Come on. I want to get out of here. Where is Dad?

Léo [*Dryly*]. Gone. He doesn't like scenes.

Michael. His inventions don't get him into lovely little surprises like this.

Yvonne. Darling—you're trembling . . .

Michael. I'm *not* trembling!

Yvonne. Yes, you are. . . . Here, come home with me . . . we'll go down together. [MICHAEL *exits. Following him,* YVONNE *says:*] Léo . . . we can't leave this child all alone in such a state.

Léo. Take Michael home. . . . I'll stay here for a minute.

Yvonne. Thank you, Léo.

[YVONNE *exits. The door of the flat is heard to close.*
Madeleine. Michael . . . Michael . . . darling . . . please don't go . . . please!!

Léo. There . . . there . . . pull yourself together. . . . Try and lie down a bit . . . ?

Madeleine. Oh, please . . . please . . . oh, God . . . I can't, I can't . . .

Léo. Listen to me, my dear . . . try and listen to me.

Madeleine. I can't . . . I can't . . . you've no idea . . .

Léo. Yes, I have. . . . I've guessed.

Madeleine. What . . . ?

Léo. That the "old bloke" and Michael's father are one and the same person.

Madeleine. Oh, my God—how could you possibly know?

Léo. Well, my dear child, not to notice you'd have to be blind, as blind as my sister and Michael. The truth hits you in the eye. I tell you, it could only have escaped people like Michael and Yvonne.

Madeleine. It would have killed me . . . if Michael had found out.

Léo. And this third person, this Number Three . . . he is a myth? I mean to say, he doesn't exist, does he?

Madeleine. Oh, no . . . he does *not* exist . . . and Michael didn't even try to find out, he didn't doubt it at at all; he swallowed this grotesque story without a moment's thought, otherwise he must have known it was a lie.

Léo. That was a bit of luck. If he'd been capable of thinking clearly, he might have suddenly discovered the truth. . . . So George bullied you, threatened to give the show away . . .

Madeleine. Yes, he did.

Léo. He would have done it, too.

Madeleine. I'd have put up with anything rather than that—even losing Michael. . . .

Léo. Funny . . . I thought George would give in to his son and implore *you* to keep quiet.

Madeleine. He tortured me . . . he threatened me all the time. . . . He wanted to "cure" Michael, he said . . . he had it all prepared . . . this lie . . . he had it all worked out. . . .

Léo [*Grimly*]. Damn it all—there are limits. [*She takes* MADELEINE'*s hands.*]

Madeleine. Thank you . . . thank you . . . I never hoped . . .

Léo. Sh—don't talk about it. I like you very much. You've made quite a conquest of me. I had no more confidence in Michael's choice of women than in George's. I didn't come here as your ally, still less as your accomplice. Now I should like to be both. I am coming over to your side.

Madeleine. Oh, what's the good . . . it's all over. . . .
Perhaps he's right . . . perhaps I don't belong to your
class. . . .

Léo. What class? Don't be silly. Now listen to me . . .
Madeleine. . . . [*She shakes her.*] Listen to me, Made-
leine: tomorrow at five o'clock, you'll come to the
Caravan . . .

Madeleine. . . . the Caravan . . .

Léo. To us. To George.

Madeleine. Who? Me?

Léo. Yes, you.

Madeleine. They'll throw me out.

Léo. No, they won't.

Madeleine. I can't believe it . . .

Léo [*Putting lipstick on, and talking with the grimaces
of a woman thus occupied*]. You know, there are moments
when love revolts me. There are others when it stirs me to
the depths of my being and gets the better of me. Who
knows what goes on inside us? That's Greek, I suppose.
Don't try to understand me, I'm a pedantic kind of person.

Madeleine. George will give away everything!

Léo. George will shut up. Leave that to me.

Madeleine. He swore he would——

Léo. He was jealous. Tomorrow he'll be the noble father
who protects his son.

Madeleine. He was a brute.

Léo [*Wincing slightly*]. No, my dear. George isn't a
brute. George is a child; he doesn't know what he's doing.
He might easily break somebody's heart without realizing
it at all.

Madeleine. You're very kind. . . .

Léo. No, I'm not. I hate disorder, that's all. I am dis-
gusted by the mess that George has left behind him. It
must be sorted out, washed, dried, and ironed. Come tomorrow!

Madeleine. But——

Léo. No buts. At five o'clock. It's an order. Swear it on
Michael.

Madeleine [*With the first faint suggestion of a smile*].
. . . on Michael. . . .

Léo. I swear . . .

Madeleine. I swear.

Léo. On Michael . . .

Madeleine. On Michael.

Léo. Splendid! Now try and get some sleep. I want you to look your very best tomorrow. Don't you get your eyes red. Here's the address. [*She gives it to* MADELEINE.]

Madeleine. After this nightmare . . .

Léo [*Getting up*]. That's all over and done with. I've adopted you. From now on you're under my very special protection. All right, child?

Madeleine. Aunt Léo . . .

Léo. That's what I wanted to hear. [*She walks toward the door.*] Don't move, I can find my way out.

Madeleine. Please let me say how——

Léo. No, dear, don't! As far as I'm concerned, all these thanks and thank-yous and thank you so much . . . [*She shrugs her shoulders significantly and shuts the door behind her, the curtain coming down already over her last words.*

ACT THREE

SCENE—YVONNE's *bedroom. The same as in Act One. To start with, the stage is in considerable darkness, but it becomes gradually lighter as if the eye was getting used to the dark. The usual state of disorder.*

LÉO [*To* GEORGE, *who enters through the door upstage left*]. Still the same?

George. Still the same. I can't bear to stay in my own room. I'm in a bad way myself, and I'm afraid I shall soon be behaving like Michael.

Léo. I can't bear it in my room either. I can hear Mick groaning and banging on the floor. I can't say I am in hysterics like the rest of you, I just feel I am at the other end of the world, far away from something that is about to happen, and I feel it's going to happen to Yvonne. Now if *I* go off the rails, that *will* be the end.

George. There's no air in this place.

Léo. Is Yvonne with Michael?

George. Yes. Impossible to get a word out of him. I never thought him capable of suffering like this. It's beastly. And I've got to control myself, when *I* feel I can hardly bear it another minute.

Léo. It's the first time he's been in love, the first time he's really suffered.

George [*A little bitter*]. Well, of course, if you manage to control yourself, you don't get any sympathy.

Léo. No one in the world, George, could understand you better and be more sorry for you than I am. But I simply refuse to compare your feelings, however tough it may be for you, to what this boy is going through. He's had no idea what it means to be unhappy, and now from one day to another . . .

George. He's got Yvonne. . . .

Léo. No, really, George. . . .

George. I mean it! He has Yvonne. He doesn't say anything to her, but he snuggles up against her. It's instinctive. And Yvonne is triumphant. She's "found him again." She's found her son again. That's all she can say. And there was I, pouring out my heart to her, making a special effort to tell her everything, making a fool of myself, and she didn't even notice. She didn't show any surprise at all. She only thinks of Michael, of the danger that he might hear something, and she keeps asking me to be careful of what I am saying. As far as I was concerned, she just looked vaguely into the distance and said: "That is your punishment, my poor George . . . that is your punishment." That is the wife I "find" again, that "finds" me again and helps me to get over it. . . .

Léo [*Sarcastically*]. That this story wouldn't upset her unduly was to be expected, I suppose. That father and son, each in turn, meet the same girl, without knowing it, and play hide-and-seek with each other, is probably an everyday occurrence in Yvonne's world. And as far as your punishment is concerned, she is perhaps not altogether wrong.

George. Well, I like that! Punishment indeed! Punishment for what?

Léo. George, I stayed behind with the girl after you'd all gone. I talked to her, and she talked to me, that is, as far as she was able to, considering the state she was in.

George. Well?

Léo. George, what you did was inhuman!

George. Say that again. . . .

Léo. George, what you did was inhuman!

George. How d'you mean what *I* did? Léo, what *you* did! It was you who told me what to do, who invented the whole plot!

Léo. I advise you never to say that again, never as long as you live to say anything which sounds like it!

George. It's in-cre*dd*ible!

Léo. You and your "incredible"! I've heard that girl say it herself and she didn't say it at all as I expected. What I heard and saw there wasn't distorted by the haze of this Caravan. I made a mistake, I admit it. Your whole story didn't look very genuine to me at the time, in fact I thought it was rather cockeyed. And perhaps you won't be very much surprised if I confess that I had precious little confidence in your and Michael's taste as far as the choice of a wife was concerned. I pictured your young woman as a tart, a little gold-digger, leading you around by the nose! I was wrong. I regret it.

George. Madeleine's taken you in, too.

Léo. No, my dear George, no. She hasn't taken me in. She wouldn't know how. She is a child, an unhappy child.

George. Oh, superb! This young lady deceives me with Michael, she deceives Michael with——

Léo. You aren't going to believe in a ghost you invented yourself!

George. That *we* invented, that *you* invented.

Léo. George!

George. All right, all right . . . that *I* invented. But, dearest Léo, perhaps neither of us invented anything: a woman who is capable of——

Léo [*Interrupting*]. Look, you're not going to believe this atrocity now, just because it suits you!

George. Superb! Superb! Now she's being canonized! Madeleine is a saint!

Léo. She is young and she loves Michael and she is quite fond of you . . . poor George. That's your share of the bargain. It suddenly occurred to me how we went to this child—yes I say that on purpose—we went there with our old habits, our selfishness, our manias, all set to wipe out youth and order . . . the future, in fact.

George. So that's how she's got you—with her order!

Léo. George, will you get into your head that there's no question of getting or not getting me. The point is to put right the wrong that I have done. . . .

George. Ah!

Léo. I'm so confused I don't know any more what I'm saying. What I mean is that we must make good the wrong that *you* have done, that *we* have done, that poor Yvonne has done without realizing it. And we must do it at any cost!

George. Go back on yesterday? Not on your life! Never!

Léo. I am sorry, but I must make you understand. Yvonne must pay for this, and so must you.

George. And you? What about you? Here you are setting yourself up as a judge and making everybody pay! Where's your share in this beastly affair? Are you sacrificing yourself the least little bit?

Léo. That happened long ago.

George. What d'you mean "that happened long ago"?

Léo. I mean: how do you know I haven't had my share and bought the right to call on you for yours?

George. What share, what sacrifice are you talking about, I'd like to know.

Léo. I was very much in love with you, George. Who knows, perhaps I still am. I believed I was sacrificing myself for the sake of your happiness. Well, I was wrong. But this time I am not wrong. It is inconceivable that you should sacrifice Michael and that poor girl just like that, so that you can all carry on as if nothing had happened. It's contemptible.

George [*Trying to take her hand*]. Léo——

Léo. No, please . . . let's have no sentimentalities, no thank-yous. I can do without them. We must make Yvonne see this, George. We must bring Madeleine here. It is essential. She must come here.

George. Bring her here? But my poor Léo, even supposing for a moment that I'd put up with the torture of having these lovers here, Yvonne would never agree to it, she'd shout, she'd scream, she's "found him again," she's "found her Mick again." You try and take him away from her.

Léo. She's found a wreck. She'll soon realize that.

George. She'd rather hang on to him dead than see him go off alive with someone else.

Léo. If that's true, you must act. I know you, you won't tolerate anything so inhuman and unspeakable.

George. But—what shall we tell Michael?

Léo. That's easy. We shall tell him that Madeleine's been wonderful—by the way, that's not saying too much—that she invented this third person to set Michael free, to return him to the bosom of his family. You'll see, he'll only love her all the more. She deserves it.

George. I didn't know you had such a big heart. . . .

Léo. My heart was no use to anybody. This is the first time it has served some purpose. I love Michael. He's your son.

George [*Slightly cynical*]. And Yvonne? Do you love her too, Léo? Do your plans include her happiness, too?

Léo [*Coolly*]. Don't search too deeply into the heart, George. That's a thing one mustn't do. You might find a bit of everything. Don't search too deeply into my heart, nor into yours.

Silence.

George. If we do this, it's a complete contradiction of everything we did yesterday.

Léo. I like contradicting myself! It's my only luxury, my own private disorder, do let me keep it. Oh, let's stop pretending, George, you know as well as I do, this family of ours is a wreck, its days are gone. It's only a shadow of that blind, idiotic force that goes crushing every dream, every hope, every chance of happiness, with its "narrow path" and its "inflexible middle-class morality." I don't want to preach, George, but let's seize our opportunity, let's salvage something out of the wreck. Let's choose our own path by all means, but don't let's prevent the others from choosing theirs. . . .

George [*Lowering his head*]. Léo—I believe you're right.

Léo [*Kindly, as if talking to a good little boy*]. George—
I love you.

On this last word, the door opens and YVONNE *enters. She
is dressed in her bathrobe of Act One, and her hair is
disheveled.*

George. We were waiting for you here. We were hoping
he'd relax being alone with you. Léo could hear him right
through the door.

Yvonne. It's hell.

Léo. Did he speak to you?

Yvonne. No. He held my hand so tightly, he nearly
crushed it. I wanted to stroke his hair. I stupidly asked him
if he was thirsty. He said: "Go away." I waited at the
door hoping he would call me back. He said again: "Go
away." It's hell. I can't stand any more. I can't!

George. Shall *I* go to him?

Yvonne. If he sends *me* away, it means he doesn't want
anybody. He doesn't want to be pitied, to be touched, he
doesn't want anybody to see him. . . .

George. He's had a terrible shock.

Yvonne. If that woman wasn't a prostitute, I'd send for
her, I'd give her to him. That's what I've come to.

Léo. That's easy to say now.

Yvonne. No, Léo . . . that's not easy to say. For me to
say it, I must be pretty well finished.

Léo. You'd give her to him . . . ?

Yvonne. Anything . . . yes. . . . I can't go on like this
any more.

Léo. Well, Yvonne, that's what I've been wanting to
hear you say. I didn't want to say it first, nor did I want
George to make you say it. Go on, tell her, George!

Yvonne. More words!

George. No, Yvonne. I don't know if you consider my
confession to you nothing but words, but what I have to
tell you is much more serious than that.

Yvonne. What can be more serious than the state we're
in now?

George. The fact that the state we're in is the direct

result of a crime, and that I happen to be the criminal.

Yvonne. You?

George. Yvonne—Madeleine is innocent. The mysterious stranger does not exist.

Yvonne. I'm afraid I don't understand. . . .

George [*Handing over to* LÉO]. Léo. . . .

Léo. As you know, I stayed alone with her yesterday——

Yvonne. And she's fooled you? My innocent sister! And George, the victim, has become the criminal.

George. Let me do it, Léo. I'd like to get the whole thing off my chest. This is it, Yvonne: I forced that poor girl to lie. I invented the whole miserable story. I made the most of Michael being ready to believe anything and of Madeleine being terrified that he'd find out the truth.

Yvonne. You did that?

George. I did that. I swear it.

Yvonne. George, you might have killed Michael!

George. What I did is not much better. That's why I said "crime." I might have killed Madeleine walking in on her like that. And after I got her into the state which you took for nerves, I took advantage of the tête-à-tête that you insisted on and completely finished her off. Nice going, eh! My best invention, the only one that really worked. And I was proud of it. Until Léo came and rubbed my nose in it.

Léo. George . . . no! I want to be fair. If it hadn't been for me——

George. If it hadn't been for you, I'd have gone on with it. No, Léo, I want to take the responsibility and I want to take it alone. It is almost as if the Caravan . . . exercises a kind of charm . . . [*He turns to* YVONNE *and kisses her.*] Yvonne's charm . . . and makes us all deaf and blind. We were just talking about it before you came in. That's why when you said you'd give her to him it took such a weight off our minds. I admit I was afraid I'd have to fight you for it.

Yvonne. George, you're indulging in a positive orgy of self-humiliation. Léo is much too clearheaded, she knows what I mean. Take care; this time it's you who are daydreaming! And I, the notorious sleepwalker and fortuneteller of this Caravan, I am the one who sees clearly for a change. What's done is done. Neither Michael nor this young woman are dead. They're going through a crisis, like yourself, like all of us. The wise thing to do is to say: "nothing has happened that we were afraid would happen" and make the most of our luck.

George. Our luck! What luck? Are you aware of the words you're using?

Yvonne. I'm using the words that come to me most naturally. I'm a mother who loves her son, and I'm not a bit sublime. I agree you did wrong, perhaps, possibly, yes, but on the whole we've been lucky, yes, lucky, to get out of it safe and sound.

George. Five minutes ago, you said with a dying voice: "It's hell, I can't stand any more, I'm finished!"

Yvonne. Exactly! It's because I can't stand any more, because I'm finished, that I've got just about enough strength to say stop before you restart something which is finished and done with. I repeat—I, the village idiot—that we've been very lucky in this unfortunate business, that we must make the most of our luck and let sleeping dogs lie.

Léo. But, Yvonne, what is this luck you're talking about?

Yvonne. Well . . . for instance . . . it was a bit of luck that the old bloke in question happened to be George.

George. Thanks very much.

Yvonne. Because if it had been someone else . . . I know you, George . . . you'd have gone all sentimental and given in.

George. Sentimental? I was trying to get my own back in the lowest possible way, pretending to myself that I was doing you a service, that I was carrying out your instructions. . . .

Léo. My dear Yvonne, your point is lost on George; I'm afraid you two misunderstand each other.

George. I don't misunderstand, I don't understand at all.

Léo. You see? [*To* GEORGE.] This is what Yvonne has in mind, if I'm not mistaken: she thinks it's a bit of luck, in spite of what has been done to Madeleine, that Michael now feels this marriage is impossible.

Yvonne. But——

Léo. Just a second——. And George, on the other hand, is trying to prove to you that there is now no reason to stop it.

Yvonne. To stop what?

George. To stop Michael and Madeleine's love.

Yvonne. What was that you said?

George. I am saying that we very nearly killed these children out of selfishness and that it is high time to bring them back to life, that's what I'm saying.

Yvonne. You are saying this . . . you!

George. Yvonne, this is the moment to tell the truth and nothing but the truth: I never had anything from Madeleine; yes I did, I want to be fair, she was very fond of me, but I pretended there was more to it than that, and I kept on pretending—I just refused to appreciate her frankness. I forced her to drag this wretched lie around, when all she did was to ask me to face up to the truth. However, all this would only be serious now, if by some misfortune Michael should hear of it. . . .

Yvonne. That would be terrible!

George. At last, we agree on that.

Léo. And you're going to agree on the rest as well.

Yvonne. George, do you honestly think, you and Léo, have you considered calmly and dispassionately, this person could bear our name, could fit into our class?

George. Your grandfather collected semicolons, her grandfather was a bookbinder; my dear Yvonne, I can see there a certain——

Yvonne. I'm not joking; I'm asking you——

George. Well, don't ask me to consider seriously anything so absurd! Classes! Families! To listen to you, one might think we were the issue of Jupiter's thigh! I am a second-rate inventor, a failure. You are a sick woman who lives in the dark. Léo has remained an old maid because . . . because she wants to be with us when we need her help. And it's in the name of all this, of all this tradition of incompetence and failure, that you would refuse Michael some air, some space, and a chance to make a success of his life. No, Yvonne. I won't have it.

Léo. Bravo, George!

Yvonne. Ah, of course! George is a god! He's infallible!

Léo. I admire him.

Yvonne. Why don't you say you're in love with him.

George. Yvonne!

Yvonne. Go on! Get married! The lot of you! I'll go away . . . you can take my place . . . no trouble at all. . . .

Léo. Are you going mad?

Yvonne [*Full of contrition suddenly*]. Yes, Léo, I *am* going mad; don't be angry with me.

Léo. I'm not angry with you.

Yvonne. Thank you. I'm sorry.

Léo. Let's cut out the thank-yous and the apologies, shall we? Listen to me, Yvonne: if I had really wanted George, I wouldn't have let you take him. It's far too late to start that up again. There's only one way to salvage our wreck and that is to save Michael, to listen to George, to tell Michael the good news and bring him back to life.

Yvonne. Is that what you call life?

George. Don't pretend you could go on enduring Michael in his present state. So what are you waiting for, Yvonne?

Pause.

Yvonne. Anyway, this girl is much too young.

Léo. I beg your pardon. . . .

George. She's three years older than Michael. Yesterday you said she was too old.

Yvonne. She is too young . . . compared with me.

George. Well, I'm damned!

Yvonne. You're asking the impossible.

George. We asked Madeleine to do the impossible, and she did it.

Yvonne. I've found Mick again, I can't let him go.

George. You won't find Michael again until you give him Madeleine. The Michael you think you have found no longer exists. If you let him go on thinking that Madeleine is deceiving him—which is abominable and which I will not stand—something inside him would doubt and go on living with her. You wouldn't benefit by the criminal thing you've done.

Léo. If I understand you rightly: your ideal would be to have an invalid son, so that he could never leave the house.

Yvonne [*Broken, bursting into tears*]. It's too much . . . it's too much for me!

George. Nothing is too much when you love somebody. You love Michael. Think of seeing him grateful and happy, instead of having him bitter and ill.

Léo. Or he'll probably marry some dreadful girl, which will be much worse.

George [*Putting his arm around her shoulder*]. Yvonne— show you've got a heart!

YVONNE *breaks away from* GEORGE *and jumps on her bed, where she hops about on her knees and points her hand accusingly at* GEORGE.

Yvonne. Leave me alone! Come off your pedestals, both of you! You aren't any better than me! Lies, nothing but lies everywhere! [*To* GEORGE.] You, try and get out of this one: Yesterday, when we got to that woman's flat, I remember perfectly—you went so far as to put on an act about the wrong floor, you pretended you didn't know her floor! You were trying to fool me, and you nearly did it. You dared to take me to your mistress!

George. You know very well——

Yvonne. Yes! To your mistress!

George. Shut up, Yvonne! You're losing your head: d'you want the boy to hear you?

Yvonne. I know what to tell him!

George [*Very quietly*]. Yvonne—it isn't very often that we can make up for what we have done. . . . We can save ourselves and two other people. . . . Darling, say you agree!

Yvonne. Again we'd have to summon the boy . . . make our way back to that woman . . . humiliate ourselves. . . .

George. For Heaven's sake! Nobody's going to "summon" Michael and tell him to "follow his father into the study"; all you have to do is to run to his room, give him a kiss, and you'll work a miracle.

Léo. As regards Madeleine, at my own risk and peril, I've been taking care of that.

Yvonne [*Going straight for* Léo]. What business is that of yours? What have you done?

Léo. My duty. I talked to her, listened to her, I consoled her. I even telephoned her.

Yvonne [*Stressing every syllable*]. You telephoned her?

Léo. To come here.   [*She quickly goes to her room.*

Yvonne. So that's what you two have been plotting!

George. That's what Léo's been plotting without my knowledge and for which I'm very grateful to her.

Yvonne. You want to force my hand.

George. We want to save you, and us, and Michael.

Yvonne. So she gets what she's been after; she'll be in possession here.

George. Please don't talk like that; it's so bad.

Yvonne. You've all become saints.

George. Yvonne!

Yvonne. Give me time. Don't rush me!

George. I thought you might realize the effort I have to make myself.

Yvonne. Poor old boy. . . .

George. Poor old girl. . . . We're not old, Yvonne, neither of us, and yet . . .

Yvonne. And yet one day one finds the children are growing up and want to take over from us.

George. That's in the order of things.

Yvonne [*With a tired smile*]. I'm afraid order isn't my strong point.

George. It isn't mine, either. [*He takes her hand.*] Your hand is like ice.

Yvonne [*Listless*]. Oh that. . . .

Léo [*Re-entering, full of spirit*]. Let's get ready for the party. Let's light the candles. That's the spirit! Mind we keep it up.

George. I am not much good at parties or surprises.

Yvonne. Oh, I don't know; I think you're doing fine.

Léo. Now then, now then, stop arguing.

George. Well, what do we do now?

Léo. It's quite simple. Yvonne, the good news must come from you, he must owe it to you.

Yvonne. But——

Léo. No buts.

Yvonne. But I'm not actually in favor of this. . . .

Léo. You mustn't show it.

Yvonne. It'll look all wrong. Besides, I'm freezing cold. Look at me! Listen! My teeth are chattering.

Léo. It's your nerves.

Yvonne. One of these days I'll die and you'll say it's my nerves. My knees are wobbly.

Léo. Make an effort. It's got to be done.

George. Yes, it's got to be done, Yvonne. Think of the present you're going to put in his stocking.

Yvonne. If I can find one of them!

A door slams.

Léo. A door bang! That's Michael. That makes things much easier. You see? A "miracle"!

Yvonne. What are you doing to me. . . ?

George [*Listening*]. What's *he* doing? Where's he going?

Léo. What if he's going out?

George. He'd slam the other door.

Léo. That's right.

Yvonne [*Very quietly, in a very clear voice*]. He hasn't eaten anything since yesterday. He's at the sideboard. Now . . . he's coming to my door. He listens . . . he puts his hand on the doorknob. . . . [*The doorknob begins to turn.*] The door's opening. . . . [*The door opens slowly.*] I'm afraid . . . as if it wasn't Michael . . . as if it was something . . . something awful. . . . Léo, George . . . what's happening to me? [*She clings to* Léo *and* George *as if in terror of something invisible; suddenly she calls out:*] Mick!

Michael *enters, leaving the door open. He looks washed out, his eyes red and half-closed.*

Michael. It's me, Sophie. . . .

Yvonne. Well, come in . . . and shut the doors!

Michael. What d'you mean the "doors"? All right, I'll shut the door. I'm going out again, anyway. I was looking for the sugar.

Yvonne. Well, you know where to find it.

Michael. Yes, I know. Are you alone?

Yvonne. My poor darling, can't you see your aunt and your father?

Michael. Oh! I'm sorry, Léo—sorry, Dad. I can't see a thing. Am I disturbing you? [*He vanishes for a moment into the bathroom and re-emerges almost immediately munching some sugar.*]

Léo. You're not disturbing us at all. As a matter of fact, your mother was just about to go and fetch you.

Michael. I wanted to talk to you, Mother. Since I'd only have to repeat it all afterwards to Léo and Dad, I'll tell you all now. First of all, Sophie, I want to apologize for telling you to go away. I was sick of myself . . . I didn't want to . . . well, you understand.

Yvonne [*Melting away*]. I understand perfectly, my poor Mick.

Michael. Don't pity me!

George. What did you want to tell us, Michael?

Michael [*Eating his sugar, a little embarrassed*]. Well . . . I can't go on like this . . . so I thought . . . Dad, you remember that job in Algiers, you said to me at the time, if I'd make up my mind . . .

Yvonne. You want to leave me?

Michael. My mind's made up.

Yvonne. Mick!

Michael. Oh, Sophie, I'm no good to anybody these days, and worse still, I'm beginning to get you all down. . . .

Yvonne. You're mad!

Michael. I'm going mad here in Paris. I can't stay here. . . . I want to go far away and to go quickly. I'll get a job. I know a bit of everything and nothing properly. Suicide disgusts me. I must have a complete change. . . .

Yvonne. What about me? What about all of us?

Michael. Oh! Sophie!

Yvonne. Give me your hand . . . listen to me, Mick. Listen to me. Look at me. What if you didn't have to go?

George. What if we had some good news for you, for example?

Michael. There's no such thing as good news any more, as far as I'm concerned.

Léo. That depends. What if the motive for your . . . departure was no longer valid?

Yvonne. What if your reasons for leaving us were no longer true?

Michael. It's no use, Sophie. I'm going back to my room. Dad——

George. No, Michael, don't go back to your room and don't ask me to see what I can do about this job.

Michael. You promised me. . . .

George. Mick, I want to tell you some news, some very, very good news. Madeleine——

Michael [*Furiously*]. Don't speak to me any more about that person! Never again! Just you leave that alone, d'you hear! Don't you see I can't take any more? So why don't you shut up!

Léo. Michael—listen to what your father has to say!

Michael [*Still more furiously*]. Stop it, will you! Leave it alone! I forbid you to mention that person, d'you hear!

George. I'm sorry, I must speak to you about her. [GEORGE *stops* MICHAEL *from leaving.*]

Michael. I'm not going to listen to you! I've had enough! [*He kicks* YVONNE'S *bed.*]

George. Would you mind not kicking your mother's bed; she is ill. And stop shouting!

Michael [*Stubbornly*]. What do you want?

George. Your aunt stayed behind yesterday, after we'd left.

Michael. You're trying to trick me into staying in Paris by inventing lies. You're trying to stop me from making up my mind. You needn't bother; my mind is made up.

Yvonne [*In an outcry*]. You're not going!

Michael [*Pointing at his mother*]. You see!

George. You're not going because it would be criminal to go.

Michael. Why criminal?

George. Because if your family doesn't count any longer, there is someone else to whom you should apologize and whom you ought to ask for permission to go, first.

Michael [*With an ugly laugh, to* GEORGE]. I see . . . how silly of me. . . . I've got it now: The lady had plenty of courage when *you* were talking to her, but she lost it

all when she was up against Léo. She realized she'd found
her match, so she turned on the charm.

Léo. I'm not easily taken in.

Michael. I shall never believe anything again!

George. Well, you'd be wrong! Yvonne. . . .

Yvonne. Do believe it, Mick! Do believe it!

Michael. Don't torture me. . . .

George. No one wants to torture you. . . . Not only is
Madeleine innocent, but she's behaved admirably.

Michael. In what way, for Heaven's sake?

George. Michael—I'm afraid I owe you an apology.
Yesterday, our attitude was too much for Madeleine. She
felt she wouldn't be able to hold out against us. So she
lied to me. I felt it but I turned a deaf ear. Mick, *she invented the whole story* to set you free, to help us to get rid
of her.

Michael. If that's true, would you have waited so long
to tell me? Mother would never have let me——

Léo [*Interrupting*]. Your mother didn't know before. We
needed proof. Actually, it was my fault, the delay. I was
plotting something . . . I was preparing a surprise for
you.

Michael. Mummy, you—you tell me.

Yvonne. I've already told you.

Michael [*Now fully convinced*]. But then we must go
to her, we must phone, we must try and find her at once!
She might have done something frightful. . . . Dad . . .
Léo . . . quickly . . . where is she?

Léo [*Pointing to the door*]. Here.

Yvonne [*Sitting bolt upright*]. Here?

Léo. She's been waiting in my room since five o'clock.

At these words, MICHAEL *stands quite still as if rooted to
the spot. He does not see that* LÉO *has opened the door
and that* MADELEINE *appears in the opening. He is covering his eyes with one hand while reaching out with the
other as if he wanted to hold onto something.* LÉO's *surprise has been a little too much for him. While* YVONNE,
LÉO, *and* GEORGE *are saying something,* MADELEINE, *who
has eyes only for* MICHAEL, *is rushing up to him. She takes
his arm, which is searching for support, and puts it around*

herself. She is holding him in her arms. All her love, all her
tenderness, are in this gesture. She does not speak.

Yvonne. Mick! Mick! Is he ill?

MADELEINE *does not speak. She tries but she can't. So she*
holds him closer still. MICHAEL *opens his eyes, as she*
gently pulls his hand from his face. He looks at MADE-
LEINE *and as he looks he slowly sinks to his knees. When*
he speaks, it is hardly more than a whisper.

Michael. Madeleine . . . my darling . . . forgive me,
please. . . .

Madeleine [*Kneeling down beside him, and smiling*
through her tears]. Michael, my love . . . will you forgive
me . . . I've hurt you so much. . . .

Michael. No, Madeleine, it was me . . . I've been such
a fool. . . .

Léo. If I were you children, I'd leave the explanations
alone and start all over again.

During this, YVONNE *is making several brave attempts to*
join the group. She even manages to smile bravely at
MICHAEL'*s happiness—but no one seems to notice her, and*
her expression changes to that of a child, lost and alone.

George. Léo is right.

Michael [*Jumping to his feet and helping* MADELEINE
up]. Léo is terrific.

George. Léo most certainly is.

Madeleine. I still can't believe this is true, this is really
happening. . . .

Michael. Nor can I. And I wanted to run away and take
a job in Algiers!

Madeleine. In Algiers?

George [*Grinning*]. Yes! While you were waiting in
Léo's room, Michael came to us, with a face like an under-
taker and sucking a piece of sugar at the same time, and
said that he'd decided to live in Algiers.

YVONNE *tries once more to join the others. But no one*
sees her. All eyes are on MICHAEL *and* MADELEINE.

Léo. When are you leaving, Michael?

Michael. All right, I've asked for it.

George. He wouldn't listen to any of us, he just wouldn't!

Michael. Dad—!

Léo. Shut up, George. . . .

George. All right, all right, I shan't say another word.

Madeleine. How kind you all are. . . .

On this YVONNE, *who has slowly walked over to the bathroom, turns away from them all, and shuts the bathroom door behind her.*

Michael [*Taking* MADELEINE'S *hand into his own*]. You're cold?

Madeleine. I suddenly turned cold when I saw you standing there like that. I couldn't help it. I think the shock was a bit too much. But it's all right now, I'm fine. I couldn't see anything at all, when I came in, except you.

George. You didn't see anything because nobody can see a thing in here. My wife detests strong light. Never turn on the top light whatever you do.

Léo [*Whispering to* MICHAEL]. Michael, your mother. . . .

Michael [*Looking around*]. Where's she got to?

Madeleine. Perhaps that's my fault. . . .

George. No, no, no! She was here a second ago.

Léo [*To* MICHAEL]. You should have made a little more fuss over her!

Michael. I thought she was here! Sophie!

George. Yvonne!

Yvonne [*From the bathroom*]. I'm not lost. I'm here. I'm doing my injection.

Madeleine [*Calling to* YVONNE]. Can I be of any help?

Yvonne. No, thanks. I'm used to being alone.

Léo. Yvonne can't bear people to help her. It's one of her manias.

They all speak in very hushed voices.

Madeleine. Perhaps in time she'll let me. . . .

Michael. That would be a major victory.

Léo [*To* MADELEINE]. Yvonne is very sensitive. Michael only had eyes for you, which is very natural, but . . . be careful, children.

Madeleine. Exactly. I was afraid she'd gone because of me.

George. Of course not. Léo, don't make Yvonne out to be such a monster.

Léo. I'm not, I'm only warning Michael. In Madeleine's interests. He mustn't make Yvonne jealous.

George. That's right, frighten her now . . .

Michael. No, Dad—Madeleine is very sensible.

Madeleine. I'm not frightened, Michael, but I'm afraid——

George [Interrupting]. Sh . . . !

The bathroom door opens. YVONNE, *standing in the shadow, leans against the doorframe. She speaks in a strange voice.*

Yvonne. You see my dear, how much I am loved? I've only to go out of the room for a second, and they're lost without me. I wasn't lost. I have to look after myself. [*She goes to her bed and drops onto it.*] Without insulin I'd be dead.

Léo [*Whispering to* MICHAEL]. Go and give her a kiss.

Michael [*Trying to pull* MADELEINE *with him*]. Come with me.

Madeleine [*Pushing him*]. No, no . . . go on. . . .

George [*To* YVONNE]. You're not ill, are you?

Yvonne [*With an effort*]. N-no. . . .

Michael [*Letting go of* MADELEINE *and coming to* YVONNE's *bed*]. Sophie, are you happy?

Yvonne. Very. [MICHAEL *tries to kiss her.*] Don't be so rough! [*To* MADELEINE.] You'll be lucky, my dear, if Mick doesn't pull your hair out every time he kisses you.

Léo [*As if struck by an inspiration*]. Michael, you ought to go and show Madeleine your famous room.

Michael. I daren't!

Madeleine. Michael! Are you refusing to show me your room?

Michael. You'll start tidying up!

Madeleine. Oh!

George. I'll come with you. . . . I'll show you my electronic underwater submachine gun.

Michael. We'll do her the honors of the Caravan. For-

ward march! [*He opens the door and turns around again.*]
Sophie, we shall leave you with the representative of
order. . . . Léo, try and stop Mummy from running us
down behind our backs.

Yvonne. Mick! Don't go! Stay with me!

George [*Rushing to her*]. What's the matter? Yvonne!
[YVONNE *falls back.*] Yvonne!

Yvonne. I'm so afraid. . . .

George. Afraid of what?

Yvonne. I'm so afraid . . . I'm horribly afraid . . .
don't go . . . don't go! George, Mick, Mick! I'm so horribly afraid!

Léo. That's not the insulin . . . she has taken something else! [*She rushes into the bathroom and returns almost immediately, shouting.*] I knew it! [*Turning to*
YVONNE.] What have you done? How could you! Yvonne!

Yvonne. My head's spinning. . . . George, I've done a
mad thing, a ghastly thing . . . I've . . .

Michael. Mummy—tell me!

Yvonne. I can't. . . . Help me . . . save me, Mick
. . . forgive me! I saw you all together, over there, in the
corner. . . . I thought I was in your way . . . I thought
I was a nuisance to you.

Michael. Oh, Mummy!

George. Oh, my God!

Yvonne. I lost my head. I wanted to die. But I don't
want to die anymore. I want to live. I want to be with you.
I want to see you both happy. Madeleine, I love you. I
will love you. I promise! Try and do something. I want to
live. I'm so afraid. Help me, please!

Madeleine. Michael, don't just stand there!

George [*Cutting in*]. Run to the doctor upstairs.

Madeleine [*To* MICHAEL, *who is in a daze*]. Go on,
darling, hurry!

George. I'll ring the specialist at the hospital!

MADELEINE *pushes* MICHAEL *gently. He runs off through
the door upstage right. A door slams. Right through to the
end of the act, there is an incessant slamming of doors.*

Léo [*To* GEORGE]. Go and ring up. I'll stay here.
[GEORGE *exits through the door.* Léo *feels* YVONNE's *pulse.*]

Her pulse is very weak, regular but weak. I knew something was going to happen. I felt it all the time.

Madeleine [*Slowly walking away from the bed,* Léo *following her*]. This is all my fault. I ought not to be here. I ought to go.

Léo. Go where?

Madeleine. I ought to leave Michael.

Léo. Don't be silly. Stay where you are. It's an order. Besides, Michael is going to need you. [*As if suddenly struck by it.*] Just as George is going to need me.

There is a moment's silence.

Yvonne [*Her voice weak but edgy*]. I can hear you, Léo.

Léo. What can you hear?

Yvonne. I heard you. You'd forgotten I could hear you.

Léo. Hear what?

Yvonne. Don't pretend you don't know. You want to get rid of me——

Léo [*Interrupting*]. Yvonne—!

Yvonne. I've poisoned myself, and I'll poison you, Léo! [*To* MADELEINE.] And I'll poison you! I saw you over there in the corner . . . I saw you all. You wanted to put me on the scrap heap . . . that's what you wanted . . . you wanted. . . . You—Mick! Mick!

Léo [*Very loudly*]. George—!

George [*Rushing in from the left*]. The specialist's in the country, they're sending someone else.

Léo. George, Yvonne is delirious. . . .

Yvonne. No, Léo, I'm not delirious. They want to get rid of me. I see it all now. I'll—tell—ev'-ry-thing.

George [*Kissing* YVONNE *on the lips, genuinely distressed.*] Quiet, Yvonne, quiet please!

Yvonne. How many years . . . is it . . . since you kissed me . . . on the lips . . . ? Are you only kissing them now to shut my mouth?

George [*Trying to quiet her by caressing her*]. There . . . there . . . there. . . .

Yvonne. I'll poison . . . your . . . lives. . . . I'll tell Mick . . . everything. . . .

Michael [*Rushing in*]. No one at home, no answer!

Yvonne. Michael, listen to me . . . listen to me, Mi-

chael . . . I don't want . . . I want you . . . I want
you to know. . . .

Léo [*As loudly as she can, while* YVONNE *is trying to
speak*]. Michael, your mother is delirious. Ring up the
hospital again. Madeleine, my dear, go and help him, will
you? He'll never find the number. Go on, hurry, there's
not much time!

She pushes MICHAEL *and* MADELEINE *out of the room
and through the door upstage left, while* YVONNE *desperately tries to make herself heard.* LÉO *returns to the foot of*
YVONNE's *bed.* YVONNE *is now madly angry.*

Yvonne [*During the above*]. Don't go, stay here. . . .
Mick, Mick . . . they're deceiving you . . . they're cheating you . . . they're sending you—away—under false—
pretenses. . . . You liars—I won't let you—get away
with it. . . .

Léo. Yvonne—!

Yvonne [*Lifting herself up with all the strength at her
command*]. It's you—it's you—it's all your doing. . . .
You wanted me to die . . . you wanted to be alone with
George. . . .

George. This is ghastly!

Yvonne. Yes! This is ghastly! And I—I . . . [*She falls
back.*]

George. If only that doctor would come. Send Michael
in a taxi!

Léo. He'd be bound to miss him.

George. But what shall we do?

Léo. Wait.

Yvonne [*Opening her eyes*]. Mick, are you there? Where
are you?

George. He is here, he is coming.

Yvonne [*Her voice sweet and charming*]. I'll be good—
I didn't mean to be unkind. I saw you all . . . over there
in the corner . . . I was so alone . . . everybody had forgotten me. I wanted to do you all a good turn. . . . My
head. . . . George, pull up my pillow a bit . . . thank
you. Is that you, Léo? And Madeleine? I'm going to love
you, Madeleine. . . . I want to live. I want to go on
living with you. . . . I want my Mick. . . .

Léo. You'll see how happy your Mick's going to be. Just try and stay quiet for a little. The doctor's on his way. We're looking after you.

Yvonne [Having a relapse]. You again! Always you! You and George! Have them arrested! I want to give evidence! Look—they're frightened to death. Don't touch me! Keep away from me! There they are! Come in! Come in! Michael! Michael! Help me! Michael! Michael! Michael! Michael! Michael! Michael! Michael! Michael! [*Screams.*] Michael! Michael! Michael! Michael! Michael! Michael! Mick, Mick, Mick . . . Mick . . . Mick . . . Mick! [*Suddenly she is still and rigid.*]

George and Léo [During YVONNE's *outburst].* Yvonne, I beg you, lie down! Don't do this! You're killing yourself! You're exhausting yourself completely! Listen to me, listen to us! Try and help us!

LÉO *is picking up one of* YVONNE's *pillows that has fallen to the floor while* YVONNE *has been having the attack. She is now about to put it under* YVONNE's *head again, but as she is lifting it,* YVONNE *ceases to shout.* LÉO *puts her head down again slowly and drops the pillow. She looks at* GEORGE.

George. It's not possible. . . . [GEORGE *sinks down and buries his face in the sheets of* YVONNE's *bed.*]

Michael [Rushing in with MADELEINE].* Can't get any information at all, don't know if the doctor's on his way or what. . . . I'll go down and see if he's coming.

Léo. It's no use, Michael. [*There is a sudden silence.*] Your mother is dead.

Michael. What . . . ? [*He is dazed for a moment, then he walks toward the bed.*]

George [Raising his head]. My poor Mick. . . .

Slowly, LÉO *moves away from the bed.*

Léo [Very bitter]. Look at you! You'd give anything to bring her back to life, but you'd go on torturing her just the same.

Michael [Furious]. You hated her!

Léo. Perhaps. And I loved her.

Michael [Going for her]. You——

George. Michael, are you forgetting your mother!

Michael [*Stamping his foot*]. Mother, mother! Sophie isn't my mother. She's my friend, the best friend I ever had! [*He rushes to the bed.*] Tell them, Mummy, didn't you tell me a thousand times . . . [*He snatches* YVONNE'S *body into his arms and covers her face with kisses.*]

Madeleine [*Rushing toward him and trying to pull him away*]. Michael, you're mad. . . .

The doorbell rings.

Michael [*Utterly bewildered*]. Oh God, I'd forgotten! I'll always forget. . . . I'll never be able to realize it . . . never. . . .

LÉO *has crossed over to open the door.* MICHAEL *looks like a little boy who is going to cry any minute.* MADELEINE *holds him in her arms.*

Madeleine. Michael . . . my darling . . . my love. . . .

Léo [*Slowly coming back*]. It was the cleaning woman. I told her there is nothing for her to do, that everything is in order.

THE HOLY TERRORS

(*Les monstres sacrés*)

English version by Edward O. Marsh

CHARACTERS

ESTHER, *a famous actress*
LULU, *her dresser*
FLORENT, *her husband*
LIANE, *a young actress*
CHARLOTTE, *a character actress*
AN ANNOUNCER
AN OLD LADY

ACT ONE: ESTHER's dressing room just after the evening per
formance.

ACT TWO. The villa at CHATOU one summer afternoon.

ACT THREE: The same, six months later.

THE HOLY TERRORS

ACT ONE

Esther's *dressing room in the theater she directs. Classic dressing room of great actress. Screens covered with muslin of all possible shades. Mirror and make-up on the left across the corner of the stage. A small Chinese screen around it. Door right, giving onto the corridor. Divan, armchairs, chairs, baskets of flowers with ribbons. Red carpet, very worn. And a mat. Lights from lamps and naked bulbs left and right of the mirror. All pearl color.*

When the curtain goes up the room is empty. Esther *is hidden behind the Chinese screen and is talking in a loud voice to her dresser, who she believes is in the room. Her arms can be seen waving above the screen, as she hangs up a riding habit at the top of the screen. It is the dress she wears in the last act of the play she is doing,* The Quarry.

Esther [*Alone and unseen behind the screen*]. Are you listening, Lulu? This time I mean it! I've had enough! I'm having the apron-stage, *and* the boxes taken away! I've dithered about too long but this is the last straw! Those boxes are driving me mad! When I think that for twelve years, through sheer idleness, well . . . and to avoid expense, if you like . . . I've put up with these conditions! It's been enough to send me into a padded cell! We close on Saturday! Sunday morning the workmen start pulling them down! Do you hear? For years we've felt people were crawling around the set all the time, and we've had to stare through leering old men and streams of women fingering our dresses . . . but tonight, really, tonight was too much! Lulu! Listen to this! Tonight one old crackpot —it was the last act—I saw it all, quite clearly, from the stage. She must have been deaf, so they bunged her into a stage box for the last act. . . . Well, there she sat, crazy old crone, shrugging and jerking her shoulders up and down like a marionette, every time I opened my mouth! André was an awful idiot and kept edging over to me and whispering asides: "Seen the old goat?" and "Couldn't they nail her down?" and so on. I didn't realize it was nerves,

at first I thought she couldn't hear the play and wanted
me to know what she thought of it. And she kept at it,
jump, shrug, jump, shrug, on and on, and I soon began
to realize that the front rows of the stalls weren't following the play at all, they were all sniggering at this old fool!
But what infuriates me is Charlotte! When she acts she
goes into a sort of ecstatic trance. Do you think she was
put out by the old goose? Not in the least! She swept up
and down, around and about, quite unmoved; and looked
at me as though there was something the matter with me
when she saw I was bothered! She didn't seem to notice
the old fool bouncing away there under her nose! I could
have murdered her! It's a good job I come off first, or I'd
have made a scene, I can tell you! I'd have stopped in
my tracks and said: "Either that old lunatic goes or I do!
And I don't say another word!" Do you hear, Lulu? That's
settled it! Those stage boxes must go! . . . Pass me my
make-up gown, will you. . . . Lulu, my make-up gown!
. . . Lulu! [*She peeps from behind the screen and then
appears in a voluminous and lovely white gown. She sees
that she has been talking to the empty room and is
astonished.*] Well I'm damned! That's the last straw! . . .
First I'm shrugged into a fury, then waste an hour talking
to thin air! Oh! [*She makes for the door and shouts.*]
Lulu! . . . Lulu! . . .

Enter LULU, *an old dresser, in black, with a silly face.*

Lulu. Did you call, madame?

Esther. I was changing behind the screen and thought
you were here. I've been talking to you for hours! Where've
you been?

Lulu. I went down to see the doorman.

Esther. Now look, I'm not an absolute idiot, am I?
When you came back from the Comédie Française you
came into my dressing room?

Lulu. Yes, madame.

Esther. Then you went straight out again?

Lulu. Yes, madame. I had to go and see the doorman.

Esther. It's those slippers. Did you go to the Comédie
Française in those slippers?

Lulu. Yes, madame. I've got tired feet.

Esther. But why in the name of God do all theater dressers wear slippers? Yes . . . yes . . . I know . . . so that you don't make a noise in the wings. Then why do you all walk plonk on your heels and make the whole stage tremble at every step you take? Pass me my wrap. I'm furious!

Lulu. There you are, madame. [*Passes her a linen wrap.*]

Esther. How is it you're back already? Did you come out before the curtain?

Lulu. Just before the end, madame. I got a bit fed up. I only went to see the master, and he doesn't come on in the last act. She telephones to him.

Esther. Telephones?! In Racine?

Lulu. Oh, I don't know *where* he was when she was phoning him. But the master wasn't on any more so I came away.

Esther. What a fool! Of course, there's a double bill! *Britannicus* first, then they're filling up the program with *La Voix Humaine.*

Lulu. I couldn't say, madame.

Esther [*Taking off her make-up*]. Did the master get a lot of applause?

Lulu. Oh, yes, madame! They were all dancing about and shouting at the end: Author! Author!

Esther. After Racine? Well . . . I suppose it's possible. Anything's possible these days! Did you like the Racine?

Lulu. Well, madame, I didn't understand what they were saying, much; 'cause they were talking a bit old-fashioned like.

Esther [*Eyes to Heaven*]. My God!

Lulu. Yes, madame. . . . Talked all old-fashioned, they did. Hm! The master was ever so funny!

Esther. Well, if he was funny playing Nero, he must have been a riot.

Lulu. He was ever so funny. He was wearing one of your old dresses . . . then, just to fool me, he went and hid behind a bit of the building——

Esther. But Lulu! That's in the play. . . .

Lulu. No, it wasn't. He was fooling me. So I said to the woman next to me, I said: "See him? The master's hiding behind that bit of building! I can see him, though, because he's got one of madame's old dresses on! I find her dresses all over the place—behind the furniture, in the fireplace, she just drops them anywhere. . . ."

Esther. What did the woman say?

Lulu. Nothing, madame. Only shrugged her shoulders.

Esther. What! Another one? Is it the shruggers' night out?

Lulu. P'raps, madame.

Esther. Anyway, you enjoyed yourself?

Lulu. Oh, yes, madame. Master did make me laugh!

Esther. He will be pleased to hear that. All right, Lulu, you can go now. I'll dress myself. I may be staying quite late. Tell the doorman not to turn out the lights; ask him to wait for me, will you?

Lulu. Madame's going to have another bad night, I can see!

Esther. You're the one who'll have a bad night, Lulu dear, looking after that sister of yours.

Lulu. Her nurse has had to go into hospital.

Esther. Hm! Nobody's safe these days!

Lulu. And you have to stay up with her all the time. Never get a wink, you don't.

Esther. You'll be exhausted tomorrow. See you're at Chatou by lunchtime and spend the afternoon in bed. Now go down to the stage door and ask the doorman for a good big cup of strong coffee.

Lulu. Oh, no, madame. I can't sleep if I have coffee.

Esther [*Fainting with laughter*]. Ohhhhhh!

Lulu. Is anything wrong, madame?

Esther. No, no . . . thank you, Lulu. . . . [*Recovering.*]

Lulu. Oh! I was forgetting. There's a young girl outside, crying, madame.

Esther. That'll be little orphan Annie!

Lulu. Oh? She didn't say her name was Annie. She's crying terrible, though. She's in the waiting room.

Esther [*Jumps*]. In the waiting room? I shall go mad! Why?

Lulu. She was nipping up the stairs, the doorman hadn't seen her. I ran after her and says: "Where you going?" "I'm looking for Mme. Esther's dressing room," she says.

She was all in tears, like, so I sits her down in the waiting room.

Esther. Where did she come from?

She opens the door. LIANE *appears in the doorway. She is young and very modern, and looks very photogenic in her neat trench coat. She can hardly stand and leans heavily on the side of the door, with her hat dangling from her hand. She runs her hand through her hair.*

Esther. Come in, young lady.

Liane. Mme. Esther! Forgive me! Won't you? I had to come! I was in the theater tonight.

Lulu. She wants your authorgraph, I s'pose.

Esther. Well, she's come at the right moment. Off you go, Lulu. After that old crackpot in the stage box I'm dying for somebody to admire me! But off you go! [*On second thought.*] No! Don't go just yet. Guard the door in the corridor and don't let anybody in! [*Smiles to* LIANE.] When the show's over, you see, I suddenly turn into the general manager. They all come with their complaints— won't I change their costume because it doesn't fit, or can they just write a little bit in because they don't like the words! No end to it. [*To* LULU.] Nobody, Lulu. Is that clear?

Lulu. Righto, madame.

Esther. And if you can manage to stop André singing *Tosca* at the top of his voice as he comes down the stairs, I'll buy you a new wrist watch. . . . Nobody can come in, do you understand? Tomorrow, Chatou, lunch! And look after your sister. [*Closes the door.*] It's really appalling! That's been going on for twenty-five years! I've been a slave to that woman for a quarter of a century! She adores me of course . . . and, oddly enough, I adore her. But she's driving me into senile decay! My husband's playing Nero this evening. . . . I sent Lulu to the Comédie Française to get rid of her, and here she is going to sit up all night with her invalid sister, so she's just refused to have any coffee because she says it always keeps her awake! Now, who's mad? Lulu or me? . . . You said you were out front tonight.

Liane. Yes, Mme. Esther.

Esther. Why did you leave before the end?

Liane. Because you weren't on the stage any longer.

Esther. Hm! Someone else who likes actresses more than she likes the theater, I can see.

Liane. But Mme. Esther . . .

Esther. No "buts," my dear. You don't like the theater. The last scene is the best in the play . . . the hunting-lodge scene. They wanted to cut it at one time and end on my exit. But it was a ridiculous idea. In that last scene I'm there, on the stage, much more effectively than if I really appeared. Of course I admit that the play . . .

Liane. I don't like the play very much.

Esther. My dear, that is the actor's dismal destiny. Either you get a magnificent part and no play, or a wonderful play that just swallows you up! When shall I ever find a good play and a good part at one and the same time? I wonder!

Liane. The play doesn't matter, anyhow. You are so magnificent!

Esther. Shame on you. Good theater should be the blending of many parts into one harmonious whole! Ah well!

Liane. Mme. Esther, it's silly, I know, but I shall have to say what I feel! I had never seen you act before . . .

Esther. You haven't chosen the best of nights! I was ghastly in that last act. That fool of a woman made me lose my head completely.

Liane. Who? Mme. de Couville?

Esther. Poor Charlotte! No, not Charlotte! Some old idiot in the right-hand stage box, who kept shrugging her shoulders all the time. A terrifying nervous tic! I didn't realize that it was nerves at first.

Liane. I didn't notice.

Esther. You're lucky! Didn't you think I was dreadful?

Liane. Mme. Esther . . . you know . . . I'm sure you just don't realize what happens. You must be so used to being admired. I don't think you understand what a state I'm in. . . . [*She sinks to the divan.*]

Esther. My poor child. . . . [*She takes her hands.*] Why, your hands are like ice! Move closer to the radiator!

Liane. I shan't be any warmer. If I weren't keeping such

a grip on myself my teeth would be chattering like mad.
Mme. Esther . . . you are "you." . . . You probably
never stop to think nowadays of what that means, and
every night you just go on and on playing the same part.
. . . But I've come from outside all that. . . . [*She buries
her face in her hands.*]

Esther. Poor darling! Don't get into such a dreadful
state about it. What can I do for you?

Liane. Nothing! Just stay where you are! Please! Let me
look at you! Let me just feel that I'm here with you! In
your dressing room!

Esther. I think I see, now. You thought I'd be distant
and grand, and you'd find me reclining on a bearskin rug,
sniffing at a bunch of orchids! Wasn't that it?

Liane. I don't know what I expected. I came up here
in a dream. Trembling like a leaf all the way! I heard your
little scene with your dresser. I heard you laugh. It needed
all the courage I could muster even to get up and stand
at the door.

Esther. Did I upset you as much as that?

Liane. Upset isn't the word. Before I saw you act I
had no idea what a great actress was like. People had
talked to me about Rachel, Duse, and Sarah Bernhardt,
of course; Greta Garbo isn't the same, she's only a shadow
on a screen. I'd seen a lot of good actresses, mind you.
Clever actresses. My grandfather used to laugh when I said
that and told me to wait till I saw a really great one—he
had his own name for the great ones: "holy terrors" he
called them. I always thought they were just ordinary good
actresses who happened to live at a time when audiences
were easy to please and that the legends about them always grew up when they died. Then, suddenly, tonight,
when I saw you and listened to you I realized that grandfather was right—great theater *is* something terrifying . . .
and holy!

Esther. Hm! I was acting like a machine . . . creaking,
too, badly in need of oil!

Liane. You thought you were, perhaps. But even the
grandeur was automatic! You just went through the wonderful things there are inside you . . . and they had the
effect they always have. Look at me.

Esther. You're bringing my courage back, my dear! I thought I'd been terrible tonight. Actors love being flattered. . . . You're very sweet.

Liane. You are wonderful, Mme. Esther, absolutely wonderful. . . . Oh, but, am I keeping you?

Esther. Not in the least! I had to stay in the theater in any case. I should have had to stay alone if you hadn't come. Actresses spend much more time alone than people think. We're told we have hosts of admirers but very few of them have the sense to come and show themselves . . . and that's where they make a great mistake. I'm very grateful to you for coming around.

Liane. I imagined your dressing room would be crowded with people.

Esther. The theater is a sort of temple, you know. We are the servants of a special god who insists on the most rigid ritual. We have a private set of prayers; we never go to other theaters ourselves; we keep playing the same silly tricks on our friends and fellow actors. And visitors from the outside world are very, very rare. Of course, by way of compensation, we have our incense and the candles of the faithful, our fans, and the bouquets. . . . But in every theater in the world the stairs backstage look just like the stairs of a prison.

Liane. Do you love your temple?

Esther. I'm wedded to it. I love my husband, and my husband's the very pulse of the theater! So I love the theater. Have you ever seen my husband act?

Liane. Yes. I admire him enormously. He's one of the "holy terrors" too.

Esther. Have you seen his Nero?

Liane. Yes, of course! He's marvelous!

Esther. You're more fortunate than his wife, then! I've heard him go through the lines of course, but it's quite impossible for me to see the show. The temple rules won't permit it!

Liane. Your dresser's version wasn't a very good description, you know.

Esther. Huh! Probably not. If you love the theater so much why don't you try to become an actress?

Liane. I am an actress.

Esther. Good Lord! . . . And . . . where do you act?

Liane. At the Comédie Française.

Esther. What?!

Liane. Only very small parts. I've only just left the Conservatoire—they've given me a year's contract at the Comédie Française.

Esther. Then, you know Florent?

Liane. Yes . . . I know him.

Esther. You must be . . .

Liane. Don't worry, I'm not at all famous. My name is Liane Boudier.

Esther. So you're Liane Boudier?

Liane. Has your husband spoken about me?

Esther. He thinks they ought to give you a chance—a really good part—Agnès, for instance.

Liane. Oh, no! He's exaggerating.

Esther [*Doing her hair*]. Liane . . . what a funny name! It means "ivy" doesn't it? Clinging ivy? Is that your real name?

Liane. No—Madeleine. Liane is my stage name.

Esther. You know, in my young days Liane was a favorite name with the tarts, I'm sorry to say. Ha, ha! All the little ladies called themselves Liane! Liane this and Liane the other! [*Varies the pronunciation.*] They used to go to the skating rink, which was very fashionable, and from five to seven in the evening you could see all the known species of ivy wrapping themselves around the skating instructor, adding the skating waltz to their wide range of accomplishments. To tell the truth . . .

Liane. About tarts . . . ?

Esther. No! Names! Take my name, Esther Ledoux— it sounds very silly. Doesn't it? But the very essence of fame is to make an impossible name widely accepted. Think of some famous names: Racine, Corneille, La Fontaine . . . Shakespeare . . . Bacon . . . All impossible, really. . . . If a young author came along and told me his name was Anatole France I'd advise him to change it straightaway! But it didn't prevent Anatole France from making his name, so to speak . . . did it? Make your name a household word, that's the secret.

Liane. You're wonderful! Wonderful . . . and so simple.

Esther. You know, after the show I never think about being an actress.

Liane. You are so very different from your reputation.

Esther. A reputation doesn't last long if you're really like it! It's lucky for us we don't bear any resemblance to what the world thinks we're like. If our enemies attacked us for being what we really are, where should we be? Listen, young lady, I'm just a woman; and I love my husband, and my son, blindly, unhesitatingly. I'm completely happy. All the rest, the dramas and intrigues, the lies and jealousy and so on, all that's kept strictly for the theater. Perhaps on the stage I purge myself of all the things I hate so much in everyday life. I don't know. Anyway, as soon as I get home I turn into a rather silly sort of woman with a very famous husband and a married son who is an engineer in Marseilles.

Liane. How old is your son?

Esther. Jean—we call him Jeannot—is twenty. I'm getting quite old, you see. You must think me decrepit.

Liane. You are as old as genius. I can't decide whether that's eight or eight hundred. Your husband is the same age, too.

Esther. How old do you think he is?

Liane. Oh! I couldn't tell. . . . Age never registers with me.

Esther. Lots of girls despise youth . . . and they all fall madly in love with Florent. Are you one of them?

Liane. Listen, Mme. Esther, I didn't come here just out of admiration, just out of love. [ESTHER *starts.*] Yes . . . I mean that. It was a calculated step. A very serious step, and terribly difficult. I was quite frightened of it before I came; now the very thought of it turns me cold. Feel my hands. All through that scene where they're insulting you and you sob and sob . . . I was in a dreadful state! . . . I kept on at myself: you will go, you won't go, you will, you won't, you will, you'll tell her, you will, you must tell her, you must!

Esther. You're beginning to intrigue me.

Liane. Mme. Esther . . .

Esther. Call me just Esther, will you? Everyone else does.

Liane. Esther! Let me tell you, with all due respect, that I think you are a child! That's why I must speak to you, whatever the cost; funnily enough, that's why I'm tongue-tied, too! Help me! Do help me!

Esther. Are you . . . in love with Florent?

Liane. Yes.

Esther. Another one! What do you want me to do about it? Don't ask me to speak to him for you. He'd simply stop his ears! Is it my fault that we're a model couple, the perfect match—husband and wife such as you never see nowadays? Every time I plead for some girl admirer of his he gently slaps my face and calls me a procuress! We simply fascinate each other. It's all terribly out of date, of course.

Liane. You're making it all much more difficult for me.

Esther. Well, don't worry, go ahead. I'm listening.

Liane [*Falls to her knees*]. Forgive me, Esther! Forgive me! . . .

Esther. Forgive you for being in love with my husband?

Liane. For not realizing what a wonderful person I was hurting. . . .

Esther. What on earth's the matter with you?

Liane. Esther, tonight as I looked at you and listened to your voice . . . I was intoxicated with your glory. You shone like a precious stone. I kept telling myself I wasn't worthy to take your place. I realized that the man who'd suggested it to me must be out of his mind . . . and that I had to, yes, I had to come and tell you.

Esther. Who suggested it?

Liane. Poor blind Esther, so wonderfully trusting, so deaf to what people say! . . . Florent suggested it . . . you simply must face it sooner or later!

Esther [*Haggard look—face covered with Vaseline*]. Florent? My husband?

Liane [*On her knees*]. Florent, your husband, who is still playing juvenile leads, and who'd do better to devote himself to you, for you are a masterpiece.

Esther [*Rises*]. You dare! . . .

Liane. I dare to criticize him . . . is that it? Yes, of course, I'm criticizing him and I make no bones about it! This evening I measured the distance that separates me from you. My love for what you are is stronger than my love for him! I was ashamed and I decided to tell you the whole story, take the load off my conscience and end all this terrible lie!

Esther. Are you Florent's mistress?

Liane. He wanted to leave you and marry me. Men are like that! That's what revolts me! This evening you uprooted me, tore me right out of myself! I may sink back again tomorrow. But now that I'm worked up into such a state, I'll turn it to good account! I'll help you! We'll work together! I was crazy about Florent before I knew you; I thought it quite natural for him to be crazy about me. But a man who's lucky enough to be loved by you can't throw it all away for someone as paltry and insignificant as me. I have no illusions, you see. I can see clearly. I'm no fool, even if Florent is a bit out of his mind. Yesterday I said to myself: "I shall marry Florent and be famous." Tonight here I am at your feet, asking your forgiveness. My excuse is that . . . I didn't know! But Florent knew, and he's the one I blame! Oh, I hate him! [*She strikes her fist on the floor.*]

Esther. I must be dreaming . . . this is impossible. It must be a dream . . . I've fallen asleep in my dressing room. [*She shouts.*] Lulu! Lulu!

Liane. No, Esther, you're not dreaming. I know this must be a terrible shock to you. But, put yourself in my place. . . . A young actress in her first job . . . and a very famous actor . . .

Esther. Be quiet!

Liane. Give me your hand, let me kiss your hand!

Esther. Don't touch me. [LIANE *falls back, crouching, her face turned imploringly up to her.*] . . . So that's what unhappiness looks like? [*Takes her by the chin.*] Let me look at you! I was so happy . . . the happiest woman in the world! Then unhappiness walks in on me with a face like this!

Liane. Esther!

Noise in wings. The door is roughly opened and CHAR-
LOTTE *comes in, wearing riding habit.* LULU *follows,
shouting at her.*

Lulu. Madame doesn't want to be disturbed, Mme. de
Couville! I'm not to let anybody in!
Esther. One moment. I'm sorry. [*Turns to* LULU.]
What is it?
Lulu. Mme. de Couville pushed past me, madame.
She said she had to see you and you wouldn't mind.

LIANE *moves away.*

Esther. This young lady was . . . rehearsing. . . .
What do you want, Charlotte? I asked not to be disturbed.
Charlotte. I'm unlucky, I can see. My mother's in the
theater, and I'd love to introduce her to you. It'd only be
a second . . .
Esther. Listen, Charlotte, I'm very fond of you and
very touched by your affection, but it's quite impossible
for me to see your mother. I'm working, and I've told
Lulu to keep everybody away! I don't want to be disturbed.
I'm sorry, but I can't be bothered just at this moment.
Charlotte. All right. I suppose it'll have to be some other
time. Mummy's so very old; she hardly ever leaves the
house, so I thought . . .
Esther. Besides, I was dreadful tonight! When I've been
dreadful I don't like people coming to flatter me. I just
want to run away and hide. My God! I envy you your
composure! How on earth did you act through that last
act at all, with that old hag jerking and twitching under
your nose all the time.
Charlotte. Did you notice her?
Esther. Did I notice? She just shattered me!
Charlotte. Poor mother! I'm out of luck with you tonight, Esther.
Esther. What?! Do you mean to say that was your
mother? That old lady in the stage box?
Charlotte. She's got a nervous tic, the poor darling.
I'm used to it, of course, so I don't realize that other
people take any notice. She's shortsighted and a bit deaf,
so the attendant moved her up into a stage box.

Esther. Now I see why you were so unperturbed!

Charlotte. Oh dear! It's always the same. I try my best to please you. And I'm terribly fond of my mother . . . but everything's against me. [*Sniffs.*]

Esther. Don't cry! Of all things, don't cry! When you've got a mother who's old and infirm, Charlotte, darling, you leave her at home. You don't risk ruining the show by bringing her to the theater. . . .

Charlotte. It's only nerves! She's got a tremendous admiration for you, Esther, and it's always the same—the more moved she is, the more her shoulders jump.

Esther. Well, let's drop the subject. But next time give us plenty of notice, or find her a seat at the back of the dress circle. Better still, leave her at home.

Charlotte. You're so unkind, Esther. . . . How can you?

Esther. I'm not unkind, but I suffer from nerves, too. My special brand is to scream when I feel I want to scream. Go away, Charlotte, go away! Take your mother home . . . and put her back to bed! You know I don't mean to be unkind, but I hate people to come pushing in here when I don't want them!

Charlotte. You are unkind to me, Esther. . . .

Goes out with a handkerchief to her eyes. The door bangs to. Lulu *can be heard through it.*

Lulu. I told you! Madame didn't want to see nobody. Now did she?

As soon as the door shuts, Esther *is shaken by a hysterical laugh.*

Esther. What a *faux pas!* Trust me! [*She suddenly remembers and puts her hand to her heart.*] Oh! I'd forgotten . . .

Liane. I . . .

Esther. Be quiet. [*Marches up and down.*] The Empress Elisabeth, when she was assassinated, felt first of all something like a violent punch. She walked on for some time with the knife in her heart. When the knife was pulled out at last she dropped dead on the spot. I am walking

now with your knife in my heart. When it is pulled out,
I suppose I shall die. But at the moment I only feel a sort
of lightness . . . I can't even say I feel hurt. Of course
it's like that when someone dies—you don't feel the loss
until after the funeral. . . . Don't speak to me! Don't
move, either! We haven't got a lot of time—let's see
exactly where we stand. Try to get it all clear. You see,
I find it difficult to understand a thing like this. Here are
a man and woman who adore each other, live for each
other, never leave one another except for their work, never
have any secrets, always confess the least little thing. . . .
[*She closes her eyes.*] Then, unhappiness comes between
them . . . in the form of a ravishing young actress who
tells you your husband has been unfaithful to you, and
then apologizes for being his mistress. I find it difficult
to adjust myself to shocks like that. Now don't cry! Am I
crying? I'm listening and thinking. . . . Am I awake or
asleep? Am I alive or dead? Is the world real any more?
. . . [*Sits.*] I can sit down. I can stand up! [*She does so.*]
Shake my leg, turn my head. Walk forward . . . backward. . . . I'm not dead. It's all true. I'm alive. . . .
And I'm still walking about, with your knife stuck in my
heart.

Liane [*In exaltation*]. Oh, Esther, Esther, I can't bear
to see you like this! I'll leave Florent! You can go on as
though I didn't exist, as though nothing had ever happened! Esther! You frighten me! Please, Esther!

*Just at this moment a deep bass voice roars out an aria
from* Tosca. *It is some way away down the corridor.*

Esther. That's saved me the price of a wrist watch!
Liane. A wrist watch?
Esther. Oh, nothing! You know, my dear, you musn't
think I'm angry with you. It's quite usual for girls to fall
in love with Florent and go crazy about him. But there's
something very unusual in a girl letting him down and
talking of giving him up!

Liane. You keep forgetting who you are! You don't
have the same reactions as other women!

Esther. Now . . . [*Polishing her nails.*] Perhaps he
doesn't love you as much as you think he does . . . and

perhaps you suspect as much and your theatrical nature made you dramatize the whole thing and play the tragic heroine.

Liane. Mme. Esther!

Esther. No need to get worked up! I'm only thinking aloud. Thinking round it. It's all so strange. How long has your . . . er . . . liaison been going on?

Liane. Since the Drama Festival at Orange. You were to join him there, if you remember . . . but you couldn't. We two stayed on. He sent a telegram saying they would be eight days rehearsing instead of three.

Esther. Yes, that's right. But . . . he wrote me a long letter full of news every day.

Liane. All lies!

Esther. That knife is as snug as if it were in its sheath. There's no deep wound, I'm not a real victim . . . just a sheath for the knife you brought with you.

Liane. I'm so sorry for you!

Esther. Sorry for me? Oh, no! You're the one to be pitied, my dear! I'm not one of your theatrical women who scream "You have betrayed me!" then sweep out of the house and vanish forever. I'm a very ordinary woman, deeply in love, and a coward. My ghost, when I die, will still be my husband's slave. So which of us is to be pitied after all? You . . . for coming so near to a love like that and seeing it slip through your fingers, because true happiness is standing at his side and has the patience to wait.

Liane. Really, he just worships you. . . .

Esther. You know that, do you? Of course he worships me, you mean nothing in his life—even if he suggests poisoning me and putting you in my place! But what I can't forget is that he's been coming home and lying to me. He acted a part, to me! What I always loved about Florent was that he acted on the stage, but, I thought, was incapable of acting at home. Losing your faith in someone is the most dreadful thing in the world. It's not our love that's ruined—love can stand much worse shocks than that—it's our happiness. I used to say: "Florent's playing Nero, what fun!" rather like Lulu. Now I shall say: "Florent is playing Nero. Just the part that would

attract him . . . with all that cunning and deceit. . . ."
I've not lost Florent, and his love. It's security I've lost,
and peace of mind. From now on I shall have to love like
they do in these dreadful plays we act in, instead of loving
innocently and trustingly, always the same and content to
be so . . . instead of loving just foolishly and wonderfully . . . as we have done till now. That's the knife
you've plunged into my heart, my child—a stage knife as
theatrical as can be, from the prop room along the corridor, and that's the worst knife of all.

Liane [*The sophisticated woman*]. How do you know
that that happiness and complacency wasn't absolutely unbearable to him? Are you sure it wasn't the very thing that
drove him away from you? You want to have it both ways:
have complicated art that you'd find unbearable if it were
real and in life itself keep your ideal as simple as an old-
fashioned picture postcard.

Esther. Beware of drama in real life. A great actor acts
on the stage. A bad actor acts in his daily life. Do you
know the worst type of actor in the world? The national
leader who is so eager to play the star part in world politics that he'll quite gaily send millions of men off to certain
death on the battlefield. The great thing about the theater
is that all the dead stand up again at the end of the play.
But the victims of the drama of life never stand up again.
You think I'm a great actress? Well, God preserve me from
playing the actress in my own drawing room. You've probably ruined my happiness now, by making me see that
Florent goes on acting when he's off the stage.

Liane. What time is it?

Esther. It's late. Florent had to see the general manager
after the show. I'm waiting for him.

Liane. He mustn't see me here! He mustn't know we've
been talking! Swear you won't tell him! And I'll swear to
give him up! I won't come between you!

Esther [*Opens the door a little*]. He's coming up the
stairs.

Liane. Hide me, Esther! Don't let him see me!

Esther. Go behind the screen, there. Under that clothes
rack! You'll see—*when I want to,* I can be one of those bad

actresses we were talking about! Stay there. You can slip
out after we've gone. I'll warn the doorman.

Liane. You're an angel!

She hides. The door opens. FLORENT *appears. He has gray
hair, wears an overcoat and scarf, and a hat on his head.
He takes off his hat after about half a minute and throws it
onto the armchair.*

Florent. Phew!

Esther. Nero, stop! A word with you!

Florent. Stay, Nero, stay! [*Corrects her.*] A word with
you! . . .

Esther. Oh, Lord! That terrible artificial verse! I never
get it right!

Florent. How did it go tonight? Good house?

Esther. Packed, as usual. But I'm getting rid of those
stage boxes. And that's final! I will not go on again and
listen to myself being cut to ribbons a mere yard or two
away.

Florent. Good! Ought to have done it ages ago.

Esther. What about Nero? Triumph?

Florent. Triumph. There were even shouts for "author"
at the end! Hm! True.

Esther. That's what Lulu said, but she told me the plot
of *Britannicus* as well . . . so I didn't really believe it.

Florent. They shouted for the author! Brrr, I'm not complaining. It was the great public, the real public, getting
excited.

Esther. Did you snap your fingers after: "Stay, Nero!"?

Florent. No, I didn't. Nor twiddle my crown around
in the final scene! I'd got a whole row of little things
ready . . . but it's no good. Fancy tricks may make you
feel you're doing something out of the ordinary, but they're
always a mistake.

Esther. What did the manager want with you?

Florent. Oh, nothing, really! Mainly money matters.
There's been some jealousy in the company about where
people's guests were seated . . . that sort of thing. "I
will not have my aunt put at the back of the stalls, while
Mlle. Tourelle's younger brother is given a seat in the

front row of the dress circle!" You know! Let's go home.

Esther. I'm nearly ready. I've been wondering whatever attracted you to play Nero.

Florent. Nero? Well . . . it's such a wonderful part.

Esther. He's so different from you.

Florent. Oh, you mean my hair. The wig they sent was ridiculous. So I gave myself a curl or two, played about with my own hair and plastered it with gold dust. And, by God, do I need a bath, it's been dropping all over the place.

Esther. I wasn't thinking of your hair. I was thinking of your eyes. Nero's so cunning and cruel, such a hypocrite. . . .

Florent. It's your system that saves me, Esther. We all carry inside ourselves the germs of all evil, a host of little corruptions! I purge away all my impurities on the stage. I follow your instructions to the letter . . . and treat the theater as a course in prophylactics!

Esther. And in real life you never, never let loose those nasty little demons you've got deep inside you? Your own special weaknesses? You never feel tempted for instance to lie, and adjust the facts a little . . . you know, simplify things now and then just to save hurting someone? . . .

Florent. Well! What ideas to have!

Esther. It's this passion for playing Nero that's made me a bit uneasy. I never did like the man—such a glib liar! Florent, have you ever lied to me?

Florent. Depends what you mean by "lie."

Esther. Oh, no! There aren't several grades of lie! You either lie or you don't! Have you ever lied to me, Florent?

Florent. Esther, you know as well as I do that I can't bear lying, that's why I'm even hesitating over answering this. Can anybody manage never once to tell the tiniest little lie?

Esther. Yes, I can.

Florent. Well, of course, you're a special case . . . you're an——

Esther [*Cutting in*]. Idiot!

Florent. Oh!

Esther. Yes, yes, I am. So, you *have* lied to me, Florent?

Florent. Is this a cross-examination? What are you getting at?

Esther. Don't get excited, darling. These . . . lies? In your eyes, I suppose they were unimportant? Sort of polite lies, generous, considerate lies? Was that it?

Florent. If you insist on it—and you're not the one to make allowances, I know—I suppose here and there I've been guilty of a few—not exactly lies—but a few minor inexactitudes.

Esther. Look me in the eyes.

Florent. You frighten me, Esther.

Esther. Look me in the eyes. . . .

Florent. Your eyes are all red . . . Esther!

Esther. Explain this!

She pulls away the screen and reveals LIANE—*who is terrified, crushed against the row of dresses.*

Florent [*Thunderstruck*]. Liane! What're you doing here?

Liane [*Suppliant*]. Florent, forgive me! I've told her everything.

Florent. Told everything?

Esther. Don't be silly, Florent. You may as well confess.

Florent. Confess what?

Liane. I was here in the theater tonight. I saw . . . Esther. I was so moved that I lost control. I ran to this dressing room . . . and told all!

Florent. I'm sorry, my dear, but I don't know what you're talking about. You told her all? All what? Esther, what did she tell you?

Esther. I thought you had more courage.

Florent. But for God's sake explain what you mean! This is a farce!

Esther. Well, let's get out of the comic groove of in-jured innocence, shall we? This girl is your mistress.

Florent. Liane?

Esther. Yes . . . Liane. And she's worth two of you—she did have the courage to admit it, and not hedge. I don't deserve hedging, Florent. Do at least be honest with me.

Florent. Am I going crazy? I must be dreaming. Liane, my dear, just tell my wife she's out of her mind, will you? She must be lightheaded or something . . .

Esther. Why bother to deny it, my poor sweet?

Florent. Why? Because it's untrue! I hardly know the girl! I've only spoken to her five or six times in my life!

Esther. You have the impudence to——

Florent. Unless . . . No! I can't believe one of our young actresses is going in for blackmail.

Esther. Well?

Florent. Nothing. I give up. We'll just wake up at Chatou, in the normal way, later on. This is a nightmare.

Esther. Would you be good enough to remind my husband of your little stay together at Orange?

Florent. Orange? The Festival? Why, the girl wasn't even there!

Esther. That's a lie.

Florent. Esther, I swear she wasn't there! I can't understand a word of all this! I hardly know her! I swear I have no mistresses at all, and that I love you and no one else and always will!

Esther. You tell him, Liane. . . .

Liane [*Collapses*]. Oh! Mme. Esther! He's right, he's telling the truth! I didn't dream what I was doing! I'm so ashamed! I've never been his mistress! I've never been to Orange! I made it all up!

Esther. Oh! I see! You have a decent impulse, it lasts a few minutes, then along comes the male of the species and the impulse is smothered again. You haven't the courage to be honest to the end, and go through with it! How mean and contemptible! . . .

Florent. Listen to me, Esther . . .

Esther. It was so simple! All you had to say was: "Esther, will you forgive me?" and I would have forgiven you. I like being cowardly in love—but your sort of cowardice revolts me.

Liane. Oh, do believe him, Mme. Esther! Do believe him! Let me explain!

Esther. Waste of time . . .

Florent. Let her explain . . .

Esther. Ah, so you admit it at last?

Florent. Don't be silly, darling! I just want her to talk because there's something funny behind all this, and we must get to the bottom of it as soon as possible. It's like an abscess, it has to be lanced or it'll burst. Liane, my dear [*as though he's talking to a very sick person*] why did you come here and tell such a preposterous lie?

Liane. It was a dreadful lie! It's all my fault! I'm to blame! Look at me, Esther! It's the truth I'm telling you now! I'm very, very sorry and deeply ashamed . . . and I'll never lie again, never!

Esther. You are not Florent's mistress?

Liane. No. I swear I'm not.

Esther. I don't believe you.

Florent. Esther . . . Esther. . . . If I swear it, myself? I swear it, by anything you like . . . will you believe me?

Esther. You'd swear anything now.

Florent. Esther . . . I swear by Jeannot and everything I hold dear—by all the happiness we have known together that it's a lie. . . .

Liane. It's all a lie! A terrible lie! You must listen! I was mad! I was longing to meet you, to get near to you somehow and play some part in your life! I invented the whole story. When I saw you on the stage I was in such a state that I just had to do something, something extraordinary! My life's so dull, very few friends, a futile party now and again—that's all. Your life was like a dream to me. It still is. I didn't know there were still people who could be so hurt, so deeply wounded, as you. Everything slides off me, I don't feel things at all in that way. So I imagined the whole thing from beginning to end! Forgive me! And try to understand. You are so good, so fine. I so rarely have a part to play at all, and when I do it's the smallest part in the play. I longed to play a great part, and equal you; I wanted to leave you dumfounded, as you did me!

Florent. Well, I congratulate you! You seem to have done pretty well.

Esther. It's unbelievable! It would be a miracle if——

Florent. Nothing like a miracle. Just coming back to

earth. This young fool's nearly given you heart failure
and ought to be spanked.

Esther. If you're speaking the truth and it was all a lie
. . . I shall be so relieved that I'll never be able to feel
angry with her. I'll only be able to think of what might
have been true, and isn't.

Liane. Love him! And hate me! You must, Mme. Esther!
I don't deserve your forgiveness!

Florent. God! What next?!

Esther. Swear it again, Florent! Look me in the eyes
and swear she was lying!

Florent. By all that we hold dear, I swear she was lying!

Liane. Do you believe him?

Esther. Yes, I believe him . . . but I don't feel as happy
as I thought I would. I'm not a young woman any longer.
The shock was rather devastating.

Florent. Liane, dear, there's nothing more you can do
here, now. You must be proud of your scene, you've done
pretty well. Now, make your exit, will you? Leave us
alone. I'll see you at the theater tomorrow.

Liane. Yes, sir. . . .

Florent. Don't call me "sir"! I can't bear it!

Liane. Mme. Esther . . . will you forgive me?

Esther. You've plunged me into hell, and pulled me
out again. I don't know what I feel about you at all. I'm
not sure what I feel. But you've won your point. I'm quite
dumfounded . . . and I shall never forget your face. . . .

Liane. I don't know what I really expected. I thought
you'd never dream of speaking to your husband about it
. . . I thought you'd feel I was being heroic giving him
up like that. . . . And I thought you'd be grateful to
him as the days went by for not showing any hard feelings
during the break with me. I thought my ghost would be
fluttering between you all the time; at any rate I'd be playing a part in your lives!

Florent. We're back at it again!

Esther. The drama of real life. Now you know why I'm
so afraid of it.

Liane. Mme. Esther . . . only the great can afford the
luxury of being simple. May I kiss your hand?

Florent. Come on. . . . Wake up the doorman on your way out, will you? You'll find he's standing up but he'll be sound asleep. Out you go! [*He opens the door and* LIANE *slips out.*] And let this beastly melodrama be a lesson to you! [*Closes the door.*] Very few things can knock the stuffing right out of me, but this, I must say . . .

Esther. Can you forgive me for believing her so easily, Florent?

Florent. Oh! It's so simple to be taken in by things like that.

Esther. Instinct's an extraordinary thing. Instead of fainting or anything like that, I listened and answered and discussed . . . acted it, I suppose. . . . Something inside me must have told me it didn't really matter . . . you know. Now I think of it, the girl was a bit . . . odd . . . all the time. . . . I rather think she's mad.

Florent. Our generation was brought up on Tolstoi and Dostoevski; they're reared on films and detective novels and psychology. She's proof enough of that. Why on earth should a tough girl like that, if her story was true, rush in here and confess to her rival?

Esther. Well, it isn't quite so silly as it looks, you know, Florent. She sees the show tonight. She's never seen me act before. I bowl her over. The girl's filled with shame . . . and rushes around to see me. . . .

Florent [*Kisses her*]. How beautifully ham!

Esther. Who's ham?

Florent. You are, I am . . . all three of us! How else could we think such an incident possible at all . . . let alone try to explain it away.

Esther. I must confess she completely bluffed me!

Florent. You'd have seen through her straightaway on the stage.

Esther. She's only a child, isn't she? She must be quite gifted. If only she works hard and develops . . .

Florent. Ah, I can see you're feeling better.

Esther. Yes. [*Silence.*] Listen, Florent. . . . Don't be cross, will you? I'm going to ask you rather a straight question.

Florent. Ask away.

Esther. Have you ever been unfaithful to me since our marriage?

Florent. Er . . . unfaithful? . . .

Esther. Stop! Don't say any more! I know what I wanted to know!

Florent. What do you know?

Esther. Nothing! I was living in a sort of half-light. That girl switched on the footlights, and took me by surprise. With all this new light on them I don't see things quite as I used to see them.

Florent. Darling, you're just terrible! It's not the same for a man as for a woman . . . I mean, you must realize . . .

Esther. I do, now! That's the main thing. Before, I was just living on and on, not asking myself any questions. Not asking you any either. I thought life was rather like . . . an old-fashioned picture postcard! I've just realized that I was wrong. I realized nothing before! Now, I realize only too well!

Florent. That damn girl's got a lot to answer for! She's worked wonders in a remarkably short time!

Esther. She's helped me. Will you see her tomorrow at the theater, Florent?

Florent. You're not going to start being jealous, now, I hope!

Esther. No, silly! . . . But I'd like you to speak to her. I've just come to a decision. I want you to tell her something.

Florent. Good! There's nothing I'm not prepared to tell her!

Esther. I've been looking for a student . . . someone who'd make me work myself, and who'd live in with us at Chatou. I've got a lot to learn from a young, modern student, I feel. Especially from Liane.

Florent [*Jumps*]. You want that girl to live in our house?!

Esther. Yes. As soon as she likes.

Florent. Esther! It's plain imbecility to play with fire like that!

Esther. Play with fire? But Florent—if you think that having a young girl in the house, a romantic, calculating, selfish little actress, constitutes a *danger*, then our happiness can't be real at all. And I hate false happiness. I know what to expect, now . . . you see, her treatment's been quite successful. Tell her I want her to be my pupil, will you?

Florent. Esther! Why don't you leave well enough alone? You will keep racing away before the pistol goes off. . . .

Esther. Well, I'm fighting against a handicap—I'm not entirely modern yet. I've got a lot to learn—and I mean to learn it!

Florent. We'll talk about it. It's getting dreadfully late. The doorman must think we've been murdered! Here's your coat. . . .

Esther. You're right, I just talk and talk, and you should get some sleep.

Florent. Me? What about you? Don't you plan to have any sleep?

Esther. Oh . . .

Florent [*Tenderly*]. Esther! [*Makes as if to take her in his arms.*]

Esther [*Moves away*]. Now don't rush me, darling! There's a knife in my heart, remember.

Florent. It's not there any longer, I hope.

Esther. Yes, darling. It is still there. . . .

Florent. Well, I'll soon pull the damn thing out. . . . [*He turns out the light and opens the door.* ESTHER *and he are in the gloomy half-light from the corridor.*]

Esther. No. Don't take it out! Please! If it's taken out, I shall die. And I want to live. . . .

They go out and the door closes. Blackness on the stage.

ACT TWO

A *red drawing room in* ESTHER *and* FLORENT'S *villa at Chatou. Typical luxury of theater stars. Angular cut across the room, with right angle in the center-back of the stage. All the reds in the room clash and harmonize at the same time. Back right, a triangular conservatory and a door in the glass leading out to the garden. Back left, triangular raised platform with balustrade out over a divan, small stairway and a door facing the top of the stairs. Front left, near the divan, a radio. In the conservatory a huge portrait of* ESTHER *dressed as an Amazon. Green plants. Front right, table where* CHARLOTTE DE COUVILLE *is playing solitaire as the curtain goes up. In front of the table and ready to go up the stairs, is* LULU. *It is a sunny afternoon.*

CHARLOTTE. I want to know exactly what happened.

Lulu. Nothing, really, madame. Mme. Esther shouted out. In the middle of the night. She was calling for the master. The master came down to her. I got up, and went to see. Madame sent me back to bed. Then, a bit later, the master came out of madame's room. . . .

Charlotte. And went back upstairs to Mlle. Liane's room?

Lulu. Yes, madame.

Charlotte. Then you went back to Mme. Esther's room? How did she seem?

Lulu. Madame thought she was ill but it was only the cramp in her leg. She told me to go back to bed. She took some of her lighting-up pills, so I came away.

Charlotte. Her lighting-up pills? What on earth . . .?

Lulu. Yes . . . "Illuminall" tablets—that's what she calls them. I say "lighting-up pills"—means the same, doesn't it?

Charlotte. Why, yes . . . I suppose so, Lulu. "A rose by any other name would smell as sweet."

Lulu [*Thinks*]. Not if you called it an onion, it wouldn't.

Charlotte. All right, Lulu. Relax. Relax.

Lulu [*Sits on the divan*]. I'm not really tired, madame, thanks.

Charlotte. Right! Right! Let's get back to the point . . . you say it was only cramp. [LULU *stands up.*] Was it very painful?

Lulu. I don't know, madame. I left madame's room straight away. Went back to bed. . . . Did what I was told.

Charlotte. Yes . . . all right . . . all right! I can see you don't want to answer.

Lulu. Not answer?

Charlotte. You're acting stupid, so that you needn't answer. . . .

Lulu. Are you calling me stupid, Mme. de Couville?

Charlotte. Not at all, Lulu. On the contrary. I think you're just acting a part, so that you needn't say a word more than you think you will. You've studied in a good school.

Lulu. Oh, you're quite wrong, madame. I never went to school at all. We were too poor, when I was a girl—couldn't afford it.

Charlotte. Go on . . . go on . . . keep it up. . . .

Lulu. Would you like me to go on?

Charlotte. Look, Lulu, darling. I'm not such a fool as I look. . . .

Lulu. No, madame?

Charlotte. No, madame. . . . Imagine that! And I'd like to ask you just one little question. I hope you won't mind.

Lulu. Excuse me, madame. . . . I've got to go and press one of Mlle. Liane's dresses.

Charlotte. One moment. . . . So you press Mlle. Liane's dresses?

Lulu. Yes, madame.

Charlotte. Are you fond of pressing Mlle. Liane's dresses?

Lulu. Oh . . . not very. . . .

Charlotte. Not very. . . . And are you fond of Mlle. Liane?

Lulu. Oh . . . not very. . . .

Charlotte. Hm. . . . And is she nice to you?

Lulu. . . . Not very. . . .

Charlotte. And last night, didn't Mme. Esther say anything about Mlle. Liane? Didn't M. Florent say anything to Mme. Esther about her? . . . Didn't you hear anything going on in Mlle. Liane's room? Didn't you hear anything, Lulu?

Esther *has come in from the garden just on these last two lines.* Lulu *has seen her and hurries out up the staircase.*

Esther. Questioning the servants, Charlotte?

Charlotte. I was trying to get some sense out of Lulu about your health. After last night's attack I have every reason to be concerned about you.

Esther. I didn't have an attack. I had cramp.

Charlotte. She was telling me you took what she calls "lighting-up pills." . . .

Esther. Oh yes! I just had to get some sleep, so that——— [*She stops.*]

Charlotte. So that you wouldn't hear *them*. I know.

Esther. Listen, Charlotte. I don't want you criticizing me and offering me your advice. The situation's quite difficult enough as it is.

Charlotte. Well, you should know! I've turned the whole thing around and around in my head, but I shall never understand why you invited the Devil to come and live with you.

Esther. My dear Charlotte! One day early in the history of the universe, God divested himself of all his faults and mistakes. He bundled them all together and made the Devil . . . then he sent him down to Hell. Most convenient! A master stroke! But only possible to the Almighty! You see, my problem is much more difficult to solve. . . . I'm afraid it's not going to be quite so convenient.

Charlotte. Well! If you're starting to go religious! . . .

Esther. Leave me alone! What about you! You don't stop at anything—you and your set—you paint the town red———

Charlotte. Me!

Esther. But you go to Mass on Sundays! That, I suppose, puts you right! I've got my own conception of morality and religion . . . and I will not be criticized by you! It's quite natural for an exceptional thing to happen to me, because I am exceptional. [*Movement from* CHARLOTTE.] Oh! don't think I'm boasting! I mean, that I am —unfortunately—an unusual person, and that—unfortunately—I can't be confined to the common laws of mankind. I must find my own. And it's far from easy, I assure you.

Charlotte. If everybody thought the same as you, the world would be in a mess!

Esther. I am not everybody, Charlotte—I'm sorry, but I'm not. What's clean for other people is just filth to me. And I want to be clean . . . in my own way. Don't you understand? I was stupidly happy, as ignorant but as blissful as a pig in a sty! But I don't want ignorant bliss any longer. I want to have time to think, reassess everything and make allowances! Yes, make allowances, that above all! But I've got to learn how! I'm not going to copy other people's mistakes and do what custom demands—just because it's what has always been done, and is sacrosanct. What do you expect me to do? I love Florent *and* I love this young girl now . . . I really love her. . . .

Charlotte. You'll never make me believe that!

Esther. Believe it or not, as you please—it's a fact! She loves my husband; he, and I, love her. I can't do anything about it.

Charlotte. But, Esther, this is absolutely shocking!

Esther. You mean wearing my heart on my sleeve, for all to see? You think I shouldn't? If there is one thing I'm determined always to be honest with it's my own emotions. I warn you, Charlotte, I shall go on doing so.

Charlotte. But before you got so mixed up with the girl, you didn't love her! Why did you drag her here and throw her into Florent's arms? That's what I can't understand.

Esther. I couldn't help myself! Sometimes you find things just dragging you on—and yet you know all the time—right up to the brink of disaster . . .

Charlotte. Ah! So you do admit it's a disaster?

Esther. Yes, it is a disaster. But I shall do my utmost to make it not like one . . . my utmost to live with it, make it acceptable, tame it!

Charlotte. Like a household pet? . . .

Esther. Why not? I can't force myself to hate Florent, or the girl. . . . It would be a lie. I love them. And I like loving people, Charlotte. I've got a passion for loving people. You hate love. Everybody hates it these days. . . . It's corrupted, and stifled, and not given a chance to live.

Everything is in league against love, there's a vast world conspiracy against it.

Charlotte. Don't expect your public to understand that!

Esther. For me the public exists in the theater! And nowhere else! We are not in the theater here.

Charlotte. Esther! You're fighting against yourself! You're trying to make a weakness, that's unworthy of you, sound courageous.

Esther. Do you think I don't need courage, then?

Charlotte. You keep contradicting yourself! If you need courage, that means you are struggling against something, you must be hurt. . . .

Esther. Of course I'm struggling, of course I'm hurt! It'd be much too simple if I weren't! I didn't have cramp last night. I cried out, because I was so miserable. I called for Florent . . . and he came. He comforted me, and wanted to stay with me. But I forced him to go, sent him back to Liane.

Charlotte. Sent him back?! But . . . You haven't got a shred of decency left!

Esther. God preserve me from that! If I'd kept Florent with me I'd have been convinced he was staying against his will . . . and then . . . Liane would have resented it, quite rightly.

Charlotte. Well, that's the giddy limit!

Esther. A deep love, like the love that exists, I believe, between Florent and me, is very like a wonderful friendship. Friendship receives great sacrifice, on everybody's part.

Charlotte. Is Florent making any sacrifice?

Esther. He's weak! It's for me to allow him a caprice here and there, to help him. The very thought of some of the things I shall have to tolerate revolts me still. But those are the symptoms of mere infatuation, not of love like ours, and I must overcome them. I am determined to stifle this nasty stupid jealousy of mine. Last night I nearly died of shame when I cried out like that. I don't want to shrink into ordinariness as I grow older, I'd hate to shrink.

Charlotte. But Esther, darling, all this might be justified if Liane loved you in return. . . .

Esther. Doesn't she love me?

Charlotte. She hates you.

Esther. You see nothing but ugliness, Charlotte, everywhere you look.

Charlotte. I'm normal. . . . Where are they, anyway?

Esther. In the summerhouse. Rehearsing. I was helping them until a few minutes ago. Liane kissed my hand, she was so grateful. She loves me all right.

Charlotte. She needed you, for her acting! That's not the same.

Esther. Well, she'll need me again! . . . She's——

Charlotte. She's got just what she wanted! At five o'clock she's playing Juliet to Florent's Romeo—only the balcony scene, it's a special matinee, and it's being broadcast. She thinks she's made! Success! Stardom! She won't need you any more. It won't be long then before she drops her mask.

Esther. What mask? I tell you the girl's fond of me.

Charlotte. She can't be!

Esther. My dear Charlotte, a girl who has studied a whole range of parts at the Conservatoire has a wider view of things than most girls of the same age. Another girl, perhaps, would hate me, but not Liane.

Charlotte. You're blind! You're completely blind! You'll see, one day!

Esther. For the last twenty years and more people have kept telling me: "You'll see," "You'll see"! I haven't seen a thing!

Charlotte. That's just what I mean! Still, you must have seen your husband was deceiving you, darling. . . .

Esther. He's not deceiving me. Things have just gone that way, little by little. I began to love Liane. She loved him. Now he loves her. We're making no secret about it. It's all quite open and above board.

Charlotte. Do you realize what people would think who didn't know how thoroughly decent you really are?

Esther. I tell you only one thing matters now—Florent's happiness. And I don't care, myself, I'm ready for whatever is best for him.

Charlotte. I give up!

FLORENT *appears from the garden.*

Florent. Esther, you're wanted! I've been given the sack. My instructions are not clear enough, it seems. Only the prima donna will do, says Liane. You'd better go.

Esther [*With a laugh*]. I'll go.

Florent. And tell her to hurry. We've got just about a quarter of an hour before we go. She's not dressed yet.

ESTHER *goes out to the garden.*

Charlotte. Florent, I'm glad we've got a minute or two alone. Esther's just told me about that business last night. . . .

Florent. Oh! . . .

Charlotte. It's dreadful, Florent! I mean . . .

Florent. Yes, it is dreadful. I sound like a thorough cad —imagine . . . I don't know what to do.

Charlotte [*Greedily*]. You tell me what happened. I'd like to see whether your versions are the same.

Florent. Esther never lies, don't worry. Her version's true. . . . She cried out . . . for me. She was unhappy. I wanted to stay with her, but there was no way of persuading her. She told me she would soon go off to sleep and insisted on my going back to Liane.

Charlotte. And you agreed?

Florent. Liane would have made an awful scene if——

Charlotte. I thought Liane was supposed to be fond of Esther. . . .

Florent. She has all the faults that go with her qualities. She is hard and hasty, and thoughtless sometimes. . . .

Charlotte. And selfish. . . .

Florent. No, Charlotte, not selfish. Just young! She doesn't realize what she's doing. And Esther does her utmost to prevent her realizing it. Oh, why did she throw me into her arms?

Charlotte. She wanted to make sure you didn't just fall into them!

Florent. A mere girl, a moonstruck child, bursts into Esther's dressing room with some ridiculous infantile story! Instead of dodging, as the most elementary sense of caution would have suggested, Esther falls right into the trap, and brings the girl here to live in our house! And of course I'm no saint, Charlotte, and the girl wouldn't leave me alone. On top of all that Esther acts as if she approved . . . and pushes us into each other's arms!

Charlotte. She doesn't know what she is doing—off her head with worry! Nothing commoner.

Florent. Do you think she's so very unhappy?

Charlotte. I think she's bluffing it out, and she'll do absolutely anything rather than break with you.

Florent. So you think she's only making believe she loves Liane? That's all put on?

Charlotte. No, strange as it may seem, I think she does love her.

Florent. This is a hell of a tangle! We'll never get out of it. . . .

Charlotte. How do you expect *her* to get out of it when you act as you are doing, Florent? You're the mystery. And what's more, you quite like it, you cultivate it. It's your special line in charm. You use silence as other men use words. Nobody ever knows exactly what's going on in your mind. You close up like a clam and keep mum, just when others would open out and talk. Do you love the girl because she excites you or because having a young mistress tickles your vanity? Do you love her enough to murder Esther for her, or only enough to torture her on the grill? Open up, darling! Tell us once and for all just what you think—I have no time for mysteries, but I'd like to understand you. You'll say I should mind my own business, of course, but I don't give a damn. . . . I've got a passion for trying to understand. . . . And that's not a passion that's shared by the younger generation, I'm sure. Let me tell you this, Florent—you may look astonishingly young, but you still belong much more to my generation than to Liane's.

Florent. Yes, yes: of course, of course! I know. I've been disgustingly weak, but Esther was even weaker!

Charlotte. Esther weak! Good Lord! Florent . . . listen! I mean—I know you're a great actor, and all that, but at the moment you're under the spell! You couldn't see the naked truth at the moment if it was sitting on the footlights, never mind about in the front row of the stalls! This girl has flattered you until you're . . . *non compos mentis!* Don't forget Esther is a great actress too . . . she's quite capable of playing a superb rendering of the noble victim, if it happens to suit her.

Florent. What would you do if you were in my place?

Charlotte. I imagine I'd do rather the same as you're doing yourself, but I would at least know that I **was** doing wrong. That's just the difference between us.

Florent. . . . Do you think I don't realize I'm doing wrong?

Charlotte. You're very contrite, of course! But that's largely because you feel you look rather ridiculous.

Florent. Ho! . . .

Charlotte. One man between two women always is ridiculous! Would you ever agree to playing a part like this in the theater? Of course not!

Florent. Well, let's forget who and what we are for **a** moment—give me some advice!

Charlotte. My advice is quite simple. There's only one Esther on this earth. I don't pretend to know how your *senses* feel about it, of course—that may be a very different story, and I prefer not to hear it anyway. I only know what *common sense* thinks about it. If I were you, I'd take that Liane girl by the scruff of her neck and throw her through the window.

Florent. I can't do that, Charlotte.

Charlotte. No, you're too well hooked! Caught! Landed! But it won't last long. Why don't you run away with her? . . . You'd be back again soon enough.

Florent. It's the theater—it distorts us, cheats us all, men and women. . . .

Charlotte. Would you like me to tell your fortune? Tell you what the future holds for you?

Florent. Future!

Charlotte. Your future . . . is in your own hands. . . .

Enter LIANE *and* ESTHER *from the garden.*

Liane. Two or three minutes with Esther and all **the** little bits and pieces fall into their right places.

Esther. There was nothing very much to it. . . .

Liane. Not for you, of course. . . .

Florent. You'll have to hurry, darling. We're on stage at five o'clock.

Liane. I am hurrying. Come and help me, Charlotte, will you?

> [LIANE *and* CHARLOTTE *disappear by the stairway.*

Esther [*Shouts after them*]. I'll see he runs through the end again while you're gone.

Florent. I think I'll go up and brush my hair and tidy up.

Esther. Wait, Florent. There is something I'd like to say to you.

Florent. There's so little time. . . .

Esther. There's very little to say, anyway. Listen, Florent. . . . Last night was deplorable, I went beyond all decent limits! . . . I hope you forgive me. . . .

Florent. Esther! You should forgive me. . . .

Esther. No, Florent. I would have found it difficult to forgive if what Liane confessed in my dressing room that first evening had been true. But this isn't the same thing at all. I brought Liane here, and drove her between us. I've loved her as I might have loved my own daughter. I even taught you to love her—it was my fault, in a way. Remember? She used to get on your nerves dreadfully at first.

Florent. Listen, Esther——

Esther. No, you listen to me, Florent. I knew all the time that this young girl was in love with you. It's all my fault. Not yours. You are a man, and you're at a critical age . . . I'm sorry to say. And I'm not a young woman any longer. . . . It was inevitable. . . .

Florent. Esther, you're making me feel most embarrassed. Please. . . .

Esther. I must say it, Florent. It's through keeping too much to ourselves these things happen. In the plays I act in, dozens of times I've said to myself: "How ridiculous all this is. . . . If only they'd talk to one another." . . .

Florent. There'd be no play then! . . .

Esther. Yes, but this isn't a play, darling. It's real . . . between you and me. So we must speak out, we musn't be uneasy and suspicious. The first thing I must tell you is that I am terribly fond of Liane; the fact is that she's young and that she's here with us doesn't irritate me in the slightest, I like it. Then there's something else I want to say . . . and that is, that I shall very soon manage not to be a nuisance to you. Well, not to be a ghost from the past, if you see what I mean, because it's so visible that I'm hurt and trying to control myself. I'm not hurt any longer, Florent. . . . I was, I must admit . . . very hurt; but I had to do some thinking. If you never think at all you can sometimes build up a stupid, bovine sort of happiness. But real happiness should be able to rise above things and leave them way down below where they don't matter any more. . . . And it can. . . . Do try, Florent. . . . But I implore you not to avoid me, or blame me, and not to be afraid of my blaming you. I shall take it all with a smile, and I promise it won't be an artificial smile specially put on for this! My one dream is to stay close to you, and not annoy you, not look like a martyr. Then, if only Liane will understand that attitude, and feel that it is genuine . . .

Florent. Esther . . . Esther. . . .

Esther. Don't let's be sentimental about this, that's not what I want at all. It would keep us away from what we're aiming at. No. What I want, and keep praying for, is to live in a way that would be condemned by society because society doesn't know what love is. I want no fuss and no show about it. . . . And I want to live that life in all simplicity—not defiantly . . . just quietly and unobtrusively, going my own sweet way. . . .

Florent. You're just wonderful, Esther! I admire you! But surely that sort of happiness couldn't last? It wouldn't be real happiness for you or me . . . or for Liane.

Esther [*In a low voice*]. She doesn't love me.

Florent. What's that?

Esther. Tell me the truth, Florent. She hates me, doesn't she?

Florent. You're mad!

Esther. Charlotte's convinced she does. . . .

Florent. Charlotte's a busybody!

Esther. Because if she did it would be . . . it . . .

Florent [*Shakes her by the shoulders*]. Now, Esther, my poor sweet! Whatever makes you think I could love any woman who hated you?

This last sentence has been heard by LIANE *who has just opened the door and appears dressed for Juliet. She stands at the top of the stairs.*

Liane. I think we must settle this now.
Florent. Liane!

LIANE *comes down the steps and speaks.*

Liane. All right, Florent. I heard what you said. We've only two or three minutes left, but that'll be quite enough. You are right, Esther. I hate you.

Esther. Liane, my dear!

Liane. I am not your dear! And as Florent doesn't seem to have the courage to tell you, I will. Listen, Esther. I don't belong to a generation that can live three in a house and share people. My generation's clearer, more precise . . . more direct, if you like. If we cheat another woman, we don't love her. If another woman cheats us, we don't love her either. We hate her. But you're a brilliant actress, Esther, and you've been giving a wonderful performance— so you fooled me . . . until now.

Esther. Me!?

Liane. You! You hate me like poison but you've been turning on the love full blast. You thought you'd get at *Florent*, being all noble and generous, all heroic. . . . Well, I've had enough of your nobility and I'm certainly not going to act noble myself! I've borne it four months, and all the time you've been trying to blow yourself up and me at the same time.

Esther. Liane! Only a few minutes ago you were kissing my hands, weeping with gratitude. . . .

Liane. You were dominating me, on purpose! As you always do!

Florent. Liane, you're not being fair. Esther has been as kind and straightforward as anyone ever could be. She could never act meanly, anyway . . . she's incapable of it.

I'm not going to let you go whipping up grievances like this—that are quite unjustified, however you look at them.

Liane. I've no need to whip up my grievances. They're only too obvious already. I'm just the simpleton who doesn't hide her motives . . . I have to say what I think, straight out!

Esther. Liane is right, Florent. You are being most unfair. There's nothing more dangerous than bottling things up inside you and never letting them out for an airing. . . . Liane will hear what I have to say and understand, I'm sure. It's quite natural for my attitude to upset her. She's young, impulsive, and passionate. She has never yet been hurt . . . and yet you want her to see her way through the absolute maze of my feelings when I'm quite baffled by them even myself. . . .

Florent. Well, let Liane listen, then—to both of us—and not keep insulting you. My point is—why all this talk of hate? There's no need to exaggerate so much—you'll only regret it afterwards. You'll never forget all this. I'd rather see you scratch each other's eyes out, than hear you bring out all these words that we shall never be able to forget. Liane doesn't hate you, Esther. Liane, you don't hate Esther, you know you——

Liane. Yes, I do hate her. Don't you think you'll smooth things over this time. That's a mania you have and it revolts me. It's the one thing I dislike about you.

Florent. Did you have to choose the day we're in a hurry and you're dressed up as Juliet to say all these unpleasant things? Anyway, you don't really mean them. You can't realize——

Liane [*Cuts in*]. I've said them before, haven't I?

Florent. Never!

Liane. Not in so many words, perhaps—I may have wrapped it up. But it ought not to have been hard to read between the lines. . . .

Florent. Do you mean to suggest, in front of Esther here, that you have told me in private that you hated her?

Liane. It gave me a good laugh seeing you dodging about, never understanding anything that didn't suit you . . . only believing what it was convenient to believe. . . .

Florent. I was convinced, and I still am, that you love Esther, just as she deserves to be loved. And I think this scene is dreadful! Pure melodrama, if you ask me!

Esther. Florent! don't be unkind to Liane. . . . She's wrong, but she's frank. She's always frank. You're being unfair again. . . .

Liane. That's right! Defend me! Go on! Pile kindness onto kindness! Wonderful acting! It only needed you to come between Florent and me, of course on my behalf!

Florent. Oh! This is awful!

Esther. Let her speak!

Liane. You must always be the woman who leaps in front of the hero and stops the bullet in her breast herself. . . . When will you stop thinking you're on the stage?

Florent. You're the one who's dramatizing this! Talk about dramatics!

Esther. Leave her alone, Florent! . . . Liane! dear! Please!

Liane. Are you bent on sending me off my head? That's enough! Do you hear? Enough! I've had more than I can stand of your sugary sentiments!

Florent. Liane, Liane! . . . Be honest with yourself! . . . Search deep down in your heart——

Liane. Don't talk to me about hearts! You and Esther are all mixed up, hearts and old-fashioned theatrical sentimentality are the same thing to you. Go on, sacrifice yourselves, cut yourselves up in pieces, commit suicide, anything! But don't talk to me about your hearts! The heart's a different thing altogether! I may have a hard heart, Florent, but I'm proud of it. Soft hearts like yours are revolting. You'd like me to love you, and go on living as though I'm as blind as a bat, with you balancing on a tightrope all the time, and Esther here just waiting for . . .

Esther. Waiting for what?

Liane. That's it! Pretend you don't know! Play the innocent! Shall I tell you what you remind me of hanging about in this house? You won't like it.

Florent. Liane! . . .

Liane. You look like somebody in a crowded restaurant,

standing near a table waiting for it to be free. The very presence of people like that in the room ruins the meal for everybody else.

Florent. Don't listen to her. . . . Liane, this is contemptible. Esther said only a moment ago that the only thing she really wanted was to live quietly here with us, the three of us together. . . .

Liane. That's because she's a coward. She daren't ask you for a plain answer! She's frightened of a straight "yes" or "no"! And so are you! You're making shift, Florent! So is Esther . . . and I'll never make shift, whatever happens!

Florent. You said you had a hard heart! . . . I don't think you've even got that! Either you've got a heart or you haven't, there's no sliding scale of qualities. But hearts are out of fashion nowadays. Like hats! Your generation doesn't wear a heart.

Liane. No, we don't! True enough! We don't parade our feelings to the world at large. We're shy about them . . . we have the modesty to keep them out of sight where they belong.

Florent. There aren't a thousand ways of loving, you know. And Esther loves you, I know. . . .

Liane. Ha! Love to the gypsy rhapsody! The sort that's only just bearable in the middle of the night, holding hands, when you've had a lot to drink. . . .

Esther. I don't understand. . . . How could she? . . .

Florent [*To* LIANE]. Can't you see what you're doing?

Liane. Esther is a specialist in tears, remember.

Esther. She hates me! . . . Florent! . . . I can't bear it! You know what I mean—can't you explain to her?

Florent. No, it's useless, Esther, she just digs her heels in. There's nothing to be done. Anyway I'm in a state of collapse.

Liane. You're in a state of collapse! Is that all you can find to say? Well, collapse, then! [*Looks at her watch.*] Oh! God! We shall be late! We're on the air in seventeen minutes!

Florent. Oh, hell! I'd forgotten that!

Esther. Hurry up, Florent. Actors must never miss an

entrance. Even when they lose their nearest and dearest, actors are always ready for their cue.

Liane. We've got all night to talk this all over and tomorrow, and the next day, and the next! I suppose there'll be no end to it!

[*She runs into the garden and disappears.*

Charlotte [*Who appears at the top of the stairway and is putting on her gloves*]. Are you driving into town? I think I'll come with you.

Florent. No, Charlotte. . . . Stay here, will you? Stay here with Esther . . . you mustn't leave her alone for a moment!

Esther. Oh! Don't be afraid! I shan't commit suicide!

Liane [*Off*]. Florent . . . are you coming or not?

Florent. Will you lend me your car? I'll be back quicker then.

Esther. "*We* shall be back quicker . . ." is what you should say. No, I'm sorry. One of the tires has a slow leak and there's no time for you to pump it up or change the wheel. You'd better take your own if you don't want to be late.

Liane [*From outside*]. Well? Have you decided?

Florent. Coming! [*Goes toward the door.*] This will drive me into the nuthouse before we're done!   [*Goes.*

Charlotte. What's the matter? . . . Has anything happened?

Esther. You were right, Charlotte. Liane hates me.

Charlotte. It's only natural. . . .

Esther. I don't know how to hate, Charlotte. It may be a weakness in me, probably is, but I don't understand hate. I'm temperamentally incapable of it. Sometimes I rush up to someone, fling my arms around their neck, and say I'm overjoyed to see them . . . and it turns out we had the most awful row the last time we met! I just forget! You see?

Charlotte. You like loving people; just as others like hating them.

Esther. But what have I done to her, Charlotte?

Charlotte. What have you done? Good Lord! You've let her take your husband away from you, then turned the other cheek and said you were fond of her! You've refused to make a melodrama out of it! You've robbed the girl of a magnificent part! Spoiled her show for her!

Esther. People never change, you know, Charlotte—though you may be surprised to hear it from me. This girl's hate hurts me more than my husband's unfaithfulness, really. Florent I've lost and yet haven't really lost, if you see what I mean . . .

Charlotte. That's what makes her so mad. . . .

Esther. Whereas Liane I've lost entirely, at one stroke —like that—in a split second. It's like a horror play.

Charlotte. Didn't Florent have anything to say?

Esther. No. He's under a charm really . . . a spell! He had lied to me. And he knew that I knew it. He could only shrug his shoulders and say: "I'm helpless. . . ."

Charlotte. All men are the same. What a breed! Did I ever tell you why Jules left me? Well, Jules, you see, had no sign of culture whatsoever, but I have always adored pictures and monuments and things, you know! Well, one day we were standing on the Acropolis, and I was just explaining Greece to him. I happened to glance at him and suddenly saw that his face was contorted with rage —hideous, my dear! He screamed into my face at the top of his voice a rude word that you probably know (but that no lady ever admits she knows) and he turned and bounded away through the huge stone columns like a mountain goat. I've never seen him from that day to this!

Esther. Poor Charlotte. . . .

Charlotte. Three years later I was sent an anonymous letter telling me he was living at a certain address with another woman. I planted myself on the pavement straight opposite the window and could just make out their shadows on the curtains. But I was there so long that a policeman came and asked me what I was doing. So I explained that those shadows on the curtain belonged to my husband and another woman. Well, darling, there are some very simple, uneducated people, you know, who are absolutely unbelievable! Do you know what he did? He just clicked his heels and gave me a full military salute!

Esther. Incredible!

Charlotte. Yes . . . I still don't know why! . . . Well, what are you going to do? You must do something! It would be just ridiculous to sit still and do nothing about it, darling! Can't you decide?

Esther. I'm going away.

Charlotte. What about me?

Esther. You?

Charlotte. Yes, me! If you go away?

Esther. Oh, I'm sorry. I see what you mean. Well— there's no need for you to go away just because of me.

Charlotte. Desertion isn't at all in my line! Besides, mother's away at the moment and the house is empty . . . and . . .

Esther. Hotels are expensive. . . .

Charlotte. Yes, very. . . . [*Realizes her mistake.*] Oh but that's a detail, of course. No, what matters is that somebody must stay here to keep an eye on things and speak up for you. . . .

Esther. Thank you, Charlotte.

Charlotte. It's the least I can do. [*Five o'clock strikes.*] Five. Time for my rest. My headaches are as good as an alarm clock . . . always on the dot. You don't mind, do you?

Esther. Of course not.

Charlotte. Florent told me not to leave you for a second. Now, no nonsense, Esther. I can rely on you, can't I? I needn't worry about you while I'm resting?

Esther. No, Of course not.

Charlotte [*Climbing up the stairway*]. Don't upset yourself. Men are just not worth it!

Esther. Will you send Lulu down? Do you mind?

Charlotte. They're brutes, all of them without exception, nasty, filthy brutes. . . .   [*Goes.*

ESTHER *lies, face down, on the divan, her head in her hands. She is motionless.* LULU *opens the door and comes down the four steps.*

Lulu. Did you ask for me, madame?

Esther [*Jumps*]. Yes, Lulu. You know the case I was packing last night? Will you finish the packing quickly, Lulu dear? And bring me my hat and coat? I'll send foi the rest of my things tomorrow.

Lulu. Is madame leaving Chatou?

Esther. Yes, I'm leaving Chatou.

Lulu. Where are we going?

Esther. I don't know, Lulu. Somewhere in town. The hotel opposite the theater, I think. I shan't feel lonely there.

Lulu. Madame won't be alone, anyway. I'll be there, as usual. We shall be together. Madame's looking very sad.

Esther. Yes, Lulu, I am sad.

Lulu. Madame didn't ought to leave Chatou.

Esther. Oh yes, Lulu, I ought. . . . Be a dear, will you . . . finish that packing, close the case, and come straight back here? [LULU *goes. A murmur can be heard of what* ESTHER *is saying.*] Not alone. . . . [ESTHER *goes round the room kissing a few ornaments and pieces of furniture. Then she comes over to the radio. She fondles the armchair close to the radio. She turns the knobs and while it warms up she kneels and puts her ear to the front of the set. The voices of* FLORENT *and* LIANE *can be heard as they play the balcony scene from* Romeo *and* Juliet. ESTHER *bursts into sobs and for the first time abandons herself to her feelings. The door opens and* LULU *appears with the case and hat and coat and comes down the stairs.*] You've been a long time.

Lulu [*Coming down*]. It's not easy, madame.

Esther [*While* LULU *helps her with her coat*]. No, it's not easy, is it? Not at all easy, Lulu dear. . . .

She takes the room in with a glance, and they go out. The "balcony scene" continues from the radio in the empty room as the curtain falls.

ACT THREE

Same set as for Act Two. A number of "modern" alterations have been made by LIANE. *It is midwinter and it is snowing. Electric lights and fires on all the time.* ESTHER's *portrait has disappeared.*

*A microphone is at the front of the stage. A reporter
keeps coming and going between the microphone, LIANE,
CHARLOTTE, and outside in the garden, where we imagine
his colleagues and technicians to be, with the recording car.*

ANNOUNCER [*Shouts in the wings*]. There. Is that all right?
Good. [*Tests mike. To the two ladies:*] Well, we're ready.
I'm sorry for causing such a disturbance. We like recording interviews at the speaker's home, if we can . . . always get better results. We don't like making a nuisance
of ourselves, of course, invading people like this . . .
spoiling the lawn, and so on. . . .

Liane. You're not spoiling it—well, no more than I do
myself. Every time I use the car I drive across the lawn!
Is the recording car just where you want it now?

Announcer. Perfect, thanks. We don't often have a
lawn, I can tell you! In town, caretakers don't even let us
use the drive when we record in apartment houses, as a
rule. We have to park in the street, and have a crowd of
people gaping around us all the time. A devil of a nuisance
they are too. Here it's marvelous for our work, like a
dream.

Charlotte. When they came to record at my place once
they had to bring the mike five floors up and trail right
through my mother's bedroom. It was torture!

Liane. Good Lord! I'd forgotten to introduce you to
Mme. Charlotte de Couville. You probably know one another already?

Announcer. Oh! Mme. de Couville! I'm sorry, I didn't
realize . . . No. I've never yet been lucky enough to interview Mme. de Couville.

Charlotte. It was a young lady announcer the last time
with me. But if it comes in your department now, you
needn't quake at the thought of going up five floors any
more. I live in a little cottage not far from here nowadays.
There's a lawn like this, and only one floor in any case,
and it's a bungalow!

Liane. Mme. de Couville was staying with me . . .
mmm . . . with us . . . I mean with M. Ledoux. She
left us only a few days ago. Her mother was taken ill. By
the way, is she better now, Charlotte?

Charlotte. She's beginning to get about again. . . .
Well . . . er . . . I'd better . . .

Liane. Are you going so soon?

Charlotte. I don't want to be a nuisance, Liane. I just
looked in as I happened to be passing. . . .

Liane. No, I won't let you go. Please [*To* ANNOUNCER.]
tell Mme. de Couville you need her . . . and that you're
very glad to see her and you'd like her to say a few words
as well. . . .

Announcer. Wonderful idea!

Charlotte. Liane, my dear! You mustn't! I'm a terrible
country clod, these days, you know that, and I look dreadful. Look at this old coat, and my nose is shining like a
traffic light. . . .

Liane. Nobody can see you, you silly . . . you just talk.

Charlotte. Of course, what a fool! I was thinking of
television! I'm terrified of photographs . . . a sort of
photophobia. I always forget the public can't see you on
the radio.

Announcer. Well, that means you've no excuse, now.

Charlotte. If I can be of any assistance to you . . .

Liane. You can, Charlotte, definitely. They came really
to see Florent, and they expected a sort of double interview, the two of us chatting at the microphone. But Florent isn't here and if I speak alone it'll be a bit thin . . .
especially as the microphone absolutely terrifies me . . .
dries me right up!

Charlotte. Well, now, what shall I say? Shall I tell them
I've played in the theater hundreds of times to cabinet
ministers and members of several royal families, and I've
never once been scared. . . . But I'm simply paralyzed
at the thought of this little mousetrap of yours.

Announcer. You must be very used to it, all the same,
Mme. de Couville.

Charlotte. Of course I'm used to it. But I still want to
run away, every time. I'm just like Florent, petrified at
anything mechanical.

Announcer. M. Ledoux is frightened of mechanical
things, is he? Will you mention that, when you speak?
It's an interesting detail. . . .

Charlotte. Well . . . I remember one evening . . . now, when was it? . . . let me see . . . about 1907, I think . . .

Liane. Charlotte! Please! The announcer hasn't the time to go back as far as that . . . and all these men are waiting for him. Tell your stories when you're on the air in a moment. Will you? [*To* ANNOUNCER.] Ready?

Announcer [*At the door, shouting to colleagues*]. Ready? . . . Right. [*Takes out his watch. Shouts again.*] Have each voice for level first, eh? Mlle. Baudier? Say anything—just a sentence or two. . . .

Liane. I am really terribly disappointed that Florent Ledoux isn't here today. I should have been——

Announcer. Good. Thank you. Mme. de Couville?

Charlotte. I'm really terribly sorry, too, that Florent isn't here . . . then I wouldn't have had this golden opportunity of boring you to death, would I?

Announcer. Ha, ha! Charming! [*Shouts.*] All right? . . . Good. Right. Now we're recording. O.K.? On the green flick. [*The green flick. He then indicates that he is starting to speak.*] Good evening, listeners, here we are this week in a delightful villa in Chatou. The villa belongs to Florent Ledoux, and we've been welcomed here by that great actor's favorite pupil, Mlle. Liane Baudier, one of the youngest and most promising new recruits to the Comédie Française. Mlle. Baudier is wearing a charming green suit—coat and slacks—that I can't help admiring. And I'm sure if they saw her now all the glamour girls of Hollywood would swallow their tonsils and resign from the business in a body, so to speak. Mlle. Baudier I hope will take that as a compliment—as it was intended, before the sentence got rather out of hand. Mlle. Baudier, don't you think your costume is a tremendous contrast to the usual costumes of musty antiquity—dare I say—that you have to wear at the Comédie Française?

Liane [*Into the mike*]. Please don't think that the Comédie Française is opposed in any way to novelty! Especially off the stage, of course! I'm sure the governors would never dream of criticizing my clothes, anyway. To tell the truth, my slacks were made from a pattern I borrowed from the director general's wife! So I'm hoping no complaints can be made on that score!

Announcer. That will interest our lady listeners, I know. And what does M. Ledoux think of your green suit? Does he think it looks too young, perhaps?

Liane. No. M. Ledoux is the youngest person I know. And . . . he rather indulges my whims . . . because (no doubt you know already) we're hoping to be married soon and go to Hollywood for our honeymoon.

Charlotte. Oh!?

Announcer [*Waves his hand for silence*]. Sh! Well, Mlle. Baudier, we had heard a rumor, of course, and we are only too glad to hear you confirm it. Are you going to Hollywood just as tourists, or do you think you will be making a film while you're there? M. Ledoux has never done a film yet and this would be news of the greatest interest to our listeners.

Liane. I can't answer that question yet. But I can say that I myself intend to do a film soon, and that M. Ledoux may surprise you all, after all. . . .

Announcer. Thank you for telling us so much, Mlle. Baudier. Well, listeners, I've had the luck to find here, visiting Mlle. Baudier, that fine actress you must all have seen in at least one of her many famous parts—Mme. Charlotte de Couville!

Charlotte [*Absolutely at her ease*]. Present sir!

Announcer. Did you know that Mlle. and M. Ledoux were leaving for Sunset Boulevard and were probably going to do a film together, Mme. de Couville?

Charlotte. Florent wouldn't like me to give away any secrets . . . and, although I'm absolutely in his confidence . . . I daren't give you any details. But I can tell you that I myself am being pressed to do a terrific film at the moment, and I'm just about to sign the contract although I confess that films have always rather horrified me. I remember my mother telling me about the early films, you know. When they used to sit in an old cellar and watch dots and squiggles dart across a spotted screen, you know. My mother's nearly blind now, and very, very deaf! And she can't remember a thing. We don't get any younger any of us, do we? Mother was only a girl, and she used to take me along with her . . . oh, I mean, of course, that was a lot later. How silly! I'm getting terribly mixed up. . . .

Announcer. Well . . . er . . . we shall soon have the chance of seeing you on the screen, then, Mme. de Couville?

Charlotte. Yes. I'm playing in the revival of *The Quarry* in a few days' time, with Esther Ledoux. We were going to open in October but Esther decided to remove the entire apron stage and the stage boxes so the theater is full of scaffolding and workmen at the moment. [LIANE, *behind* CHARLOTTE, *is desperately making signs to the* ANNOUNCER *to stop her talking.*] We shall be starting *The Quarry*, though, soon. . . . That'll be in the theater, at night, of course . . . and in the daytime I shall be filming. One thing. I'm particularly intrigued to——

Announcer. We are intrigued, too, Mme. de Couville, at the thought of seeing you at last on the screen. [*He pushes* LIANE *to the mike.*] Don't you think so, Mlle. Baudier?

Liane. It is a great thing for actors to agree to work for films. And I'm very proud myself to have helped the cinema by overcoming some of Florent Ledoux's scruples. Now his genius will be on permanent record with the help of filmic art.

Charlotte [*Puts her head close to* LIANE'S]. Hoorah!

Announcer. Mme. de Couville shares our enthusiasm. It was her charming "hoorah" you have just heard.

Charlotte [*Seizes the mike*]. Yes, hoorah again! Hurrah for anybody who is ready to try something new! Three cheers for Florent Ledoux! It shows tremendous courage. [LIANE *signs to her, but she goes on.*] To launch into entirely new territory at this point in his career. Hoorah for him! Hoorah for me, too . . . I don't hesitate to say so! And while I'm here—hoorah for France, hoorah for Old England, hoorah for——

Announcer. Thank you, Mme. de Couville! Thank you! You have said wonderfully what I know all of us feel. Well, that brings us to the end of our weekly interview with the Stars of Stage and Screen. [CHARLOTTE *tries to speak again. He raises the mike to his own mouth to get it away from her.*] Listen to "Come to Stardom" again at the same time in next week's program. Good night, ladies and gentlemen, good night.

Charlotte. God Almighty! [*They sign to her to be quiet.*] Oh!

Announcer. There! Don't you worry, we'll cut your "God Almighty!" We can do wonders with things like that. Now, it only remains for me to thank you ladies for your help. And do forgive all the trouble we've caused you.

Charlotte. No trouble at all. I'm the one who . . . er . . . I thought I'd never manage to say anything at all! [*Casually and distantly.*] It's all rather fun, I think. [LIANE *raises her eyes to heaven.*]

Announcer. Don't bother to see me out, Mlle. Baudier, please. It's snowing. I'll just get the mike out of the door and that'll be that. Thanks again. Very many thanks.

Liane. Thank you, too. Mind those stone steps—they're very slippery. And you know . . . [*Looks meaningfully at him*] if the recording isn't very good after all, just give me a ring and I'll come and do another for you.

Charlotte. Yes, ring me too, won't you?

Liane. Of course, Mme. de Couville as well—if you need her. Good-bye!

[ANNOUNCER *goes out through door to garden.*

Charlotte. Isn't it fun? Things come into your head for no reason whatsoever. I was amazed at the things I said.

Liane. I should think so.

Charlotte. You don't seem very pleased, Liane. . . .

Liane. You know, Charlotte . . . Florent's been here all the time, in his room. Hiding!

Charlotte. Florent!

Liane. Yes. You know how he hates radio. I wouldn't like him to know you'd been here and we'd talked any sort of nonsense into the mike, you know. . . .

Charlotte. I don't think you talked "any sort of nonsense." . . .

Liane. Well, I don't think he'd approve of our impromptu sketch, let's say.

Charlotte. Oh! I must fly! I ought to have been home hours ago! My poor mother always imagines I've been run over by a bus when I'm late.

Liane. Mind the steps out front, they're very treacherous.

Charlotte. I may call again later on . . . may have a surprise for you. . . .

Liane. What surprise?

Charlotte. If I told you, it wouldn't be a surprise any more. Don't bother to come with me. It'd be silly in this snow. I'll run through it. So glad to have been of some assistance. I'll find my own way.

[*She opens the door and disappears.*

Liane [*Raises her arms to heaven*]. Ooooooooooooooooooooh! [*She then turns and shouts.*] Florent! Florent!

Florent [*Appears at the door over the stairway*]. Have they gone? Can I come down?

Liane. Yes. Come down. They were very charming young men, and they came in all this snow just for our convenience. It was a pity to be rude to them.

Florent. It was to avoid being rude to them that I shut myself in my room.

Liane. It was you they really wanted to see, of course. Quite rightly.

Florent. You told them I hated radio, all reporters and all journalists without exception, I hope?

Liane. Why hurt their feelings? I told them you weren't here.

Florent. Did they interview you?

Liane. They wanted to know what my plans were. . . . Well, our plans . . .

Florent. What did you say?

Liane. Oh, the microphone always scares the wits out of me. I didn't say exactly what I would have liked to say. I'm afraid you'll be angry with me. . . .

Florent. Did you say anything about me?

Liane. You're the one the public's interested in, not me. I don't kid myself, you see. I said you were coming with me to Hollywood.

Florent. Liane!

Liane. And it's sweet of me to confess, because you

never listen to the radio. You would never have known.

Florent. What about the newspapers? Do you realize how dangerous it is to talk too early, to say anything at all before——

Liane. You're always so afraid of publicity. You should like publicity, Florent. It's our profession. . . .

Florent. Publicity likes me, that's quite different. I don't object to publicity when it's in praise of a job well done, and the success is earned. But that's the sort of justified fame that grows with time. It proves that the public isn't forgetting us. What maddens me is this sort of artificial publicity that people plan and arrange for themselves . . . without doing anything at all!! Modern publicity, machine-made fame, mass-produced counterfeit reputations, not worth the paper they're printed on!

Liane. You've got stuck tight in the old type of system. Everything handmade.

Florent. Yes . . . and I'm glad of it. When a thing's handmade it gives me confidence; and I don't like machines, I must admit. On principle. Handmade everything, even handmade publicity, real, natural sort of stuff, that's what I like. I feel warmed by things like that. Your machine-made stuff revolts me.

Liane. Well, don't blame me! It's not my fault the world moves forward. This is the age of films and such things, the telephone and radio! I think these men are wonderful coming to ask me questions here at home and carrying my voice away in a little box!

Florent. It's astonishing how much your generation adores potted art.

Liane. You . . . and Esther! . . . Aren't you a bit pre-Waterloo?

Florent. Maybe we are. Don't ask me to change at my age, though. When they're as old as me, men just don't change.

Liane. A pity. A great pity. When you think what a great actor like you could bring to the screen.

Florent. You're quite wrong, Liane. The theater and the screen turn their backs on one another, and look in opposite directions. The beauty of the theater, the magic of the theater, is that you can be carried right away by an absolutely massive Tristan or even a doddering old Isolde. On the screen, Tristan must have almost the exact age of the real Tristan, and so must Isolde. All their youth is cut up into little strips, and sliced, and stuck together again until they get it right. In the theater you have to act, really live and die; Oedipus, Cassius, Cyrano, Britannicus, Romeo, Juliet, and all the others demand years of experience on the stage. Esther and I are just beginning to feel we can tackle those juvenile leads after all these years! It's a great pity perhaps, but that's how it is. On the other hand, real youth, with all its hardness and cruelty, ought to play all the old-age parts in the theater. So it's only natural for youth to be attracted by the cinema—it's trying to find itself all the time.

Liane. A pure paradox.

Florent. What of it? When truth comes out, paradox is the name it goes under.

Liane. Remember that—don't waste it.

Florent. Remember what?

Liane. All we needed was a few bright cracks—then you could turn author in your old age!

Florent. I'm basically old-fashioned, Liane. You'll have to resign yourself to that.

Liane. I won't. . . . You're doing it on purpose.

Florent. Don't let's quarrel, darling, please. I was only explaining, as pleasantly as I could, why I'm turning down that American film offer. That's all. Don't let's talk about it any more.

Liane. You're ruining my career!

Florent. Your best career is to stay with the Comédie Française and do some hard work! Get bored and irritated beyond measure, wear yourself out playing the classics, and then——

Liane. Wait a hundred years for the chance of playing Juliet. . . .

Florent. I didn't wait a hundred years for the chance to play Romeo. . . . And you played Juliet only a month or two ago! . . .

Liane. That was a special matinee for students! You

can't call that playing Juliet! And you are *you*. Still I think I'd rather see Romeo played by a young man of the right age in any case. . . .

Florent. Esther would explain, better than I can, how difficult it is to solve the eternal problem of these Romeo parts on the stage. . . .

Liane. So that final, Florent, is it? You're turning away thousands of Hollywood dollars? You won't go? And won't let me go, either?

Florent. Why don't you go alone? There's nothing to stop you. I'll be waiting for you.

Liane. It's only to get you that they've asked me at all! You know that well enough! I'm not worth a cent to them without you!

Florent. They love discovering new stars.

Liane. You've made me too famous for anybody to discover me now.

Florent. Do you blame me for that?

Liane. I wouldn't blame you if you accepted their offer, and gave me the chance of going to Hollywood—but if you condemn me to . . .

Florent. Condemn you to what? Working for your reputation? Growing worthy of your fame? Really deserving some of the fortune they'll offer you?

Liane. No! To rotting away in your futile Comédie Française!

Florent. Liane!

Liane. To moldering away in that old-fashioned death-trap I was fool enough to get caught in!

Florent. But it's the only place you can play Racine, Corneille, Molière, Shakespeare. . . .

Liane. I don't care a damn! I want to do films! And I will!

Florent. You don't want to be an actress—you want to be a dark, flat shadow. . . .

Liane. You're the shadows, if you only knew . . . ghosts, in fact!

Florent [*Kisses her*]. I'm being silly. I'm sorry! Youth will flame and sparkle. . . . I always forget the years there are between us.

Liane. There would be no years between us at all if only you'd have confidence in yourself, and in me! If you weren't so downright obstinate, and stood up out of that old armchair you're glued to all the time. Oh, Florent! . . . You're being ridiculous. Suppose I took you at your word? Would you really let me go alone to America. Leave me to career around Hollywood by myself? You know you'd hate it and never put up with it!

Florent. If it meant you'd be happy, and famous. . . .

Liane. Happy? Without you? No, Florent, I'll stay here. And I'll work, but I won't give in. I'm going to keep at you about this. I'll convince you someday!

Florent. I doubt it.

Liane [*Listens a second*]. That was the garden gate.

Florent. Are you expecting any more mechanical men?

Liane. Yes . . . as a matter of fact, you'd better hurry back into hiding.

Florent. Who is it this time?

Liane. Someone who always makes your hair stand on end.

Florent. Not your film agent?

Liane. Yes. Come on, hurry off! Quickly!

Florent [*Goes up the stairs four at a time, turns at the top.*] Don't let her think she has the faintest chance of persuading me into films, ever!

Liane. I can't hear her—it must be the snow. But she'll be here in a second. [*He pulls a face.*] Oh! Shame on you! Why do you make such faces? . . . Now, then . . . Begone, Macbeth! Hop it! The witches are after you! Double, double! Toil and trouble! . . .

Florent. "How now, you secret, black and midnight hags!" They were the journalists of their time, you know!

Liane. That's pure prejudice. I was right—you're old-fashioned!

Florent. Farewell, Garbo.

They put out their tongues at one another. LIANE *hurries to the door from the garden and opens it. Enter* ESTHER *in a white gust of snow.*

Liane. Come in! Quickly!

Esther. Is Florent ill?

Liane. You're smothered in snow! Come up to the fire. That stove of yours was a museum piece, I swept it out as soon as I could. There are electric fires all over the house now. . . . And I moved all the potted ferns. They made the place look like a junk shop, they went with the stove. . . .

Esther. I asked you if Florent was ill.

Liane. No. He's wonderfully fit.

Esther. Oh! When they gave me that telephone message I was quite frightened. I thought he must be ill. "Florent wants you urgently at Chatou." Why urgently? What does he want? Where is he?

Liane. It wasn't Florent who wanted you. I did. I lied.

Esther. What, again?

Liane. What do you mean, again?

Esther. I was thinking of that rather memorable lie you told in my dressing room, the first time we met. . . .

Liane. Oh, Esther—don't! You remind me of that stupid story of the man who bought a new hat on Armistice Day in 1918 and walked into exactly the same shop on V-E Day 1945, and said gaily: "Here I am again! Remember me?!"

Esther. Does it feel as long ago as that to you?

Liane. It's ancient history. Life moves so fast nowadays . . . for us young people at least. . . .

Esther. Your hearts don't beat any faster, Liane. So Florent doesn't know I'm here?

Liane. Sh! Let me explain. He knows there's somebody here but he doesn't know it's you. He's barricaded in; he thinks I'm talking to an American Woman who horrifies him, a film agent. . . .

Esther. Liane, I find these little maneuvers very distasteful. [*Rises.*] And I won't stay another minute.

Liane [*Forces her to sit again, puts her hands on her shoulders*]. In this snowstorm? Esther, don't be silly. I'll go and tell Florent you're here. He's sure to find out anyway. You must see him now. But I really had to warn you first

Esther. Don't try to drag me into any plot against Florent! You might as well realize from——

Liane. No, it's just the opposite! It's helping him, not working against him. . . .

Esther. All right. . . . If that's really the case I'm prepared to listen.

Liane. Why that tone of voice, Esther?

Esther. Well really! You're a bit incredible, Liane! No one would ever think you knew it was the first time I've been back to this house since——

Liane. Since the night you ran away. . . .

Esther. Yes . . . I ran away. . . .

Liane. Can you imagine what it was like when we got back from the matinee that day? Florent was driving like a drunk, to start with. When he found out you'd gone he rushed into the Couville woman's room and shouted: "So you left her alone? I told you not to leave her alone! Where is she? Where's Lulu?" And he shook her so violently that she wanted to call the police. He ran out to the garage and found your car was gone. Then he had a sort of brainstorm and started banging his head against the wall. . . .

Esther. What did you do?

Liane. Me? It wasn't long before I realized that what I was in love with was not Florent alone, but the two of you, the wonderful sort of atmosphere that surrounds you when you are together.

Esther. I had to go. It would have dragged on and on, we'd have washed our dirty linen in front of one another time and time again. . . . Florent's weak, weak but obstinate. . . .

Liane. That's it, Esther. You're quite right. He is— weak and obstinate! But I acted disgracefully! I admit it frankly. I was absolutely disgraceful that day, from the word "go." Just like a devil who'd jumped out of a box. But I've got some excuse. The Juliet dress didn't fit me properly and—I'm not a complete fool—I knew I was bad in the balcony scene, a mere beginner compared with you! That burst of fury, that sort of nervous hysteria I had . . . was really aimed at myself . . . well, at me and Florent.

I thought he was being ridiculously weak. He ought to
have made a scene with you, and then another one with
me! But he dodged them both, slipped away, cheated us
of them. I wasn't annoyed with you, Esther, I was annoyed with him . . . and with myself, and a lot of other
things—this red plush curtaining, this dreadful nightmare
of a house of yours, like a set for some crazy crime play!

Esther. I could hardly know that, could I?

Liane. I suppose you always picture me in the Juliet
dress, throwing a rather vile temper on the stairway there.

Esther. The past, Liane, is the present grown a little
older. And as you grow older you begin losing your
memory.

Liane. You seem to remember the smallest details of
that night in the theater.

Esther. It was our first meeting. And in those days you
hadn't done me any harm. Whereas after that night . . .
You know me now, Liane. I forgot harm easily enough,
I even forget hate. I can't harbor resentment however
much I try. And this forgetting the harm people do to
me isn't a virtue in me . . . it's more like a disease.

Liane. Esther, if I go on my knees, and beg you to forgive me . . . will you like me again, just a little?
Please . . . ?

Esther. I never like people just a little. I either love them
or I don't love them. I once learned to love you, Liane.
Then I had to set to and learn not to love you any longer.
If this means starting and going through that all over
again, I think it's asking too much of my old bones. I'd
rather not run the risk.

Liane. You are terrible, Esther.

Esther. And you are quite disarming. Let's talk about
something else, do you mind?

Liane [*Pause*]. Are you opening the theater again soon?

Esther. The play was really doing very well but I just
had to take it off because of the heat. The atmosphere in
the theater was unbearable. Now the workmen are in and
I can't reopen for about three weeks. Poor old theater.
The apron and boxes were very solidly built. They had to

be pulled out, extracted, like wisdom teeth. What are
your plans exactly?

Liane. That's why I sent you that message. I want to
ask your advice.

Esther. Surely not.

Liane. Florent believes in no one but you. He has no
faith in anyone else's views. . . .

Esther. Please don't. . . .

Liane. But it's true. Every five minutes he says "Esther
would explain that for you" or "Esther could tell us, of
course . . ." and so on. All the time. Your opinion's the
only one in the world that counts for him. I have no illusions about that. . . . You belong to the same family.

Esther. The same generation. . . .

Liane. It's this eternal question of age that's at the root
of it all! Esther, what would you say if the film people
made you a big offer?

Esther. They've been making me big offers for years.
I always refuse. No, Liane, I've spent much too much time
learning my job. I haven't got the time or energy to waste
on learning another. Besides, it's not my idea of art. The
radio invades the drawing room and even the bedroom
. . . the cinema splashes its huge eyes and heads with
monstrous ears and noses across a massive screen. . . .
What I like in the theater is the mystery, the remoteness
of everything. I like all the things that make the theater
solemn and impressive, and that actually separate us from
the public. I like the sudden way the house lights go out,
the hush, the rising curtain, the great arch of light above
the footlights, and the darkness everywhere else. I like the
purring cars that glide up to the theater before the show
and hurry the audience away right afterward. . . . All
those things. That's why I had those stage boxes removed.
They intruded.

Liane. And you think films have no mystery about them?

Esther. They're different. Though I do see that the
screen demands a certain type of sincerity. Your eyes are
like windows onto your soul. On the screen the audience
can see right through into the house—so you do need
things to be straight, inside.

Liane. Don't you think Florent's wrong to refuse all these American offers?

Esther. He has plenty of sincerity, of course. But, my dear Liane, I wouldn't dare say any more. Florent is terribly weak, except about things connected with the stage. But he does know his own strength. When it's a question of his work he never hesitates—he knows exactly what he wants.

Liane. He wants me to get on—but he just won't give me this wonderful chance of going to Hollywood.

Esther. Now, really, Liane! Do you mean to say that you've brought me out here to Chatou to get me to persuade Florent to take you to Hollywood?

Liane. Yes.

Esther. Well, I'm damned!

Liane [*Eagerly*]. Do it, Esther! Do it for his sake! They think he's wonderful in America. They'll rave about him! He'll make film history!

Esther. And . . . he'd be a wonderful springboard for you.

Liane. Esther! You're so bitter!

Esther. I'm slowly getting back into the fashion.

Liane. Be kind, Esther. Try to persuade him! Help him! And help me, too. Speak to him!

Esther. If that's what you really want, I'm willing to have a try. But I think you're making a mistake. Anyhow, I'm not at all sure I can persuade him, you realize that?

Liane. Promise?

Esther. I promise.

Liane. Oh, marvelous! I'll run and fetch him. I'll tell him I asked you to come.

Esther. I promise to do my best. That's all I can do.

Liane. You're an angel!

Esther. Haven't I heard that before somewhere?

Liane. Today I really mean it. Wait here.

She runs up the stairs and disappears. ESTHER *looks around the room and sees the empty place where her portrait used to be.*

Liane [*Opens the door and stands aside*]. But I keep telling you it wasn't my agent after all, it was . . . someone else . . . someone totally different. . . .

Florent. You!

Liane. I'll leave you. . . .   [*She goes out. Door closes.*

Florent. You!

Esther. Yes, me. Are you so surprised?

Florent. I don't understand. Liane was expecting some American woman. . . .

Esther. It was me. . . .

Florent. You mean you were . . .

Esther. No, Florent, I "wasn't" . . . I came because Liane rang the hotel. She left a message that I was urgently wanted at Chatou.

Florent. So you came.

Esther. Yes. I thought you were ill. . . .

Florent. Esther!

Esther. I'm relieved to see that you're in the best of health. That's a comfort—it's the main thing.

Florent. But what did Liane mean by her message? Why did she ring you?

Esther. I wonder.

Florent. Didn't she tell you why?

Esther *points to the little door and puts her finger over her lips.*

Florent. Liane isn't the sort to listen at keyholes. She does do worse things, I admit, but not that. What did she say?

Esther. Invented an excuse. . . .

Florent. What?

Esther. She said she wants me to persuade you to take her to Hollywood.

Florent. But that's absurd!

Esther. Yes, quite. But remember, I said it was an excuse.

Florent. What did she really want?

Esther. Oh! . . . She's a very complex little thing, Liane. Very deep. I'm not telling you anything you didn't know, of course. . . .

Florent. No, Esther. I know her well enough.

Esther. Are you happy?

Florent. Please, do you mind not talking about me? I only wish I could see why Liane should bother you to come out here in this snow. . . .

Esther. Oh! Bother me! . . .

Florent. Yes, Esther. Why did she? I was the one who should have made this move, because it is a new move. . . . [*Gesture.*]

Esther. I think I see why. . . .

Florent. You're cleverer than I am.

Esther. I've spent a long time by myself lately, you see. I've had oceans of time to think things over. . . . [*Steadily.*] And I've devoted a lot of that time to thinking about Liane. . . .

Florent. Come and get warm, Esther, you must be frozen. Would you like a hot rum, a grog or something?

Esther. No, nothing, thank you. Listen, Florent. I can guess at things I would never have dreamed of before. . . . I think I can see the reason for that telephone call.

Florent. She was sorry. . . .

Esther. No, Liane's never sorry about anything. I don't think I'd better say any more. I don't want to hurt you.

Florent. Please go on. I promise not to interrupt again. . . .

Esther. Well, Florent, I'm quite sure I see the reason for it: I keep getting in her way.

Florent. What do you mean, you get in her way? You've not given a sign of life since you left here!

Esther. That's just it. My ghost keeps getting in her way. Florent, I know what I mean to you. I know. There are all our old habits . . . and you must often talk about me, quote me, when odd things turn up wonder what decision I'd come to. She's taken my portrait down from the wall, but she hasn't been able to take my ghost away! I haunt this house—every room, all the junk, as she calls it, absolutely reeks of me. She must have felt that all the time I was away from here I was growing in importance, getting younger, more attractive, all the time . . . getting more and more in her way!

Florent. Oh!

Esther. Yes, more in her way than ever! So she tried to lay the ghost, break the spell and open your eyes again . . . so she used the first pretext that came along, to bring you face to face once more with reality, the actual me—this old ruin you see in front of you now.

Florent [*Thinking*]. I suppose it's possible. Poor Liane. But if it's true, her calculations were all wrong. . . .

Esther. Calculations always are.

Florent. Because . . . Esther darling . . . I've never seen you looking so wonderful and so young as you're looking now! You're magnificent!

Esther. Did you think I'd got one foot in the grave already?

Florent. Esther! Of course not! But Charlotte's been a bit upsetting. She kept saying you were looking like a living corpse since you'd left Chatou. She terrified me.

Esther. Charming person, Charlotte. Mind you, when she met me I was going through a bad spell. . . .

Florent. You can't think how glad I am to find you looking so splendid. Charlotte said you just refused to go to a doctor.

Esther. What do you expect, Florent? I have about as much faith in pills and electric shocks and all their other newfangled ideas as you have in machines. There's only one thing that does miracles with your looks, and that's love.

Florent [*Jumps*]. You mean you're in love?

Esther. I'm in love. You're not shocked, are you?

Florent. Me? No, no, no. But . . . I . . . er . . . didn't expect it, that's all. . . . It's no more than I deserve, I suppose.

Esther. You can't have everything, darling.

Florent. No . . . I realize that. Pity. . . . And God knows, I can't blame you! Well . . . mm . . . are you opening again soon?

Esther. I was going to open early this month, but the theater was not ready. Still full of scaffolding. What are your plans?

Florent. Me? Oh . . . Liane has plans, I have none.

She wants to drag me off to America.

Esther. Why don't you go?

Florent. I will not go! That is, I said I wouldn't go. But now, I . . . er . . .

Esther. Why don't you make the girl happy, then, and accept?

Florent. Listen, Esther. I did have a plan of my own . . . but it'll have to go overboard now. But there's no reason why I should keep silent any longer. Esther . . . I'm dreadfully unhappy. . . .

Esther. I thought as much.

Florent. And because I know how kind you are I was screwing up courage to telephone you. I was looking for some pretext to invite you back to Chatou and say: "Esther, I've been a fool. Forgive me. Let's send this little girl off to Hollywood . . . she'll be a thousand times happier there. And let us live on till the end side by side, together."

Esther. Only, there we are. Now you see . . . I'm in love.

Florent. Yes. There we are.

Esther. You haven't even asked me who it is I'm in love with.

Florent. No, Esther. I don't particularly want to know. When you don't know, you can just about put up with it. But it's impossible when you know the names and everything else, all the details.

Esther. You never know—it might be quite the opposite. You sometimes find it hurts just as much just *not* knowing the details. You might find it helps to know the name and a few other things. If you could say: "It first began hurting on the twelfth of August," for instance!

Florent. Esther . . . I suppose he's a young man?

Esther. Yes . . . very young.

Florent. What amazes me, Esther, is that this obvious mistake of mine hasn't been a lesson to you. . . .

Esther. Your mistake?

Florent. Don't let's mince words. Liane was the mistake of my life. I'm astounded to see you fall into what is certain to be as big a mistake. You can see what it has meant for me!

Esther. You've taken plenty of time to come to the conclusion that Liane was a mistake.

Florent. No, you're wrong there. I knew it from the very beginning. But there was something unreal about the happiness I felt with you, Esther—it was somehow unsubstantial, because nothing could cast the slightest shadow on it at all. I had no realization of it, I was just gliding along in it, didn't feel it. This little fool of a girl brought something distinct, with sharper outlines . . . and deeper shadows. Brought everything into relief. Then you kept urging me on, pushing me toward her. . . . It seemed almost as if you wanted this to happen. . . .

Esther. A husband can be as faithful as a dog, Florent—but that doesn't mean he isn't diseased. Faithful dogs often are. Liane's lie, in my dressing room that night, opened my eyes. I saw at once what threatened us, and I also saw that sooner or later it had to come. So I thought I'd better provoke a crisis straightaway—like a violent inoculation—let you get over it quickly, and then have done with it!

Florent. And you wanted to get your own crisis over in the same way, too, I suppose?

Esther. Yes . . . that's what I wanted. . . .

Florent. This . . . young man . . . Does he love you?

Esther. I'm weak enough to think so.

Florent. When I think that we had happiness in our hands all the time and it slipped through our fingers—we let force of habit take control and wipe everything out! We should have watched and studied every minute and kept telling each other how wonderful they were! "What incredible luck!" we ought to have kept saying: "Esther's in love with Florent! And Florent's in love with Esther! There's one miracle. And the public's in love with them both! That's two miracles." That's what we should have kept saying—over and over again! But you see, miracles that last and keep going on soon stop being miracles. Men are stupid enough to begin thinking they're normal. Can't this silly escapade of mine open your eyes? Doesn't its meaning stare you in the face? You must see how impossible your future is?

Esther. Oh, I think it will open my eyes . . . it has done so already.

Florent. And in spite of that you're still going to risk it? It's sure to turn out the same. . . . You'll waste your time and hurt yourself and . . .

Esther. If we took any notice of what other people do, we'd just never do anything ourselves . . .

Florent. All right, Esther, no need to insist! It's an easy victory for you! But your little *affaire* will be just as short-lived as mine, you mark my words! It's a kind of dark tunnel we have to get through somehow or other at our time of life. . . . Only . . . Esther . . . let me wait for you at the other end of the tunnel.

Esther. I think I told you Florent—I'm afraid this isn't just an *affaire*, in the ordinary sense of the word. I think it's going to last a very long time—I think it will last forever.

Florent. It can't! It just doesn't sound like you. . . .

Esther. All the better, Florent. Now you can see me as I really am! Before, I was wrapped up in the mist of habit and you never saw me properly at all. I've changed my habits, you've changed yours, and you can see me now with fresh eyes, probably better than you've seen me for many a long year.

Florent. I'd give all the riches in the world for you never to change again. And for the chance of seeing you as clearly as this forever, Esther . . .

Esther. Well . . . you may. . . .

Florent. Esther! How?! Is there any possible way?

Esther. Oh, yes. A very simple way, really; as simple as a miracle . . . miracles are always simple. . . .

Florent. I'll do anything, anything. . . .

Esther. Close your eyes and ask me who he is. . . .

Florent. Who who is?

Esther. The man I'm in love with. . . . Go on . . . ask. . . .

Florent [*His eyes closed*]. Esther . . . who is the man you're in love with?

Esther [*Low laugh*]. You, of course, stupid. . . .

Florent. Say that again!!!

Esther. I love you! I always did, of course—but I used to love you touched up, like a tinted photograph. Now I know better. I love you real.

Florent. It's not fair! I don't deserve such luck!

Esther. You see—you really believed I was in love with someone else. You were just as stupid as I was that night I swallowed Liane's ridiculous story.

Florent. Esther, I'm going to arrange Liane's trip to Hollywood and see that she has an absolute torrent, a Niagara, of publicity! I'll leave the Comédie Française and we'll do a play together again——

Esther. Oh, no! Anything but that! You stay where you are and I'll stay where I am. When we're both dead we'll find Molière and get him to write us a new play . . . for the two of us! Of course, he'll probably write a better part in for himself, but you'll have to put up with that.

Florent. I'm sure I'm dreaming.

Esther. You have been dreaming. You're just beginning to wake up.

Florent. What about Liane? How shall we tell her? She's capable of being absolutely murderous sometimes when she's——

Esther. I'll look after her. . . .

Florent. You can't, Esther! I know you. . .

Esther. I wouldn't hurt a fly? Well, Liane isn't a fly. And your whole future's at stake. . . .

The door opens at the top of the stairs and LIANE *appears.*

Liane. Well?

Esther. I've succeeded. You're going to Hollywood.

Liane [*Mad with joy*]. No?!

Esther [*Curtly*]. Yes, you're going to Hollywood, Liane, dear. But you're going alone.

Liane. What was that you said? [LIANE *stops at the bottom of the steps.*]

Esther. Florent has agreed to your going to Hollywood, but he's staying here. With me. He's going to marry his wife. He's too old to discover America.

Liane. Florent, is this true?

Florent. Yes, it's true. You see, Liane, we had a misdeal

—the game just couldn't work out. You and I were holding cards that didn't correspond at all. We had to throw in our hands. Our actors' vanities were living together, not our real selves. Don't worry, I'll see you get to Hollywood.

Liane [*To* ESTHER]. And I thought I could trust you.

Esther. I've been learning a lot recently.

Liane. Is that your last word, Florent?

Florent. It's my last word. You go. I stay.

LIANE *runs to the stairway and then turns around on the second or third step. She backs up the stairs as she talks.*

Liane. All right. Nothing could have pleased me more. I wish you joy of each other! Barnstormer and busker get together again! Pretty picture: tenor and prima donna assemble for curtain! It's only logic after all. Well—now I can breathe again. You two can stay here and dodder on till you're no good for anything except charity shows and garden fêtes! You and your kind are out of date! I for one find Europe stifling. I must go somewhere I can have more scope, more air, more light.

Esther. Spotlights?

Liane. Oh, nuts!! [*She disappears and slams the door. Silence.*]

Esther. Well . . . if that's the Hollywood type, I congratulate you on deciding not to go and meet any more.

Florent. Let her go. Don't talk about her. I've got you back. Esther! You! You! [*He presses her to him.*] And that knife she plunged in your heart—that's not there any longer?

Esther. People have been known to live for years with a bullet in their hearts. Yes, darling, the knife's still there, but I find it's getting integrated . . . it's fusing with my body. I can hardly feel it at all. What I do feel is something I rather like. I never used to think about having a heart at all, just took it for granted. Thanks to that knife, I do think about it now. And it's quite wonderful!

Florent. I'll never let you go again!

Esther. Oh! I am an idiot! Lulu's waiting outside in the car with my luggage!

Florent. Ho! What foresight! What generalship!

Esther. Well, you wouldn't have expected me to come

all this way just for Liane. . . . No, I had a very good reason for coming to see you.

Florent. What reason?

Esther. A telegram from Jeannot! [*Takes one from her bag and hands it to him.*] Read it.

Florent [*Reads it, then . . .*]. A grandson!

Esther. We're ripe for playing *Pélleas and Mélisande . . .*

Florent. You . . . a granny! [*Then, less happily:*] And me . . . a grandfather!

She laughs. Just at this moment CHARLOTTE's *voice is heard in the wings.*

Charlotte. Hello, there! Florent! . . . Liane! . . . Liane! . . . Liane! [*Then she enters.*] There you are! This snow blinds me, Liane. I was just passing in the car and I thought I'd . . . [*She recognizes* ESTHER *and stops short.*] Esther!

Esther. Yes, it's me, Charlotte. I'm going to marry my husband.

Charlotte. Well! It's about time! And . . . er . . . what about . . . her?

Esther. She's packing her bags. . . . She's off to Hollywood.

Charlotte. Oh! How appropriate! Long live the New World!

Florent. Sit down, have a drink!

Charlotte. No! No! This is a heaven-sent opportunity! You're not going to dodge it this time, Esther. . . .

Esther [*Doesn't understand*]. Dodge what? . . .

Charlotte. Mummy! She's in the car outside. I'll go and fetch her! I'll make you meet her this time!

Florent. But it's snowing! I'll come with you.

Charlotte. You mustn't . . . it might give Esther time to think! It's now or never! I'll fetch her!

Esther [*Shouts to her as she goes*]. All right! Bring her in! I'd love to meet her. . . .

[CHARLOTTE *runs out through the garden door.*

Florent. Oh, what a bore!

Esther. Not at all. Quite the contrary! You'll see. [*He starts to speak but she puts her hand over his mouth.*]

Don't. I want you to. It'll be an experience for you. . . .

Florent. An experience? . . .

Esther. Yes. Then straight afterwards I'm taking you away. We're off to Marseilles. . . .

Enter, floundering and flustered because of the snow, CHARLOTTE *and a very old lady dressed in black.*

Charlotte [*Radiant with joy*]. Mummy, may I introduce Esther and Florent, the two greatest artists of the living theater!

The OLD LADY *is down front right, with her back to the audience.*

Esther [*As* FLORENT *bows politely and seriously, she speaks to* OLD LADY]. I'm delighted to meet you! You shall be the first to hear some wonderful news I've just had! [*She waves the telegram.*]

Old Lady. Oh, no, no! Quite warm, thank you!

Esther. Oh, Lord, of course! I forgot! [*she suddenly roars out the words.*] I'm a grandmother!

The OLD LADY *is astonished, shrugs her shoulders vigorously and shakes her head . . . as though she were saying:* "No, no, no!"

Florent [*To* ESTHER]. You see . . . she won't believe it. [*Turns to* OLD LADY.] I was only saying to her a moment ago——

But he is interrupted by ESTHER's *roar of laughter. She obviously loses control as she watches the* OLD LADY's *shrugs, and her laughter infects* CHARLOTTE. CHARLOTTE's *laughter spreads to the* OLD LADY, *who laughs like a madwoman, shrugging her shoulders all the time.* FLORENT *doesn't understand, of course, but begins to laugh in spite of himself.* LULU *comes in from the garden with all the suitcases. The sight of her makes them roar. She puts the cases down and begins laughing too. The hysterical laughter of* ESTHER *and* FLORENT *is above the rest . . . it is a sort of release, a theatrical farce after five months of the strain of tragedy.*

THE EAGLE WITH TWO HEADS

(*L'Aigle à deux têtes*)

English version by Carl Wildman

CHARACTERS

THE QUEEN, *aged thirty-one*
EDITH VON BERG, *aged twenty-three*
STANISLAS, *or* AZRAEL, *aged twenty-five*
FELIX VON WILLENSTEIN, *aged thirty-six*
COUNT VON FOEHN, *aged forty-five*
TONY, *a Negro deaf-mute, in* THE QUEEN's *service*

ACT ONE: THE QUEEN's bedroom in Krantz Castle

ACT TWO: THE QUEEN's library in Krantz Castle

ACT THREE: The same

The tragedy of Krantz will always remain an enigma. How did the assassin manage to enter THE QUEEN's *rooms? Under cover of what threat did he manage to spend three days with* THE QUEEN?

THE QUEEN *was found stabbed in the back, at the top of the library staircase, by the open window. She was wearing a riding habit and had just taken the salute from her soldiers. She had appeared for the first time unveiled.*

The assassin was lying at the bottom of the stairs, struck dead by poison.

This tragedy has inspired several accounts—historical, scientific, poetic, passionate, sectarian—and all of these could be true.

THE EAGLE WITH TWO HEADS

ACT ONE

SCENE: *one of* THE QUEEN's *bedrooms in Krantz Castle.*
Not only does THE QUEEN *rarely stay long in residence in*
one castle but she changes her bedroom every night—she
never sleeps in the same room. Perhaps, having abandoned
her first room and used several others, she might return to
the first. I mean to say that she never sleeps in the same
room on two nights running.

This particular bedroom is spacious, and in the middle
of it stands a canopied bed. In the section of a wall that
stands obliquely across the right-hand side of the stage is
a high window opening onto a park and on a level with
the treetops. On the opposite wall (set obliquely on the
left) hangs a huge portrait of the King; there is also a fire-
place which flickers with light and shadow. It is dark. A
night of thunder and silent lightning. Chandeliers. THE
QUEEN *likes only candlelight. In the foreground, not far*
from the fireplace, is a small table over which a cloth is
spread, and this is the only splash of white in this scene of
moving shadows, dim light, gleams from the fire, and light-
ning flashes. On the table a light repast has been prepared.
There is wine in an ice bucket, goat cheese, honey, fruit,
and some of those country-made cakes shaped like the
entwined letters of a monogram. A silver chandelier orna-
ments the table and concentrates the light on the cloth, on
the two places set opposite each other, and on the two
empty chairs.

A secret little door, hidden by the King's portrait, on the
left of the bed, opens onto the corridor which THE QUEEN
uses to reach this bedroom. In the right foreground is a
double door. When the curtain rises, EDITH VON BERG,
Reader to THE QUEEN, *is holding a chandelier ready for*
the table, while the Duke, FELIX VON WILLENSTEIN, *is*
about to put a log on the fire. EDITH *is wearing evening*

dress. She stops, standing with the chandelier in her hand.
FELIX *is in court uniform.*

EDITH. Felix, you're clumsy!

Felix [Turning around a little but keeping the log in his hand]. Thank you!

Edith. Don't you even know how to set a log on the fire?

Felix. I was wondering whether to put it on or not. I don't see the point of having a fire. There's thunder about and it's so sultry.

Edith. Nobody asked your opinion. Keep it to yourself, and put on a log. The Queen likes to see a fire. She likes a fire and an open window.

Felix. Well, I'd prefer to have the window closed and not light the fire. If you have the window open, the fire attracts the insects and the bats.

Edith. The Queen loves the insects and the bats. Felix, do you love the Queen?

Felix [Dropping the log and straightening himself]. I beg your pardon!

Edith. Whatever's the matter? I merely asked if you love the Queen and obeying her, or if you prefer your own ideas and hope to win her over to them.

Felix. Can you never open your mouth without saying something unpleasant?

Edith. You always ask for it, my dear Felix.

Felix. What can I do to make you like me?

Edith. Nothing.

Felix. There must be something. Tell me. I'd be curious to know what it is.

Edith. Your job!

Felix. So that's how it is! Have I done something wrong?

Edith. You do nothing else. You're an arrant blunderer. Where are your brains? You always look as if the court etiquette and ceremonial were new to you.

Felix. Her Majesty does not care for etiquette or ceremonial.

Edith. That is precisely why her mother-in-law, the Archduchess, insists on my always maintaining them.

Felix. You serve the Queen on behalf of the Archduchess. I serve her on behalf of the King.

Edith. The King is dead, my poor Felix, and the Archduchess is living. Remember that. [*Pause. Then,* EDITH *signs to* FELIX *with a movement of her head:*] The chairs.

Felix [*Uncomprehending*]. The chairs? . . . [EDITH *shrugs her shoulders.*] Oh, of course! . . . [*He moves each one away from the table.*]

Edith. The candles. . . .

Felix. Which?

Edith. Is it my place to remind you that, if the Queen sups in her bedroom, only a Duke may touch the Queen's table? You have deigned to put one chandelier in the correct place. Where is the other?

Felix [*His eyes searching the room*]. How stupid of me!

Edith. You said it yourself, Felix!

Felix [*Rushing toward her*]. Good Lord! [*He relieves her of the chandelier she has been holding and places it on the table.*] I was thinking how beautiful you were with those candles, Edith, and gazing at you, I forgot that I should take them from your hands.

Edith [*More and more sarcastic*]. You thought me very beautiful with those candles, did you?

Felix. Very beautiful. [*A pause. Distant rolling of thunder.*] I don't like storms.

Edith. The Queen will be glad. She adores storms and laughs at me because I hate them as much as you do. Do you remember the storm here a year ago, the night before we left for Oberwald? The Queen would not come away from the window. After each flash of lightning, I begged her to come back into her room, but she continued to laugh and shout: "Another one, Edith, another!" I had the greatest difficulty in preventing her from rushing out into the pouring rain in the park where the storm was uprooting the trees. This morning she said to me: "What luck, Edith! A storm is brewing for my first night at Krantz!"

Felix. She likes nothing but violence.

Edith. You could do with some yourself, Your Grace.

Felix. She does not care for *your* violence, Edith.

Edith. She says so, but if I were soft and docile, she would not tolerate me for a minute.

Felix. Which is as much as to say you find me docile and soft, and that she cares little for my presence.

Edith. Oh, my dear Felix, for Her Majesty you are a piece of furniture, an object. You had best resign yourself to that role.

Felix. I was a friend of the King's.

Edith. That is probably the sole reason why she bears with you.

Felix. During the journey here, in the coach, she spoke to me four times.

Edith. Mere politeness on her part. She wears it like her fur gloves—for the journey. She spoke to you of mountains, snow, and horses, limiting her conversation to what you have in common. Don't imagine there is any reason to get foolishly excited!

Felix [*After a pause and a roll of thunder*]. But . . . Heaven forgive me, Edith . . . are you jealous?

Edith [*With a laugh like a madwoman's*]. Jealous? Me? Of whom, of what? Well, would you believe that! Jealous! I demand an immediate explanation of that insult. Did I understand aright? . . . I hesitate to think so, I really do.

Felix. Calm yourself, Edith. In the first place, it's you who are always insulting me, not me you. Furthermore, if you want to know the truth, it seemed to me that my irritation at the sight of that empty chair [*he points to one of the chairs*] annoyed you to such an extent that you lost your self-control.

Edith. You really amaze me! So, I was not mistaken. Doesn't the Duke von Willenstein realize what this day is? Exactly ten years ago, your master was assassinated on the morning of his wedding day. You were a witness to that murder. Where were the King, the Queen, and their escort bound for? This very place where we are now! Your memory is not good, nor is your knowledge of the Queen. It is with the King's ghost that Her Majesty sups on this wild night in the room which was to have been their wedding chamber. And that is the mysterious guest of whom you dare to be jealous. And that is the kind of man you are. One who dares moreover to be fond of the Queen, to love her, and to be jealous of the King's ghost.

Felix. You're crazy!

Edith. That's a nice thing, coming from you! I am not crazy. I was once. I was foolish enough to be crazy about you.

Felix [*Trying to calm her*]. Edith! . . .

Edith. Let me be! The Queen is dressing and can't hear us. I will have my say out.

Felix. The Archduchess opposed our marriage.

Edith. The Archduchess has an eagle eye. She saw through you before she did me. And if you wish to know the reasons for my changed feelings toward you, well, it was she who opened my eyes. "That young fool doesn't love you. Watch him closely," she said. "He is only looking for ways of approaching the Queen." It was a bitter blow. At first, I put it down to the Archduchess' being afraid of one of her ladies-in-waiting coming under the influence of one of the King's friends, one of those companions whom she holds responsible for his marriage with a princess whom she never liked. I tried to be blind and deaf. But I saw and I heard.

Felix. What did you see and hear?

Edith. I saw you gazing at the Queen. I saw you blushing like a schoolgirl when she spoke to you. And before me, you didn't even have the courage to continue your lies. In less than a week, you gave up all pretense, you treated me as a rival, as a person whose clear-sightedness was becoming a hindrance to you. Deny it, if you dare.

Felix. What need had I of your good offices to approach the Queen, since, unless I am mistaken, I can approach her as freely as you?

Edith. As freely as I! I am her Reader and her only confidante. Don't confuse my post with that of one of her household servants.

Felix. But that is what we are.

Edith. The Queen does not love you, Felix. You had

best admit that fact. She does not love you and I don't love you any more.

Felix. One piece of frankness for another. I must confess I don't like your spying and being in the pay of the Archduchess.

Edith. How dare you! . . .

Felix. As things stand between us, it's better to say everything. I loved you, Edith, and perhaps I love you still. You maintain I don't love you any more because I love the Queen. Maybe. But why should this affect the Queen, or you? I worship her as a divinity. She is beyond our reach. I dreamed of our loving her together. That is impossible, because you are a woman and the Queen is not a woman. Since you refuse to understand me and since the Archduchess refuses to let you share my life, I shall share it with no one—I shall content myself with serving at your side, and my happiness will be watching and waiting for a smile from the Queen.

Edith. You forget that, since the King's death, I am the only person to whom she shows her face.

Felix. A veil and a fan cannot hinder the effect of her beauty, nor diminish its impact on my heart.

Edith. One day, when I asked you if you thought it were possible to love me in the lustrous orbit of the Queen—yes, I foresaw your folly!—did you not explain that you could not love a woman who hides her face, a phantom?

Felix [*Going close to* Edith *and speaking in a very low voice*]. I have seen her face, Edith. [*Thunder.*]

Edith. What?

Felix. I have seen it.

Edith. Where? . . . How? . . .

Felix. It was at Wolmar. I was crossing the Achilles gallery when I heard a door slam. And no one else but she dares slam doors like that. I hid behind the pedestal of the Achilles statue. Achilles' ankles and legs formed a great lyre-shaped opening, and through this lyre I could see the whole length of the gallery in perspective and the Queen at the far end growing bigger as she came toward me. She was coming toward me, Edith, perfectly alone.

I was like a hunter aiming at game which believes itself
unseen and does not think men can exist. She was
coming nearer without either fan or veil. A long, long,
black dress, and her head so high, her face so pale, so
small, so unattached that it looked like one of those heads
of aristocrats which the crowds in the French Revolution
bore aloft at the end of a pike. The Queen appeared to
be suffering intensely. Her hands were pressed hard against
her bosom. They seemed to be forcing to the open lips of a
wound calling for help. She stumbled. She drew near.
She looked at my hiding place. For one unbearable moment she stopped. Had she wished to keep some rendezvous
with a memory of Frederick and courage suddenly failed
her? She, who had never lacked courage before, leaned
against one of the great mirrors, staggered, straightened
up, hesitated, and then I saw her from the back, with
that somnambulist gait, returning to the door from which
she had come. Truly, Edith, I saw that which should not
be seen. Through that marble lyre, I saw that which cannot be seen without dying of love and shame. My criminal heart beat so loudly I was afraid. Would she hear it,
turn back, discover me and fall dead, uttering a cry? No.
I gazed intently and she went away from the pedestal.
Imagine a hunchback jockey and the injured thoroughbred
which he brings limping from the race. Imagine the figure
of a poor woman carried away by the current along this
golden-mirrored canal. The door slamming. That was the
end. I have seen the Queen's face, Edith. I have seen
the Queen. And neither you nor anyone else has ever
seen her.

Long pause. Faint thunder.

Edith [*Hissing*]. A hunchback jockey, a limping horse!
The Queen's deportment is well known all over the world!

Felix. She was suffering greatly, Edith. I shall never
forget that sight. She looked like one of those Spanish
virgins bristling with daggers. Her face had such beauty
—it was frightening.

Edith. Well, it does seem more serious than I imagined.

Felix. Confessing to a crime would not have been harder for me.

Edith. At least, we share one secret now.

Felix. If the Queen heard of it, I should kill myself.

Edith. She would kill you. She's quite capable of it. She is a first-class shot.

The prolonged ringing of a bell is heard.

Felix. The Queen is coming!

Edith. Leave before she rings the last time. I must be alone when Her Majesty announces her coming. Go quickly.

Felix [*In a whisper, as he is about to leave*]. I've seen the Queen, Edith. She is dead.

Edith [*Stamping*]. Will you go?

She opens the door on the right and shuts it as soon as FELIX *has gone.* EDITH *goes to the window. A louder roll of thunder is heard and a flash of lightning lights up the tops of the trees in the park. The rain begins to fall among the leaves.* EDITH *steps back fearfully. The bell rings a last time. She goes to the table, checks the way it is laid, the chairs, the fire. The portrait pivots around. The* QUEEN *appears. She is hiding her face behind a black lace fan. She is wearing full court evening dress, her decorations, gloves, jewelry. She slams the door behind her. A flash of lightning accompanies her entry and the candles flicker in a gust of wind.* EDITH *curtsies.*

The Queen. Are you alone?

Edith. Yes, Your Majesty. The Duke von Willenstein left when you rang first.

The Queen. Good. [*She snaps her fan shut and throws it onto the bed.*] What a wretched fire! [*She leans in the direction of the fireplace.*] That looks like Felix's handiwork. He must have been gazing at you and put the logs on any which way. I am the only person who knows how to build fires. [*She pushes a log into place with her foot.*]

Edith. Your Majesty!

The Queen. How tiresome you are, young woman. I am going to burn my shoe and catch my dress on fire. That's what you're going to say. I always know what you're going to say. [*The storm becomes worse.*] A magnificent storm!

Edith. Does Her Majesty wish me to close the shutters?

The Queen. That is something else I was expecting to hear. [*She goes up to the window.*] The shutters! Close the windows, draw the curtains, shut yourself in, hide behind the wardrobe. Deprive yourself of this splendid spectacle. The trees are wrestling with sleep and panting with fear. They fear the storm as cattle do. It is my own special weather, Edith—weather fit for no one. My hair is sparkling with electricity. My lightning and that of the clouds are at one. I breathe at last. I should like to be on horseback and gallop over the mountainside. And my horse would be frightened and I should mock him.

Edith. May the lightning spare Your Majesty!

The Queen. Oh, lightning has its whims, and I have mine. Let it come in, Edith, let it in my bedroom! I'll chase it out with my horsewhip.

Edith. Lightning destroys great trees.

The Queen. But it would not be interested in my genealogical tree. That is too old. And it knows well enough how to destroy itself. It needs no one's help to do that. Ever since this morning, those trees out there have felt the storm in all their old twisted branches and told me of its wonders. The King had Krantz built before he knew me. He also loved storms and that is why he chose this meeting place of mountains where the heavens relentlessly war and fire their cannon. [*Very loud thunderclaps.* EDITH *crosses herself.*] Are you afraid?

Edith. I am not in the least ashamed of letting Her Majesty see I'm afraid.

The Queen. Afraid of what? Of dying?

Edith. Just afraid. I can't explain it.

The Queen. It's strange. I have never been afraid of anything but quiet. [*The* QUEEN *returns to the table.*] Everything is ready?

Edith. Yes, Your Majesty. I kept an eye on His Grace.

The Queen. Call him Felix. How irritating you can be when you call him "His Grace."

Edith. According to the book of etiquette——

The Queen. The book of etiquette! Do you know why

I love a storm so much? Because it scatters the leaves. Because its disregard for order unsettles ancient rites of the trees and animals. The Archduchess, my mother-in-law, is etiquette personified. I am the storm. I can understand why she fears me, opposes me, and keeps her eye on me from a distance. You will probably write to tell her I am supping tonight with the King.

Edith. Oh, Your Majesty. . . .

The Queen. Tell her. She will just exclaim: "Poor thing. She's mad!" And yet I am creating a new ceremonial practice. She ought to be pleased. You can retire, Edith. Put your head under the bedclothes, say your prayers, and try to sleep. You must be tired out after the journey. If I need the least little thing, I'll ring for Tony. He is also scared of storms. He'll not be going to bed yet awhile.

Edith. The Archduchess would punish me if she heard the Queen was left on her own.

The Queen. Edith, are you under the Archduchess' orders, or mine? I command you to leave me alone and to get some sleep.

Edith [*After a prolonged curtsy*]. I'm sorry, but I fear that, on the last point, I shall not be able to obey the Queen. I shall stay awake. I shall be ready to serve her, should my presence be required.

The Queen. It is clearly understood, isn't it? According to court etiquette, you are permitted to enter my room at any hour of the day or night. But by *my* etiquette, by mine, not a soul is allowed to come into my room this night, even if the castle is struck by lightning. That is our royal pleasure. [*She laughs.*] Our royal pleasure! The last refuge of sovereigns. Their last hope. Their free will, as it were. Good night, Fräulein von Berg. [*She laughs.*] I was joking. Good night, my dear Edith. My women will undress me. Go and lie down, hide your head under a table, or play chess. [*She waves her hand.*]

[EDITH *makes three bobs, retires and leaves by the door on the right.*

As soon as she is alone, THE QUEEN *stands still by the door. She listens. Then she breathes the smell of the park in the storm and of the rain in front of the window. Lightning*

*and thunder greet her. She goes to the table, examines the
candles, and sees that everything has been done according
to her instructions. She pokes the fire. She stops in front of
the King's portrait. In it, the King, aged twenty, is dressed
like a mountaineer.* THE QUEEN *stretches her hand toward the portrait.*

The Queen. Frederick! . . . Come, darling. [*She pretends to lead the King by the hand to the table. The
whole scene is mimed by the actress as if the King were
in the room.*] We well deserve having this moment together. Alone, with the storm raging around us to protect
us from the rest of the world. All is set: thunder in the
sky, flames in the hearth, and a country meal like the ones
we used to have after those wonderful times stalking the
chamois.

Drink, my angel! [*She takes the bottle from the ice
bucket and fills the glasses.*] Let us toast each other. [*She
clinks her glass against the King's.*] It's real mountaineer's wine. What a change for us after that awful ceremony.
Frederick, you were pulling such a face. . . . What? . . .
It was the crown. It was not made for you, my love, and
the Archbishop had great difficulty in preventing it from
wobbling on your head. You nearly burst out laughing.
And then there was the Archduchess telling me every five
minutes to stand straight, to remember my bearing. I did.
I passed, as in a dream, straight through the crowd, the
acclamations, the fireworks, and the bombardment of
flowers. Nothing was spared us in that interminable apoth-
eosis.

In the evening, we took a post chaise . . . and here we
are. We are no longer the King and the Queen. We are
a husband and a wife, madly in love with each other, and
supping together. It is hard to believe. In that chaise, I
said to myself: It will never be! We shall never be alone.
[*The storm becomes more violent.*] And now, Frederick,
since you drink and eat and laugh, and since the Archduchess is not here to forbid it, I am going to take my
cards and tell your fortune. During our hunting expedi-
tions, we secretly got gypsies to do this for us. Don't you
remember, dear? . . . And I learned to be a fortuneteller

from them. . . . And you used to lead me up into the palace attic, so that I could tell your fortune without being discovered. [*She rises and takes a pack of cards from a corner of the mantelpiece. She shuffles them.*] Cut! [*She places the cards on the table and acts as if the King were cutting. Then she sits and arranges the cards fanwise.*] Let us see what the cards have to say. [*Despite the storm, a distant gunshot is heard, then another, and a third. THE QUEEN raises her head and listens, motionless.*] The crowd will send those fireworks after us right to Krantz. Shooting, Frederick. Is there anything new? [*She finishes arranging her semicircle of cards.*] I doubt it. However much we shuffle and cut and fan them out, the cards invariably tell us the same thing. I use a black fan to hide my face. Destiny uses a black and red one to show hers. But hers never changes. Look, Frederick. You, me, traitors, money, trouble, death. Whether we tell our fortune in the mountains, in the attic, or in Krantz, the cards never reveal anything we don't already know. [*She counts with her index finger.*] One, two, three, four, five—the Queen. One, two, three, four, five—the King. One, two, three, four, five . . . [*More shooting in the distance.*] Frederick, listen. . . . [*She starts again.*] One, two, three, four, five. A bad woman . . . you know her. . . . One, two, three, four, five . . . a dark young woman: Edith von Berg. . . . One, two, three, four, five—money troubles. [*She laughs.*] Still your ruinous theater and my ill-fated castles. One, two, three, four, five: a bad man. Greetings, Count von Foehn. You're there at roll call, of course. One, two, three, four, five: death. One, two, three, four, five: death. One, two, three, four, five . . . [*Shooting nearer at hand. THE QUEEN, keeping one finger raised, looks at the window. She starts once more.*] One, two, three, four, five: death. One, two, three, four, five. And here is the fair young man who intrigues us so much. Who can it be, Frederick? I wonder. . . . One, two, three, four, five . . .

Brighter lightning and louder thunder than previously. A vivid flash. Suddenly, someone is seen to be clinging

*to the other side of the balcony and to climb over it and
drop down inside. He gets up in the opening of the window and steps down into the room. He is a young man,
closely resembling the portrait of the King. He is wearing
mountaineer's dress. He is haggard, disheveled, soaked
with rain. His right knee is smeared with blood.*

The Queen [*Uttering a fearful cry*]. Frederick! [*She
leaps up behind the table. The young man stands motionless in the room.*] Frederick! . . .

*She pushes the table away, sweeping aside the cards. Just
as she is about to rush toward this apparition, the young
man falls in a heap on the floor. Without a moment's
hesitation, she rushes to the young man who has fainted,
snatches a napkin on the way, dips it in the ice bucket,
kneels by the young man and strikes his face with the wet
napkin. She raises him up. He opens his eyes and looks
about him.*

In the following scene, THE QUEEN *acts with decision, and
with a certain muscular strength which she seems to possess despite her frail appearance.*

The Queen. Quick! Make an effort. Stand up. [*She
tries to raise him.*] Do you hear me? Stand up. Stand up
at once. [*The young man manages with difficulty to raise
himself on his knees. At that moment, the bell rings.*]
I'll lift you up. [THE QUEEN *puts her arms under his and
helps him. The young man stands swaying like a drunken
man. She shakes him by the hair. He then takes a step
forward.* THE QUEEN *speaks to him in a low voice as she
drags him toward the canopied bed.*] Understand this.
You only have a second to hide in. Someone is coming.
[*The bell rings a second time.*] Come on! [*She pushes
him behind the canopy.*] And stay there! [*Someone knocks
on the door on the right.*] If you stir, if you collapse, you
are a dead man. You have left blood everywhere. [*She
snatches a fur rug from the bed and throws it over the
carpet. Aloud:*] Who is there? Is it you, Edith?

Edith's voice [*From behind the door*]. Your Majesty!

The Queen. Come in. [EDITH *enters and shuts the door*

*behind her. She is pale, upset. She can scarcely get the
words out.*] What is it? I give you orders and you disregard them. Explain. Are you ill?

Edith. It was so serious. I thought I might venture to

The Queen. What is so serious? Have you seen a ghost?
What is wrong? It is certainly serious to disobey me.

Edith. Did Your Majesty hear the shooting? . . .

The Queen. When you left me you were dying with
fear because of a storm, and here you are almost fainting
with fright because of some firing. That is excessive! So,
Fräulein von Berg, the storm upsets your nerves, you
hear some shooting going on in the park—who it was or
at what it was I do not know—and you take it upon yourself to come and disturb me in my room.

Edith. Will Your Majesty permit me to explain?

The Queen. Explain, Fräulein. If you can.

Edith. The police——

The Queen. The police? What police?

Edith. Your Majesty's police. It was they who were
shooting. The men are below.

The Queen. I don't understand your explanations in
the least. Try and be more explicit. Von Foehn is below,
is he?

Edith. No, Your Majesty. Count von Foehn is not with
this detachment, but their officer is recommended to Your
Majesty by the Count.

The Queen. What does he want?

Edith. A regular manhunt had been organized in the
mountains after a malefactor. He had entered Krantz
Castle park. Has Your Majesty noticed anything suspicious?

The Queen. Go on. . . .

Edith. The police officer begs Your Majesty's permission
to search the park and the castle offices.

The Queen. They may search and shoot as much as
they like, provided they don't come and bother me any
more with such nonesnse.

Edith. Oh, Your Majesty, it's not nonsense. . . .

The Queen. And what may it be, then?

Edith. Will Your Majesty allow me to explain it all?

The Queen. That is what I have been asking you to do for the last hour.

Edith. I didn't dare.

The Queen. You didn't dare! Why? Does it concern me?

Edith. Yes, Your Majesty.

The Queen. Really? And who is this strange individual for whom the police organize man hunts?

Edith. A murderer.

The Queen. He's killed someone?

Edith. No, Your Majesty, he wanted to. . . .

The Queen. Whom?

Edith. You. [*Correcting herself.*] I mean . . . the Queen.

The Queen. Better and better. The police are well-informed and assassins have second sight. Edith, are you not forgetting that I move from castle to castle without telling anyone beforehand? I decided yesterday at Wolmar to spend tonight at Krantz. I made the whole journey without a break. Is it not strange that assassins and the police should be informed of my most secret moves? Even if I wished to give an alarm, the swiftest courier would not reach my police before tomorrow.

Edith. This is what the officer explained to me. A dangerous society is plotting against Your Majesty. A young man has been chosen to carry out their orders. As this young man did not know where to find the Queen, he first went to the cottage of his mother, a peasant woman living in Krantz. Count von Foehn—if Your Majesty will forgive my saying so—knew of, or foresaw, Your Majesty's anniversary trip to Krantz, and he thought the criminal was making for Krantz to try to find Your Majesty and make his attack. A police detachment trailed him. But, just as they began to surround the cottage, the criminal managed to slip away. He is at large. They are looking for him. He is on the prowl and lurking in the park. Your Majesty may now understand my anxiety and that there was good reason for my incurring her displeasure and disobeying her. [*She bursts into tears*].

The Queen. Oh, please, no tears! Am I crying? Am I

dead? No. And Count von Foehn's men are guarding my
castle. They are mounting guard under my windows. [THE
QUEEN *walks about the room with her hands clasped behind her back.*] More and more peculiar. . . . A criminal
attempt is being made on the Queen's life and Count von
Foehn does not bother to come himself. He sends a detachment! And . . . may I know if the officer in charge
has any knowledge as to the criminal's identity?

Edith. Your Majesty knows him.

The Queen. Could it be Count von Foehn himself?

Edith [*Very shocked*]. Your Majesty is joking. The
criminal is the author of a poem which was secretly published, and which the Queen showed the great weakness of
liking and learning by heart.

The Queen. Do you mean "The End of Royalty"?

Edith. I'd rather I did not have to pronounce that title,
Your Majesty.

The Queen. You are really incredible. . . . Well, my
dear Edith. . . . You have found me safe and sound, the
storm is passing, the police are watching, and you can at
last go and sleep. You look like death. Let the police be
served with drinks and their officer act as he may think fit.
Don't disturb me again. I might take it amiss next time.

Edith [*About to leave*]. Your Majesty. . . . Would
Her Majesty . . . permit me at least to close the window?
Anyone could climb the ivy. It has grown into ropes. I
shouldn't sleep if I felt Her Majesty was right over here
and had that great window open onto the unknown. I beg
this favor of her.

The Queen. Close the window, Edith. Close it. It does
not matter now, in the least.

EDITH *fastens the shutters, closes the window, draws the
curtains. She makes her three bows and leaves* THE QUEEN's
bedroom, slowly closing the door. THE QUEEN *listens to*
EDITH VON BERG *departing and closing the doors on the
way to her room.* THE QUEEN *advances four paces into
her bedroom.*]

The Queen [*Addressing the bed*]. Come out! [STANISLAS
comes out from behind the canopy. He stays motionless

at the corner of the head of the bed.] You have nothing
to fear. [STANISLAS' *knee is still bleeding. He does not
raise his eyes toward* THE QUEEN, *who paces up and down.*]
Well, my dear sir, did you hear all that was said? I suppose
there is not much we don't know about each other. [*She
picks up her fan from the bed, but does not open it. She
will use it as a stick to strike the furniture and to mark
the rhythm of her words.*] What is your name? [*Silence.*]
You refuse to tell me your name—all right, I'll tell you.
A sovereign's memory is amazing. You are called Stanislas.
Your surname I don't know and I don't wish to know.
You published, under the title "The End of Royalty" . . .
and under the pseudonym of Azrael—a good name!—
the angel of death . . . a short poem which was meant
to be an attack against me. It achieved some notoriety.
This clandestine publication passed from hand to hand.
I admire this poem. And I admit that I know it by heart.
Tediously long poems have been published against us.
They have all been of a very mediocre quality. Yours was
short and it was good. I noticed also, and I congratulate
you on this point, that your poem scandalized more because of its form than because of its matter. People thought
it obscure, and, in fact, absurd. It was neither in verse nor
in prose, and—I am just quoting—it was like nothing at
all. For this very reason I liked it. To be like nothing—
like no one. No praise could move me more. To me, there
is no such person as Stanislas. You are Azrael, the angel
of death, and for me you have no other name. [*Silence.*]
Come here. [STANISLAS *does not move.* THE QUEEN
stamps.] Come here! [STANISLAS *takes one step forward.*]
This is the King's portrait. [*She points to it with her fan.
STANISLAS *raises his eyes, sees the portrait and immediately
lowers his eyes.*] That portrait was painted during our engagement. The King is in your attire. He was twenty. How
old are you? [*Silence.*] You must have been about ten at
that time. And I suppose you were one of those scapegraces
who threw firecrackers and ran after our coach.

You are, of course, aware of this extraordinary likeness
between you? I expect there is some connection between
that likeness and your appearance here. Don't pretend!

Probably, your accomplices considered—very astutely—
that this resemblance would throw me off my guard, would
paralyze me, and help you to carry out your deed. But,
my dear sir, things never happen as one imagines. Am I
wrong? [STANISLAS *keeps silent*.] This is the third time
the Queen addresses you. [*Silence*.] As you wish. There
is no precise etiquette to cover our present situation. We
will therefore do without it and make up the rules as we
go along. [*Pause*.]

Did you know I was staying in Krantz Castle? [*Silence*.]
I see. Your lips are sealed. It's not for lack of talking in
your society groups though, is it? How you must have
talked! What things you must have said, and heard others
say! Well, my dear sir, it so happens that I have been
silent for ten years. For ten years, I have forced myself to
keep silence and to show my face to no one save my
Reader. I hide it under a veil or behind a fan. Tonight,
I am showing my face and I am talking. Whether on
account of the storm or of a presentiment, I do not know,
but at nine o'clock this evening, I began talking to my
Reader. I admit I only told her things I want her to
repeat. I talked to my Reader, then I talked to myself.
And I am not stopping. I talk. I talk. I talk to you. I feel
quite capable of asking the questions and giving the an-
swers. And to think I was complaining that nothing new
ever happened! There is something new in Krantz. I am
free. I can speak and show my face. It is marvelous. [THE
QUEEN *goes toward the armchair by the table*.]

Tell me about your adventure. . . . [*She is going to
sit. She suddenly changes her mind, dips a napkin in the
ice bucket and goes toward* STANISLAS.] Here . . . bandage your knee. The blood is running down your legging.
[STANISLAS *moves back*.] So, I'll have to bandage your knee
myself. Hold your leg straight. [STANISLAS *moves farther
away*.] But you're impossible! Either dress your wound,
or let someone do it for you. [*She throws the napkin to
him*.] I can easily support silence, but I don't like the
sight of blood. [STANISLAS *has taken the napkin, and band-
ages his leg with it.* THE QUEEN *returns and sits in her
chair*.]

Well, tell me your adventure. [*Silence.*] I must have been dreaming. I was forgetting I have to tell *you*. [*She settles down and fans herself.*] You are given the order to kill me. You are given arms. You are told your first duty is to discover in which castle I am staying, for I am constantly changing my place of residence. Perhaps Wolmar is suggested . . . perhaps Krantz. But, even supposing a clever member of your organization had guessed—though I very much doubt it—that I would be staying in Krantz tonight, that person could not have told you which room I would sleep in. I have four here. You climbed straight into the right one. [*She waves the last fortune-telling card.*] I can do no other than salute you as fate! [STANISLAS *has finished tying his bandage. He stands up and stays motionless in the same place.*]

You leave my town. You are sure of the conclusion of your venture. It will lead to my death and to yours. Before setting out, you want to kiss your mother. She is a peasant woman living in Krantz. The police follow you. They surround the cottage. You know every nook and cranny of that place. You hide and you escape. The storm assists you. Then there begins the stalking, the pursuit, the rocks, the brambles, and the dogs, coming under fire from the sky and from men. That exhausting chase of the hunted beast brings you to this very castle. [*Pause.*]

In this room—just imagine—I was celebrating an anniversary. The anniversary of the dead King. I was dining with the King, with the ghost of the King. This empty chair was his. This honey and this goat cheese were the kind of fare he liked. Down below, in the dark, your wound was bleeding. You were almost fainting with exhaustion. A gun was fired. The dogs barked. You had to exert yourself once more. An open window! You grasp hold of the ivy, climb up, scale the wall, appear before me. I confess, I did think I was seeing the King's ghost. I did think your blood was his. I uttered his name. You sank to the ground. But that is not how ghosts melt away. They can only do that at cockcrow. [THE QUEEN *closes her fan and taps it sharply. She rises.*] Warm yourself. Come closer to the fire. Your clothes must be wringing wet [*As if hypnotized,*

STANISLAS *crosses the room and crouches by the fire.* THE QUEEN *goes around the table and places herself behind the King's chair.*]

The King—you know this—was assassinated in a post chaise. We were going to Krantz after the wedding ceremony. A man leapt onto the footboard with a bouquet in his hand. I thought he was pressing the flowers warmly to Frederick's breast, and I laughed. The flowers concealed a knife. The King was dead before I realized what had happened. But here is a detail you would not know. The King was dressed like a mountaineer, and, when the knife was pulled out from his breast, the blood spurted onto his knees. [THE QUEEN *goes up to the table.*] Eat. Drink. You must be hungry and thirsty. [STANISLAS *remains crouching by the fire, his expression more and more wooden and inscrutable.*]

I am not asking you to speak to me; I am asking you to sit down. You have lost a lot of blood. Take this seat. It is the King's. And if I offer it to you, that is because I have decided—*decided*—to treat you as an equal. As for me, I can no longer consider you as a man. What? You ask me who you are? But, my dear sir, you are my death. It is *my* death I am saving; *my* death I am hiding; *my* death I am warming; *my* death I am caring for. Make no mistake about that. [STANISLAS *rises, goes to the King's chair, and seats himself quietly in it.*]

Good! You have understood me. [*She pours him out some wine.*] They killed the King because he wanted to build a theater, and they want to kill me because of my building of castles. But it was only natural on our part. Our families are madly devoted to art. Through so much writing of poor verse and painting of poor pictures, my father-in-law, my uncles and cousins tired of these pursuits and changed their methods. They wanted to become showpieces themselves. My dream is to become a tragedy. And that is no easy matter, you will agree. I am working hard on myself, scratching out, tearing to pieces, and starting afresh. Nothing worth while is created in the bustle of the world, so I shut myself off from it in my castles.

Since the King died, I have been dead. But mourning, however great, is not true death. My death must be like the King's. And to achieve that, I must not take any road that chance offers and on which I might lose my way and not reach him. [THE QUEEN *shows* STANISLAS *a locket she wears.*] I have even procured from my chemists a poison which I keep here at my neck. It is marvelous. The capsule takes a long time to dissolve. It is slowly absorbed into the body. You smile at your Reader. You know you are carrying your death within you and no one is aware of it. You put on your riding habit, you mount your horse. You leap over obstacles. You gallop and gallop. You get flushed with excitement. A few minutes later you fall from your horse. The horse drags you along. The trick has worked. I have kept this capsule out of mere caprice. I shall not use it. I soon realized that destiny must act by itself. For ten years, I have been consulting a ghost whose mouth never utters a sound. For ten years, nothing has been said from without. For ten years, I have been cheating. For ten years, everything that has happened to me originated from me and it is I who decided what it should be. Ten years of waiting. Ten years of horror. I was right to love storms. I was right to love lightning and its terrifying mischief—the way it undresses a shepherd and bears his clothes miles away; prints a tree leaf on his shoulder. It enjoys these pranks. The lightning cast you into my room. And you are my destiny. And I like that destiny. [STANISLAS *opens his mouth, as if to speak.*]

What are you saying? [STANISLAS *shuts his mouth again, tautening his whole frame to keep silent.*] Don't try and be so stubborn, you obstinate mule! Your veins are bursting, look at your fists and your neck! Shed your silence, it's killing you. Who but I could hear you? Shout! Stamp! Insult me! You stubborn mule! Stubborn mule! Do you realize what is happening? [THE QUEEN *passes quickly to the window. She turns around and speaks standing in front of the curtain.*]

Supposing, instead of lurching about in this place where you have discovered me, instead of being exhausted by your race for life and your wound, supposing you had recognized me and struck me down? . . . Tell me, who were you? Tell me! Say that word which is tied to your tongue: "Assassin!" You fainted. Is that my fault? I lifted you up, hid you, saved you, made you sit at my table. In your honor, I have broken all the rules of propriety and etiquette which govern the conduct of sovereigns. To kill me will be more difficult, I grant you that. You will have to become a hero. To kill suddenly, on an impulse, is nothing. To kill deliberately, in cold blood, requires a far stronger character. You can no longer avoid your deed. It is within you. It is you. Your crime has been working upon you. No human strength could spare you its conclusion. None! Save the worst of all: weakness. And I won't insult you by thinking you capable of such a ridiculous failure. Though I should very much dislike being the victim of a murder, it would suit me admirably to be killed by a hero. [STANISLAS, *who is clinging to the table, snatches off the tablecloth and sends the cutlery and crockery, etc., flying.*]

That's more like it! Upset things, break them, send them flying! Be a storm! [*She goes toward him.*]

A Queen! "What do I know of a Queen? Only what she says, and that may be nothing but deception. What do I see of a Queen? A woman in ceremonial dress playing for time. All that luxury, those chandeliers and jewels are an affront to me and to my companions. You despise the crowd; it is from the crowd I spring." [THE QUEEN *stamps.*] Enough! Enough! Or I'll strike you in the face! [THE QUEEN *passes her hand over her eyes.*] What do you know of the crowd? I show myself. The crowd acclaims me. I hide. The crowd adopts the policy of the Archduchess and of Count von Foehn. [THE QUEEN *sits on the end of the bed.*]

About Count von Foehn, there is much to say. He is the head of my police. Do you know him, little hero? He does not cut a very pretty figure. He is always plotting. He dreams of a regency state with himself at the helm. The Archduchess urges him on. I believe she is in love with him. How amusing if, unwittingly, you were his secret tool? That would explain your escape, the slackness of the police, and with what ease you slipped out of their clutches. It is unusual for Foehn to miss his man. To be sure, he did not deign to stir when his Queen's life was threatened. Poor Count! If only you knew what service you have just rendered me! . . . [*During these last remarks,* STANISLAS *has been gazing at one object after another around the room. Then his gaze returns to the table and he lowers his eyes.*]

But enough of that person. Let us settle our own affairs. [*In a voice of command.*] You are my prisoner. A free prisoner. Have you a knife? A pistol? . . . You may keep them. I give you three days to do me the service which I expect of you. If, however, you spare me, I shall not spare you. I hate weakness. Your only regular contact will be with me. You will meet Fräulein von Berg and the Duke von Willenstein, who see to my personal needs. That will be as far as your contacts with the world will extend. Fräulein von Berg is my Reader—it would be difficult to find a worse. I will say that you are my new Reader and that, to introduce you into Krantz, I contrived the romantic happenings of this night. Nothing I do surprises them. They will hate you, but they will respect you, because I am the Queen. The day after tomorrow Fräulein von Berg, who keeps the Archduchess informed, will have divulged this scandal. So you see, we haven't a day to lose. And I repeat: if you don't kill me, I shall kill you. [*While* THE QUEEN *has been speaking without looking at* STANISLAS, *like a captain, the following has occurred:* STANISLAS, *because of so much inner tension, has almost fainted away. He has wavered, supported himself on the armchair. He raises his hand to his eyes and slumps into the chair.* THE QUEEN *has not realized what is happening and thinks* STANISLAS *is forcing himself to commit an act of rudeness. She shakes her head sadly and looks at him.*]

No, sir, thank you. I never feel tired. Allow me to remain standing. [THE QUEEN *goes to open the curtains and window, unlock the shutters and open them. The night is now calm. Gleaming wet earth, glaciers in the mountains, the sky bright with stars.*]

The storm is over. Such peace! The smell of trees. The

stars. And the moon circling our ruin with its own. The snow on the mountains, and the glaciers. How brief are storms! How brief is violence! Everything subsides and sleeps. [THE QUEEN *gazes at the stars a while. She slowly closes the shutters, the window, and the curtains. When she turns around, she thinks* STANISLAS *has fallen asleep. His head is bowed till it touches the table. One of his hands is hanging down.* THE QUEEN *seizes one of the candlesticks and holds it near* STANISLAS' *face. She touches his brow lightly with the back of her hand, from which she has removed the glove. Then she opens the secret door.* TONY *appears. He is a Negro in the uniform of a Mameluke. He bows and stops on the threshold. He is a deaf-mute.* THE QUEEN *says something by moving her lips.* TONY *bows.* THE QUEEN, *at this moment, is behind* STANISLAS' *chair. She picks up her fan from the table and strikes him on the shoulder. He does not react. She goes around the chair and shakes him gently, then more vigorously.*]

But . . . may Heaven forgive me! . . . Tony! Since you can't hear me, I am going to tell you the truth! The poor fellow faints every five minutes because he is dying of hunger. [*She calls him.*] Hello! . . . Hello! . . . [STANISLAS *stirs. He opens his eyes. He blinks. He stands up suddenly with a haggard expression.*]

Stanislas [*Like a madman*]. What is it? . . . What is it? . . . What's the matter? . . . [*He looks around him and sees* TONY *in the shadow.*] My God!

The Queen. What is wrong? . . . Really, little hero! Are you afraid of Tony? You need not be. He is the only being whom I can trust implicitly. He is a deaf-mute, and *he* is a real deaf-mute. [*She laughs delightedly.*] We talk to each other by signs. He lip-reads. I was able to give him my orders without disturbing your sleep. [STANISLAS *feels unwell again. With his head thrown back, he supports himself by leaning against the table, which slips away from him.*] Now, now! . . . But you are not at all well. [*She supports him. And with motherly graciousness says:*] I know what is wrong with you, you stubborn mule. And as you refuse what is on this table, Tony will serve you a meal in your

room. He is going to take you there now. He is strong.
He will care for you, cram you with good things, he will
put you to bed and tuck you in. He will dress you.
[TONY *comes down to the table, takes one of the lighted
chandeliers and goes toward the little door. He opens it
and discreetly disappears into the corridor.* STANISLAS
*prepares to follow him. He turns around before disappear-
ing.*] Have a good meal and go to bed. Refresh yourself
. . . Good night. You have a hard day before you. Till
tomorrow!

ACT TWO

THE QUEEN'S *Library in Krantz. A large room with shelves
and tables loaded with books. At the back, a broad wooden
staircase rises, opposite the audience, to the upper gallery,
which is also covered with books and ornamented by
horses' heads. At the top of this staircase, with its brass
banister rail and knobs, a small landing and a great window looking onto the sky above the park. On the right
and on the left of this window are busts of Minerva and
Socrates. In the right foreground, on a large round table,
is a chandelier and a globe of the heavens. Near the table,
a chair and a broad armchair. Upstage of the table, a sort
of easel or frame on which targets for shooting can be
fixed. On the floor, running from this frame to the extreme left where there is an opening in the bookshelves
leading to a door, is a linoleum track. By the targets is
a gun and pistol rack. On both sides, there are doors
set in the bookshelves. Downstage left of the door, the
wall above a white glazed earthenware stove is covered
with a huge map. In front of the stove, chairs and comfortable armchairs. Shining parquet floor and red rugs.*
Afternoon light.

As the curtain rises, FELIX VON WILLENSTEIN, *helped by*
TONY, *loads the guns and pistols and arranges them on
the rack. He works the frame, which runs forward and*

*backward on rails, into an opening out of sight of the
audience.* TONY *is going to pass* FELIX *the targets for
him to fix on the frame.*

FELIX [*Keeping his mouth out of sight of* TONY, *who
lip-reads*]. Here, filth! Rub these barrels! [*He gives* TONY
a chamois leather.] And they'd better shine! The Duke
von Willenstein at the beck and call of an ape! It's scandalous! And the Queen tolerates it, in fact she encourages
it. And the Queen shows you her face. It's true, it's only
to a monkey she shows it. Don't imagine that is a
privilege, because it is the perfect expression of her
disgust.

*While he is finishing checking and putting the arms in
order,* EDITH *enters along the right-hand gallery and comes
down the stairs.*

   Edith. Talking to yourself, Felix?
   Felix. No. I am taking advantage of the fact that Tony
can't hear me to say a few nice things to him.
   Edith [*At the bottom of the staircase*]. Mind, Felix.
He can follow by watching your lips.
   Felix. I'm making sure he can't see them.
   Edith. He might even hear through his skin.
   Felix. Let him, after all. I don't care.
   Edith. The Queen wants us to show him proper respect.
   Felix. But I do, Edith. I do. Look. [*He bows to* TONY.]
You can clear off, filth! I have seen enough of you!
[TONY *bows gravely, looks a last time at the arms and
departs. He mounts the staircase and disappears along the
                        left-hand gallery. A door is heard.*
Edith [*In a low voice*]. Do you know what is happen-
ing? . . .
   Felix. I know the whole castle is in a turmoil since last
night's alarm. Hasn't the man been found?
   Edith. He is in the castle.
   Felix [*Starting*]. I beg your pardon?
   Edith. Felix, it's an incredible story. The man is here
in the castle. He is living here. And it's the Queen who
made him come here.

Felix. Are you mad?

Edith. Who wouldn't be? Her supper for the King, her desire to remain alone, all that happened during that anxious night, was nothing more nor less than one of the Queen's little games.

Felix. How do you know?

Edith. She told me this morning. She was bursting with laughter over it. She told me that she would never forget my expression, it was too comic for words; that Krantz was a sinister place; that she certainly had the right to enjoy herself occasionally.

Felix. I don't understand a thing.

Edith. Neither do I.

Felix. The Queen knows you are easily frightened. She was poking fun at you.

Edith. The Queen never lies. That man is in Krantz. She is hiding him. He had hurt himself in the park. There is blood on the carpet.

Felix. I must be dreaming. You say that the Queen has introduced into Krantz an anarchist who wanted to kill her?

Edith. That was all part of her game! The Queen thinks I am the worst Reader in the world. She wanted another and she knew perfectly well which. When the Queen decides something—I don't have to tell you this—she allows no one to influence her decision and she always gets what she wants.

Felix [*With an angry gesture*]. Who is this man?

Edith. You may well ask! Felix, you'll have to turn a blind eye and hold your peace. These are the Queen's instructions for you: if this man has come to Krantz and entered the castle, it is because the idea has appealed to the Queen's fancy; he is her guest and she asks you to consider him as such.

Felix. But who? Who is he?

Edith. I have several surprises for you. He is the author of a notorious poem. The Queen has often sung its praises to us. How was it I didn't guess that this wild admiration was in fact a piece of bravado and that it would not stop there?

Felix. Do you mean the fellow who signs himself Azrael is in Krantz? Is staying in Krantz?

Edith. The Queen had been attacked and she wanted to gain the upper hand. At least, I suppose that was it. She gave me no details. It was "Her royal pleasure" to everything. Poets, it appears, are mere starvelings, writing to order for anyone who will pay them. It didn't take her long to unearth this poet and make him transfer his allegiance. Only, as she imagined that the whole court and all the police and castle household would be opposed to her in this and put innumerable obstacles in her path, she thought it exciting to act in secret.

Felix. And what about the police? Are you not forgetting that a detachment was sent?

Edith. Was Count von Foehn with them? No. Well, then? The officer in charge was on the side of the Queen. His alarm was a false one. His men shouted, fired their guns, but they had orders to miss their target. Once in the castle, your courteous friend Tony merely had to take this fellow by the hand and lead him into Her Majesty's presence.

Felix. By the time the Archduchess hears of this and has intervened, anything may have happened.

Edith. Whatever we do, we must not lose our heads. You're only too apt to lose yours. I advise you to be circumspect. You know how suddenly the Queen can switch from laughter to anger. We are the only people in Krantz to share this secret. Whatever indignation it may arouse in our breast, we must hold our peace and take our lead from her. Leave the rest to me.

Felix. And does Her Majesty count on bringing me face to face with this person?

Edith. Undoubtedly. And I have kept the biggest surprise for the last. This person is the very image of the King.

Felix. The image of the King!

Edith. I was about to leave the Queen's bedchamber, when she called me back. "Edith! You'll probably receive a shock when you see my new Reader. It would be kinder if I warned you and you warned Felix. You'll think you're seeing the King. The resemblance is extraordinary." I couldn't move for stupefaction, and she added: "The King looked like one of our peasants, so there's nothing surprising if one of our peasants looks like him. In fact, that was what decided me, that resemblance."

Felix. Monstrous!

Edith. Felix! I am not in the habit of judging the Queen.

Felix. And Heaven forbid I do so. Only the mind boggles at this.

Edith. I agree.

Felix. A peasant! What peasant? What can a peasant have in common with a holder of office replacing the Countess von Berg, Reader to the Queen?

Edith. Don't be silly. A peasant from Krantz could very well have studied in town and know more than we do.

Felix. Be that as it may, we must protect the Queen. In this amazing caprice of hers, there is a constant threat of danger.

Edith. That is true.

Felix. What can we do?

Edith. Not talk and let me manage things. Do you suppose a new Reader is going to oust me without my feeling some resentment?

Felix. Are you keeping your post then?

Edith. You surely don't imagine for a moment that the Queen will admit this new Reader into her inner sanctum and let him come to her at any hour of the day or night? There is no provision for a supplementary Reader, and I doubt whether Her Majesty's innovation will be long-lived.

Felix. The Queen *did* want to appoint that vile Tony Governor of the Castle of Oberwald.

Edith. Yes, Felix. And she didn't quite succeed. [EDITH *has pricked up her ears and in the same breath whispers.*] Not a word!

THE QUEEN *appears, coming from the left-hand gallery and followed by* TONY. *As soon as she appears at the top of the staircase,* EDITH *turns toward her and bows.* FELIX, *by* EDITH's *side (with his back to the audience), clicks*

his heels and bows his head with the sharp movement
which is customary in court salutes. THE QUEEN *is wearing*
an afternoon dress with a very full skirt. A veil hides her
face.

The Queen [*Veiled, descending the stairs*]. Good day,
Felix. Edith, have you explained to him?

Edith. Yes, Your Majesty.

The Queen [*On the last steps of the staircase*]. Approach,
Felix. [FELIX *goes up to the banisters.*] Edith will have
told you what I expect from you. I have, for personal motives, introduced to Krantz a new Reader, and I have every
reason to believe he is excellent. This Reader is a young
student who was born in the vicinity. His likeness to the
King is most strange, and was more persuasive to me than
any recommendation. He is poor. He has no titles. I'm
wrong. He has the finest of them all: he is a poet. One of
his poems is known to you. Under the name of Azrael,
which I wish him to keep, he has published a work aimed
at ourselves and which I like. Youth and anarchism go
together. Youth rebels against the existing order. It dreams
of being "other" and of itself bringing about that change.
If I were not a Queen, I should be an anarchist. In fact, I
am both Queen and Anarchist. That is why the court de-
rides me and the people love me. And that is why this
young man very soon found an affinity with me. I owed
you this explanation. You are in personal attendance on
me and I would not for the world have you misunderstand
my actions. That is why I should be grateful if you would
show this young man that people of your class possess an
inward graciousness.

Are the targets set up? Yes. The guns are clean. Tony
gave you the new bullets, I expect. You may go now.

FELIX *bows, goes toward the door on the right, opens it,*
stands back and turns toward EDITH.

Edith [*Motionless*]. Your Majesty needs me perhaps?

The Queen. No, Edith. I told you you could go. And
never enter without ringing first.

Edith *bows, retires and goes out in front of* Felix, *who closes the door. As soon as the door is shut,* The Queen *taps* Tony *on the shoulder. He bows, climbs the staircase, and disappears toward the left.* The Queen *is alone. She raises her veil. She lifts a gun off the rack, walks away from the target corner along the linoleum track, stops on the extreme left, raises the gun, takes aim and fires. She returns to the target, looks, replaces the gun in the rack and takes another, returns to her shooting position and fires a second time. Same business. But this time she takes a pistol and goes back to fire it. She lowers the weapon when* Stanislas *appears at the top of the staircase.* Tony *stops on the landing and then returns whence he came.* Stanislas *comes down. He is wearing a dark town suit, with a jacket buttoned up high—one of the King's suits.*

The Queen [*Who is on the left of the staircase, invisible to* Stanislas *and with her weapon raised*]. Is that you, young man? [Stanislas *comes down the last three steps and sees* The Queen *coming forward, still holding her weapon in the air.*] Don't be surprised at seeing me armed. I was target shooting. I like shooting game less and less, but I like shooting. Are you a good shot?

Stanislas. Not a bad one, I believe.

The Queen. Have a try. [*She goes to the big table, places her pistol on it, goes to the rack, takes a gun and hands it to him.*] Stand where I did. It is a bad position for anyone coming down the stairs, but Tony usually keeps watch. And besides, I have sharp ears. I can hear the servants listening behind the door. I hear everything. Fire! [Stanislas *fires.* The Queen *goes to the target corner and works the mechanism which brings the target in on its frame out of the shadow.* The Queen *detaches the target.*] A bull's eye! Congratulations. I had fired slightly high and to the left. [Stanislas *replaces the gun on the rack.* The Queen *keeps the target in her hand and will fan herself with it.*]

Be seated. [*She points to an armchair on the left, in front of the stove. She sits near the large table, fanning herself with the target and playing with the pistol.*] I hope your knee is getting better and that Tony's bandage doesn't bother you too much. Were you able to sleep in Krantz?

Stanislas. Yes, Ma'am. I slept very well and my knee doesn't hurt any more.

The Queen. Capital. One sleeps well at twenty. How old are you?

Stanislas. Twenty-five.

The Queen. Six years separate us. I am an old woman in comparison with you. Were you a student?

Stanislas. I worked alone, or nearly so. I didn't have the means to go to college.

The Queen. Lack of means is not the only thing which forces people to study alone. The first time my father killed an eagle, he was amazed to see that it did not possess two heads, as on our arms. That was the type of man my father was: rough and charming. My mother wanted to make a queen of me, but I wasn't taught how to spell. Fräulein von Berg can scarcely read in her own ᐧ language. I shall not lose by this change. I would like to hear you read. After all, you have been appointed Reader.

Stanislas. At your pleasure.

He rises. THE QUEEN *rises and goes to take a book from the table. She places the target on the table near the pistol.*

The Queen. Look, sit here. [*She points to the armchair she has just left, near the table.* STANISLAS *remains standing. She hands him the book. Then she goes to sit in the chair* STANISLAS *has left.* STANISLAS *sits.* STANISLAS *places the book on the table and pushes away the pistol.*] Be careful, it's loaded. Open your book and read. You can read anywhere in Shakespeare.

STANISLAS *opens the book and reads.*

Stanislas [*Reading*]. "Scene IV. Another Room in the same Castle. The Queen's Apartment. Enter QUEEN and POLONIUS.

   Polonius. He will come straight. Look you lay home to him:
     Tell him his pranks have been too broad to bear with,

And that your grace hath screen'd and stood between
Much heat and him. I'll sconce me even here.
Pray you, be round with him.
Queen.   I'll warrant you;
Fear me not. Withdraw, I hear him coming.
                         [POLONIUS *hides behind the arras*].

Enter HAMLET

Hamlet. Now, mother, what's the matter?
Queen. Hamlet, thou hast thy father much offended.
Hamlet. Mother, you have my father much offended.
Queen. Come, come, you answer with an idle tongue.
Hamlet. Go, go, you question with a wicked tongue.
Queen. Why, how now, Hamlet!
Hamlet.   What's the matter
       now?
Queen. Have you forgot me?
Hamlet.   No, by the rood, not so:
     You are the queen, your husband's brother's wife;
     And—would it were not so!—you are my mother.
Queen. Nay then, I'll set those to you that can speak.
Hamlet. Come, come, and sit you down; you shall not
       budge;
     You go not till I set you up a glass
     Where you may see the inmost part of you.
Queen. What wilt thou do? thou wilt not murder me?
     Help, help, ho!
Polonius [*Behind*]. What, ho! help! help! help!
Hamlet [*Drawing his sword*]. How now! a rat? Dead,
       for a ducat, dead!"
The Queen [*Rising*]. I don't like blood and Hamlet is
too much like a prince in my family. Read something else.
[*She moves some books, takes a pamphlet out and hands
it to* STANISLAS.] Here! [STANISLAS *has put down the vol-
ume of Shakespeare and is about to take the pamphlet.
He starts back.*] Here. . . . You will not refuse to read
me your poem. I know it by heart. But I should like to
hear it read by you. [STANISLAS *takes the pamphlet.* THE
QUEEN *goes up to the map on the extreme left.*] Read.
[THE QUEEN *has her back turned to* STANISLAS *and seems*

to be consulting the map. STANISLAS *still hesitates.*] I am
listening.

    Stanislas [*Beginning to read in a muffled voice*].
    "And the Archbishop warned the Queen:
      'You must prepare yourself.
      For Death is at your door.'
    Wincing and grimacing, the Queen began confessing
    To the Archbishop a list of crimes
    In which murder, incest, and treachery counted for
      but little. . . ."

Pause. THE QUEEN *continues consulting the map. She
completes the incomplete verse.*

    The Queen. " . . . Stopping her mouth, her nose,
    Death stalked in on high chopínes . . ."
    Stanislas. " . . . On high chopínes and stitched up in
      black oilcloth.
    Then began an endless business.
    Twenty times she started her act afresh and failed.
    The gathered courtiers, princesses, ladies-in-waiting,
      clergy and even the Archbishop couldn't keep their
      eyes open.
    Fatigue racked their limbs. Under this torture, their
      features flagged and gave them away.
    At last, Death looked round.

Pause. STANISLAS *looks at* THE QUEEN. *Then proceeds:*

    And, as she bowed her way out,
    The stench and the candles in the windows showed it
      was all over.
    Then the fireworks blossomed in the sky,
    The wine flowed over the little dance floors hastily
      erected in the streets,
    And everywhere the heads of drunks went rolling
      merrily about."

STANISLAS *jumps up and throws the pamphlet angrily into
the middle of the library.*

Enough of all this!

    The Queen [*Swinging around*]. You surely can't be a
coward?

Stanislas. Coward, did you say? Do you call me a coward because I won't pick this pistol up off the table and shoot you in the back?

The Queen. We made a pact.

Stanislas. What pact? Tell me. You decided, as you decide everything, that I was your destiny. These are heady words. You decided that I was a killing machine and that my role on earth was to send you to heaven, and by that you mean, of course, the heaven of history and legend which belongs to you. You dare not commit suicide—that would not be grand enough—you want me to do it for you. What are you offering me in exchange? A priceless reward: implementing a historic case, sharing with you the aura of fame surrounding a mysterious and fatal crime.

The Queen. Did you not come to Krantz to kill me?

Stanislas. Have you stopped a moment to think I might be a man? to ask yourself where I came from, and why? You have understood my silence not a jot. It was fearful. My heart beat so loudly I could scarcely hear you speaking. And how you spoke! You couldn't possibly understand that there are other people, that they exist, and think, and suffer, and live. You only think of yourself.

The Queen. I forbid you——

Stanislas. And I forbid you to interrupt me. Did I interrupt you last night? I appeared out of the dark, out of the darkness of which you know nothing, of which you can guess nothing. You probably think my life began at the window of your castle, here in Krantz. I didn't exist before, save for a poem which stirs your senses, and suddenly I become a specter which is your death. Rubbish! Your room was warm, luxurious, cut off from the world. In it, you played with suffering. And then I arrived. Where do you think I came from? From the outer darkness, from all that isn't you. And who sought me in the darkness, who dispatched to me signals swifter than commands, who made of me that creeping sleepwalker tiring himself out and only hearing the dogs, the shots, and the pounding of his heart? Who dragged me on from rock to rock, from crevasse to crevasse, from bramble thicket to bramble thicket? Who hauled me up as on a rope to that cursed window where I fainted? You! You! For you are not of the kind that chance visits. You told me so. You dream of being a masterpiece, but there is no masterpiece unless God has a hand in it. No, you make decrees, issue orders, maneuver, build, and instigate what occurs. And even when you imagine you don't do this, in fact you do. It was you who unwittingly gave me a spirit of revolt. It was you who unwittingly led me to make acquaintance with the men among whom I hoped to find violence and liberty. Unwittingly, it was you who dictated my companions' vote and led me into a trap! In truth, these are things no court of justice would admit, but they are known to poets, and I am telling them to you.

I was fifteen. I came down from the mountains where everything was pure, like ice and fire. In your capital, I found poverty, lies, intrigue, hate, the law, and thieving. I dragged on, from one shame to another. I met some men who were nauseated and attributed this state of things to your rule. And where were you? In a cloud, where you lived your dream, spending whole fortunes and building temples for yourself. You were superbly unaware of our miseries. Someone killed your King. Is that my fault? It's one of the dangers of your trade.

The Queen. In killing the King, they killed me.

Stanislas. So little, that you now hope destiny will kill you. You adored the King. But what sort of love was it? You were destined for the throne from your earliest childhood. You were turned into a monster of pride. You were led before a man of whom you knew nothing beforehand. He occupied the throne. You liked him. Even if you had disliked him, that would have altered nothing. And you became engaged and went hunting together, galloping together, then you were wedded and he was killed.

Now take me. Since my childhood days, I have been choking with love. After so much watching, waiting, and seeing nothing turn up, I decided to seek it out. I was no longer content to be ravaged by a countenance, I had to be ravaged by a cause, to give myself up to it, plunge into it and disappear.

When I entered your room, I was an idea, a crazy idea, the idea of a madman. I was an idea confronted with another idea. I made the mistake of fainting. When I came to, I was a man with a woman. And the more he became a man, the more she was determined to be an idea. The more I was won over by this luxury to which I am quite unaccustomed, the more I gazed at this striking woman, the more that woman treated me as if a were a mere idea, a death machine.

I was crazed with hunger and fatigue, crazed through anxiety, crazed by the storm and by that silence which was more heartrending to me than a cry. And then I managed to pull myself together and become again that fixed idea which was what I was meant to be, and which I ought never to have ceased to be. This room was going to become my wedding chamber—for a blood wedding.

I reckoned without your profound cunning. Scarcely had I ceased to be a man when you had become a woman again. You are certainly expert in spells and enchantments! To make a hero of me, you used all the powers which a woman normally brings into play when she wants to make a man fall in love with her.

And the worst of it was, you were successful. I ceased to know or to understand; I fell asleep for what seemed ages but was in reality only a second; I dreamed dreadful dreams; I awoke and saw you and heard you; I trembled and I struggled and strove, wondering how anyone could endure such suffering and not die.

The Queen [*Drawing herself up to her full height*]. I command you to say no more.

Stanislas. I thought one of the things you had decided was that we should ignore etiquette and treat each other as equals.

The Queen. That was a pact between my death and me. It was not a pact between a Queen and a young man who climbs in at windows.

Stanislas. Someone has climbed in at your window, has he? What a piece of villainy! Well, then. . . . Shout! . . . Ring your bell! . . . Call out! . . . Let your guards take me. Hand me over to justice. These are also the reactions of a Queen.

The Queen. It is you who are shouting. You'll stir up the whole castle.

Stanislas. Shall I? I don't care if I am arrested and executed. Can't you see I'm going mad?

The Queen [*Who is at this moment behind the table, seizes the pistol and holds it out to* STANISLAS]. Shoot me!

Stanislas [*Recoils.* THE QUEEN *keeps the pistol in her hand*]. Don't tempt me!

The Queen. In a few seconds, it will be too late!

Stanislas [*His eyes shut, facing the audience*]. All the love which impelled me toward killing is surging back into me like a wave. I am finished.

The Queen. Must I repeat my words? If you don't kill me, I shall kill you. [*She has gone in a quick movement to the bottom of the stairs.*]

Stanislas [*Shouting to her*]. But kill me, kill me, then! Finish me off! Let's get it over. Does the sight of blood upset you? My heart would know one joy, if my blood could arouse in you one feeling.

THE QUEEN *lowers the pistol. She turns around and fires toward the targets. The whole maneuver takes place in a flash. A prolonged ringing is heard.* THE QUEEN *keeps the pistol in her hand and rushes toward* STANISLAS. *She forces the volume of Shakespeare into his hands.*

The Queen. Sit down. Start reading. Read with the vehemence you put into those last insults. [*The bell rings more violently.*] Read! Quick! [*She seizes him by the hair, like a horse by its mane, and forces him to sit.*] You must.

Stanislas [*Having dropped into the chair, opens the book and shouts the scene from* Hamlet].

"Thou wretched, rash, intruding fool, farewell!
I took thee for thy better: take thy fortune;
Thou find'st to be too busy is some danger." . . .

He stops reading and shuts his eyes.

The Queen [*Shaking him*]. Go on!

STANISLAS *proceeds with his exaggerated reading.*

Stanislas [*Reading*]. "Hamlet, to the Queen:
Leave wringing of your hands: peace! sit you down,
And let me wring your heart: for so I shall,
If it be made of penetrable stuff;
If damned custom have not brass'd it so,
That it is proof and bulwark against sense.
The Queen. What have I done that thou dar'st wag
thy tongue
In noise so rude against me?"

The door on the right opens. EDITH VON BERG *appears.*

The Queen [*Having gone back to her post and lowered
her veil*]. What is it, Edith?
Edith. Forgive me, Your Majesty. . . . But I was in
the park when I heard such loud cries . . . and a shot.
. . . I feared . . . [*She stops.*]
The Queen. What did you fear? Will you ever stop
fearing? Feared what, Edith? I was target shooting, and if
you had dared to come closer still, you would have learned
something of the art of reading from a Reader who
knows how to read. [*To* STANISLAS, *who has risen on the
entry of* EDITH *and who is standing, book in hand, against
the table.*] Please excuse Fräulein von Berg. She is not
used to it. She reads in such a low voice, I sometimes
wonder if I am not deaf. [*To* EDITH.] Edith, I find it
distasteful—supremely so—to have people listening either
at doors or windows. [TONY *enters through the little door
on the left opposite the targets, at the end of the linoleum
track.* THE QUEEN *sees him and turns to* EDITH.] Will you
excuse us? [TONY *speaks with his fingers.* THE QUEEN
replies. TONY *leaves.*] I am very displeased, Edith. The
growing indiscretion of your conduct forces me to place
you under arrest. Tony will bring you anything you may
need. [EDITH *bows and mounts the staircase. She disappears through the left door. To* STANISLAS.] And now I
would like you to hide. I am going to receive a visitor and I
don't want you to miss a word of what is said. May I call a
truce? We will talk afterwards. The gallery makes a won-

derful observation post. [STANISLAS *passes slowly in front of* THE QUEEN, *goes up the stairs, and disappears to the right. As he disappears, the little door on the left opens.* TONY *enters, looks inquiringly at the* QUEEN. *She nods her head.* TONY *steps back and lets in* COUNT VON FOEHN. *Then he withdraws and shuts the door.* VON FOEHN *is in traveling dress. He is forty-five. An elegant and astute man of the court.*] Good day, Count.

Von Foehn [*Bowing his head while at the door and then advancing a few steps toward* THE QUEEN]. Greetings to Your Majesty. I hope she will excuse my appearance before her in this guise. It is a long road and a rough one.

The Queen. I wanted to have it repaired a long time ago. But I feel this expense should figure on the civil list. Our ministers consider it is incumbent on me. The road will stay as it is.

Von Foehn. The state is poor, Your Majesty, and we are practicing economy.

The Queen. You are speaking to me like my Minister of Finance. I shut my eyes and he goes over the accounts, imagining I am listening. But I'm not following at all.

Von Foehn. It's very simple. Wolmar is on a height and its upkeep must be an expensive item. People say that this little jewel has cost Your Majesty a fortune.

The Queen. Now, Foehn, you're neither the Archduchess, who thinks she is infallible, nor the said Minister, who thinks I am insane.

Von Foehn. The Archduchess may fondly deprecate the fact that Your Majesty has debts and that she is unable to come to your assistance in this matter, but everyone knows that these expenses only affect your own purse, and that the people have never had to suffer for them.

The Queen. Everyone knows that, do they? My dear Count, you make me laugh. What, then, is the source of the absurd rumors which are constantly spread about me? When I was young, the Archduchess so often drilled into me the need for a straight bearing that it has become second nature to me. And yet, what don't they accuse me of? It appears I horsewhip my grooms, smoke a pipe in front of the servants, am exploited by a circus acrobat for whom I hang trapezes in the throne room itself; and I'm only quoting the amusing things. The others are so depressing I would not waste my time recounting them. I despise the people, I ruin them. That's the kind of malicious tale which is circulated about me.

Von Foehn [*Bowing*]. Your Majesty, the dark side of the legend concerning you——

The Queen. Is there any other to a legend nowadays? Formerly, a legend took a hundred years to strike its medals, but they were struck in bronze. Now, it strikes them off daily and at random on the cheapest newsprint.

Von Foehn. Your Majesty! The press would never permit themselves to . . .

The Queen. Wouldn't they, indeed! These things are said in the form of advice. And there are innumerable clandestine pamphlets besmirching my good name. What have you done about that? The police seem to tolerate it. Von Foehn, you are the head of my police, are you not?

Von Foehn. Your Majesty! . . . Your Majesty! . . . The Archduchess is the first to deplore this state of affairs, and if she weren't I should not have the honor of being here in Krantz today and presenting Your Majesty with my humble respects.

The Queen [*Changing her tone*]. At last we're coming to the point. I knew it. You have come to scold me . . .

Von Foehn. Your Majesty is joking!

The Queen. . . . about the ceremony of remembrance.

Von Foehn. Your Majesty guesses everything before it can be put into words. But there is the clearest indication that the Archduchess is in despair at this . . . misunderstanding between the Queen and her people. If the Queen would deign to show herself, this deplorable misunderstanding would soon disappear.

The Queen. My absence from the ceremony created, as the newspapers would say, a very bad impression.

Von Foehn. I had the post chaise driven at all speed, Your Majesty can be sure of that. But the crowd must have been very disappointed on seeing this empty coach. The Archduchess feels, if I may repeat her words, that the Queen owed this effort to the memory of her son.

The Queen [*Rising*]. Von Foehn, is she not aware that the reason for my voluntary exile is precisely my grief at the death of her son, and that it is not my way of mourning to ride in a coach in a procession?

Von Foehn. The Archduchess knows all that. She is quite aware of it. She is by nature explosive, if I may say so, but she is clear-sighted, and a shrewd politician.

The Queen. I hate politics.

Von Foehn. Unfortunately, Your Majesty . . . politics is the business of monarchs, just as mine is to keep watch over the kingdom, to make investigations, and to do the unpleasant jobs.

The Queen. What does the Archduchess want?

Von Foehn. She doesn't *want* . . . She *counsels*. She counsels Your Majesty to break a little with your habit of going into seclusion.

The Queen. You can't do such a thing "a little," Count. You either hide, or you show yourself. There's no such term as "a little" in my vocabulary. It is by doing things "a little" that people finally do nothing at all. If my motto had not been "I cleave to the impossible," I would have chosen the saying of a Red Indian chief when someone criticized him for eating "a little too much" at an Embassy dinner: "A little too much is just enough for me!"

Von Foehn. Will Your Majesty authorize me to repeat that saying to the Archduchess?

The Queen. Let it serve as my reply.

Von Foehn [*Changing his tone*]. Krantz is a wonderful place . . . wonderful! You arrived here yesterday, Your Majesty?

The Queen. Yesterday morning.

Von Foehn. And Your Majesty came from Wolmar. The journey must have seemed endless. And that storm! I fear Your Majesty must have had a very bad night.

The Queen. I? I adore storms. Besides, I was dead tired and I slept in one of those rooms in the north tower. I heard nothing.

Von Foehn. I'm glad. I feared my manhunt might have

caused some disturbance and interfered with Your Majesty's repose.

The Queen. Oh, fancy my forgetting! Of course, Fräulein von Berg came to ask me if I would allow the police to search the park. But . . . weren't you there?

Von Foehn. We are too apt to forget Your Majesty's fearless courage, and that we don't have to pander to her nerves, as we do for other princes. However, I should not have liked to give undue importance to this little affair by my arrival at the castle in the night. I came the night before and stayed in the village, at the inn.

The Queen. Foehn! It's not nice of you to come to Krantz without staying at the castle. Did you catch your man? He wanted to kill me, I believe.

Von Foehn. My police are talkative. I see my men have been gossiping in the castle.

The Queen. I don't know whether your police are talkative. Fräulein von Berg certainly is, and she adores minding other people's business.

Von Foehn. We had been shadowing him since the previous day. I wonder how he knew—I mean how his organization knew—that Your Majesty would sleep at Krantz? I didn't know that myself. Anyway, we lost track of him after he had gone to one of the cottages in the village where some of his family live. He had slipped away, or perhaps someone had tipped him off. We organized a regular manhunt. I'm sorry, as this hunt forced us to disturb Your Majesty's solitude. I am relieved to learn, however, that Your Majesty was not unduly affected.

The Queen. And, of course, you drew a blank, your man is still at large. . . .

Von Foehn. My men do not deserve your reproaches, Your Majesty. They have captured their man.

The Queen. But, how wonderful!

Von Foehn. Yes, at dawn. He was trying to get away through the passes. He must have been exhausted. He gave himself up.

The Queen. What sort of man was he?

Von Foehn. A young hothead in the service of one of

those organizations whose subversive activities Your Majesty was deploring a moment ago. So, Your Majesty will realize that the head of her police force has not remained criminally inactive.

The Queen. Has he been questioned?

Von Foehn. I questioned him myself.

The Queen. What was he, a laborer?

Von Foehn. A poet.

The Queen. No?

Von Foehn. Your Majesty really should not encourage poets. They always end by introducing their disorder into the social machine.

The Queen. Foehn! You said a poet wanted to kill me, is that right?

Von Foehn. Oh, it's just their way of responding to the Queen's praises.

The Queen. What praises?

Von Foehn. Your Majesty, if I am not mistaken—I suppose it is a sort of heroic contrariness—but you seem to affect a great liking for a certain subversive poem published in one of those pamphlets of which you so rightly disapprove. This man, this young man, is the author of it.

The Queen. Do you mean Azrael? How extraordinary!

Von Foehn. He was nearly all in. In five minutes, he was blowing the gaff—as my men would say. I mean, he confessed everything. He's a hothead, but not incorrigible. He gave me the names of his accomplices and the address of their meeting place. A nice little haul for me on my return, I fancy.

The Queen [*Who had been sitting, rises*]. Count von Foehn, I must congratulate you. And thank you for this capture. I did think your absence yesterday surprising, and I might have wondered if this afternoon's visit were not for the purpose of certifying my death.

Von Foehn [*Smiling*]. Your Majesty is unsparing.

The Queen. I can be. Especially toward myself. [*She holds out her hand*]. My dear Count. . . .

Von Foehn [*Is about to kiss her hand, when she withdraws it and places it on his shoulder*]. I apologize for my untimely visit, which must appear very irksome to the

Queen in this atmosphere of contemplation and study. [*He bows.*] May I ask the Queen for news of Fräulein von Berg?

The Queen. She is unwell. Nothing serious. She is confined to her room. She'll be pleased to know you thought of her. Tony will show you out. [*She goes to the door and opens it.* TONY *appears.*] Tell the Archduchess how deeply grateful I am for her concern over my popularity. Farewell. [THE COUNT *bows, passes in front of* TONY *and goes out.* TONY *looks at the* QUEEN. *He follows the* COUNT *and shuts the door.* THE QUEEN *slowly, pensively, unveils.*] You may come down. [STANISLAS *comes around the gallery from the right and descends the staircase in silence. He goes up to the round table, leans on it, and bows his head.* THE QUEEN *faces him, as she stands in front of the stove.*] There!

Stanislas. It's monstrous!

The Queen. That's the court. I am in the Archduchess' way. Foehn promotes a murder. You fail. Foehn has ceased to be interested in you, you realize that, don't you? If you hadn't been concealed in this castle, his men wouldn't have been long in doing away with you. It is, in fact, because the Count is so sure of making you disappear, that he didn't hesitate to speak to me about you. [*Silence.*]

Stanislas. I'm going to give myself up.

The Queen. Don't be ridiculous! Stay here. Be seated. [STANISLAS *hesitates.* THE QUEEN *sits.*] Take that chair. [STANISLAS *sits.*] Foehn is looking for you. The purpose of his visit was to keep watch on me and on the castle. Although I took steps to prevent his meeting Fräulein von Berg, he seems to suspect something. I can rely on von Willenstein. He will divulge nothing. Our present situation is such that any police on earth would be baffled by it. I drew you into it. It is up to me to try and find a way out.

Stanislas. I am an object of shame!

The Queen. No, of isolation. And your solitude has encountered my solitude, that is all. [*She turns toward the stove fire. The flames light up her face. Night begins to fall.*]

What is so beautiful about tragedy and gives it such human and superhuman interest is that all its characters live beyond and above laws. Who were we last night? You said this: one idea confronted by another. And now, who are we? A hunted man and woman—equals. [*She rakes the fire.*]

Does your mother live in the village?

Stanislas. I have no mother. The Krantz peasant woman is my stepmother. She turned me out when I was sixteen. Yesterday evening, I returned to her cottage for private reasons. I had hidden some papers there. I had to burn them.

The Queen. Have you friends?

Stanislas. None. I know only the men who drew me into a trap. If there are any sincere ones among them, my God save them from their blindness.

The Queen. Foehn won't arrest anyone. You needn't worry about that. He'll just make them believe you betrayed them, and leave it to them to get rid of you.

Stanislas. It's all one to me.

The Queen. Could you see Count von Foehn from the gallery? Could you see his face?

Stanislas. I could.

The Queen. Had you seen it before? I mean, have you by any chance been in his presence before?

Stanislas. He is too clever a man for his innumerable agents to realize that they are his agents.

The Queen. I was glad you did not betray your presence.

Stanislas. Oh, I was so afraid my heart would be heard pounding, like last night in your room. It was all I could do to stop myself from leaping from the gallery. I could have strangled him.

The Queen. You wouldn't have caught him unawares. He was on his guard. Foehn thinks that I am a crazy woman and that you are a madman. Yesterday in Krantz, at the inn, I am sure he smiled to himself and said: "The Queen believes she is a poem, and her murderer believes he is a poet. How very entertaining!" Note that your companions probably have an almost identical way of seeing things. I refer to the sincere ones. Many talk and few act.

Nothing is more conventional than a community, of whatever kind it may be. [*The light is fading more and more.* THE QUEEN *turns around to the fire, the glow of which is reflected upon her.*]

Why did you burn your papers yesterday in Krantz?

Stanislas. For fear a search would be made.

The Queen. Were they poems?

Stanislas. Yes.

The Queen. What a pity.

Stanislas. If I hadn't burned them yesterday, I should today. [*Silence.*]

The Queen. And after burning your poems . . . what were your marching orders?

Stanislas [*Rising*]. Really!

The Queen. I thought there were to be no more scruples, civilities or hypocrisies between us!

Stanislas [*Sitting down again, in a low voice*]. I was to assassinate the Queen in Wolmar.

The Queen. Assassins should kill swiftly and out of doors, kill swiftly and be stoned to death by the crowd. Otherwise, there is a tailing off, and any tailing off is unbearable. [*Long pause.*] The newspapers would have said: "The Queen, victim of a brutal crime." The Archduchess and Count von Foehn would have been present at your execution and led the court in mourning for me. There would have been funeral rejoicings! The bells would have rung, and the regency been established as prescribed in the constitution at present in force. The prince is there ready, under the Archduchess' broad wing. And so, the trick would have worked. The Archduchess would have been ruling, or, rather, Count von Foehn. You see what politics is.

Stanislas. The ignoble wretches!

The Queen. So, you were to kill the Queen in Wolmar. Well, you have fulfilled your mission in Krantz. You were to kill the Queen, Stanislas. It is done, you have killed her.

Stanislas. Me?

The Queen. Does a queen accept the idea of someone's entering her bedroom and swooning there? Or of hiding the man who climbs in through her window at night? Or of anyone's refusing to answer when she questions, or not addressing her by her proper title, or offering her insults? If she does, then she has ceased to be a Queen. I tell you, Stanislas, there is no Queen now in Krantz, you have killed her.

Stanislas. I follow you perfectly. You tell me that there is no need for politeness between us, but the politeness of princes obliges you to try and elevate my solitude up to yours. I am no dupe.

The Queen. Do not imagine I would accept the idea of your failure. . . . I would have turned you out long ago, if I had.

Stanislas. I am nothing. The Queen remains the Queen. A Queen whose court is envious because she eclipses it. A Queen whom thousands of humble subjects hold in affectionate esteem. A Queen in mourning for her King.

THE QUEEN *seats herself in the chair near the stove, looking toward the audience. One can scarcely distinguish anything except the stove, which lights up their faces. The library is full of shadows.* STANISLAS *slips behind* THE QUEEN's *chair and stands there.*

The Queen. You have killed that queen, Stanislas, more completely than you intended. When I was a little girl, there were people always pestering me, preparing me for the throne. That was how I was brought up, and I hated it. King Frederick was a revelation. I no longer thought of anything but love. I was going to become a woman. I was going to live. I did not become a woman, I did not live. Frederick died the day this miracle should have occurred. I buried myself in my castles. On a stormy night, you climbed through my window and disturbed the whole delicate balance of my life. [*Long pause.*]

Stanislas. How peaceful it is after the storm! Night is falling in such silence . . . you cannot even hear the cowbells.

The Queen. From this corner of the castle, you can't hear anything, you seem cut off from the whole world. I used not to care for this quiet. Now I do.

Stanislas. Wouldn't you like me to ask for candles?

The Queen. No, don't move. I don't want anything. I only want the night to stop falling, the sun and the moon to stay where they are now, this castle to remain exactly as it is at this moment and live for ever thus, as if under a spell. [*Silence.*]

Stanislas. Sometimes, a balance comes from such an intricate assembly of parts, it seems incredible and one wonders if the slightest breath would not destroy it.

The Queen. Let us stay quiet a while. [*Silence.*] Stanislas, pride is a wicked fairy. She must not come near. She might touch this minute with her wand and transform it into a statue.

Stanislas. Pride?

The Queen. It is a woman who is speaking to you, Stanislas. Do you understand? [*Long pause.*]

Stanislas [*Closing his eyes*]. God . . . make me to understand. We are adrift on the high seas. Fate, chance, the waves, and the tempest have thrown us together on this wreck which is the Krantz library—and which is adrift upon eternity. We are alone in the world, at the utmost limit of all that is insoluble and extreme—where I thought I should be in my element but about which I knew . . . nothing. Our discomfort is so fearful that the discomfort of the sick and dying, of the poor and starving, of the prisoners covered with vermin, of the explorers who get lost in the polar ice, is but comfort by comparison. There is no high or low, no right or left. We do not know where to set our eyes, our souls, our words, our feet, our hands. O God, enlighten me! Let an Angel of the Apocalypse appear, sound his trumpet and shatter the world around us!

The Queen [*In a low voice*]. O God, snatch us out of this miasma! Take from me the supports which hold me to one course. Destroy the rules of kingly conduct and especially that of caution, which I took for modesty. Give me the strength to acknowledge my errors. Overcome the monsters of pride and habit. Make me to say that which I do not wish to say. Deliver us. [*Silence.* THE QUEEN

lowers her veil. Awkwardly and artlessly:] Stanislas, I love
you.

Stanislas [*In a similar fashion*]. I love you.

The Queen. Nothing else matters.

Stanislas. Now is the time when I should kill you.
Then I should never lose you.

The Queen. My little hero, be gentle, come close to
me . . . come. . . . [Stanislas *kneels beside her.*] Lay
your head upon my knees. Ask nothing further of me.
Your head rests upon my knees and my hand upon your
head. Your head is heavy. As if severed from the body.
This is a minute all on its own, of limpid ecstasy. I loved
you when you appeared in my room. And, to my shame,
I was ashamed. I loved you when, through exhaustion,
your hand dropped like a stone beside you. And, to my
shame, I was ashamed. I loved you when I seized you by
the hair to make you read. To my shame, again I was
ashamed. [*Silence.*]

Stanislas. Some dreams are too intense. They awake
the sleeper. We must take care. For we are the dream
of one who sleeps so profoundly that he is not even aware
that he is dreaming us.

*In this moment of silence and shadows lit by the fire, a
knocking is heard several times at the little door. Stanislas jumps up.*

The Queen [*Quickly, in a low voice*]. It's Tony. Don't
move. [The Queen *goes up to the little door and opens
it. Tony appears. He is holding a candle in his right hand.
He talks with the fingers of his left hand. Tony places
the candle on the table.*] Fräulein von Berg has thrown
a letter out of the window for Count von Foehn. He must
know everything by now. [Tony *goes out by the little door.*]
You have nothing to fear for the coming night. Fräulein
von Berg shall remain under arrest, while I consider what
is to be done. No one but she has the right to enter my
room. You will stay here under my protection. Tomorrow
morning, Tony will lead you by a mountain path to my
old shooting lodge. This lodge overlooks a farm and I am

sure I can depend on the keepers there. . . . Then——
Stanislas. No.

The Queen. Stanislas!

Stanislas. No, listen. I prayed that God might hear me
and he sent me his angel. For a day and a night, we have
been a prey to his thunder. He has knotted us together.
Don't think that I regret my words, or that I put yours
down to a moment's obscurity and to the confusion into
which our souls were thrown. I believe you and you must
believe me. Tomorrow, you will cease to love a poor skulk-
ing fellow waiting to steal into your presence. Assassins are
made of other stuff. You have not lived. I must come to
your rescue. You have saved my life, I will save yours. A
ghost was killing you and preventing you from living.
I have laid that ghost, I have not killed the Queen. The
Queen must come out of the shadow, a Queen who rules
and accepts the burdens of a sovereign. Plotting against
you is rife. It's all too easy; you make no reply and the
ministers know this. Answer them. Change your mode
of life completely. Return to your capital. Be radiant.
Speak to the Archduchess as a Queen, not as a daughter-in-
law. Crush Foehn. Appoint Duke von Willenstein Com-
mander in Chief. Get the support of the military. Review
them on horseback. Astound them. You won't have to
dissolve Parliament even, or appoint new ministers. They
bow to the iron hand of authority. I have seen yours. I
saw you last night wielding your fan as a scepter and
striking the furniture with it. Strike the dusty furniture
of your offices crammed with old files. Sweep away all
those papers, all that dust. The people would worship
you on their bended knees for such an act. Lift your veil.
Show your face to them. Display yourself. No one will
show you disrespect. That I can assure you. I will watch
your work from afar. I'll live in the mountain ranges. I've
known them from childhood. No police would catch me
there. And when my Queen is victorious, she will fire a
salvo that will tell me of her victory. And when the Queen
wants to call me to her, she will give an eagle cry and I
will fly to the peaks where she built her castles. I do not

offer you happiness. The word is debased. I offer you our forming together an eagle with two heads, like the one that you bear on your arms. You built your castles as eyries. They were awaiting such an eagle.

There must be no tailing off. That would be unbearable. You asked God to save us. Heed his angel who speaks through my voice. [THE QUEEN *pulls three times on the bell cord*.] Now, say this after me:

O God, admit us into the kingdom of your mysteries.
Let our love avoid the staling contact of men's eyes.
Wed us in heaven.

The Queen [*In a low voice*]. O God, admit us into the kingdom of your mysteries. Let our love avoid the staling contact of men's eyes. Wed us in heaven. [*The door on the right opens.* FELIX VON WILLENSTEIN *appears, shuts the door behind him, salutes*.]

Oh, Felix, how astonished you look. What is the matter? Oh yes! . . . I was forgetting. I'm showing myself naked before two men. I'm giving up the veil, Felix, and I'm ten years older. You will get used to it. I have to give you some orders.

I am returning to the court. We will all leave tomorrow at one o'clock. Order the carriages, my post chaise. Only the castle staff will remain in Krantz.

Fräulein von Berg is no longer in my service. The Archduchess will adopt her as one of her ladies-in-waiting.

As soon as you arrive in the town, you will take command of the forts. Organize the journey and its stages immediately. I will brook no delay. You will go before me in my capital with a hundred and fifty men and you will fire a salute of a hundred rounds.

Tomorrow at noon, you will assemble my light cavalry in the park behind the lake. You will watch this window closely. [*She points to the window at the top of the staircase.*] As soon as I appear there unveiled, the Guards band will play the royal anthem. That will be the beginning of my reign.

I depend upon your devotion to me and your loyalty to my cause. You may go now.

FELIX VON WILLENSTEIN *clicks his heels, salutes, and leaves.*

The Queen [Going to STANISLAS, *places her hands on his shoulders and gazes intently into his eyes].* Stanislas . . . are you pleased with your pupil? [STANISLAS *shuts his eyes, tears well from them.*] Tears?

Stanislas. Yes. Of joy.

ACT THREE

The same as Act Two. It is about eleven o'clock in the morning. The library window overlooking the park is wide open. When the curtain rises, STANISLAS *is seen standing on a step of one of the library ladders. He has some books under his left arm and is holding in his right hand a book which he is reading. After a moment,* FRÄULEIN VON BERG *comes along the left-hand gallery and down the staircase. She comes close to* STANISLAS, *who, being absorbed in his reading, does not see her.*

EDITH. Good morning.

Stanislas [Starting, and shutting the book]. Oh, excuse me, Fräulein.

Edith. Did I disturb you?

Stanislas. The Queen wants to take some books with her, and, instead of getting them ready, I was reading them.

Edith. But that is a Reader's duty.

Stanislas. To read them to the Queen, yes. Not to read them to himself.

Edith. Has the Queen gone riding?

Stanislas. When the Queen gave me her instructions, she was in riding habit. She had had Pollux saddled. I should think she has gone for a gallop in the forest. She does not expect to be back before noon.

Edith. Well! . . . You even know the names of her horses. How clever of you!

Stanislas. The Queen happened to mention that horse's name in front of me. Haven't you seen Her Majesty yet?

Edith. My dear sir, I have been locked in my room. It was already about ten o'clock when Tony deigned to let me out. I knew nothing of this unexpected journey for which the castle is busy preparing.

Stanislas. Yes, I believe the Queen is returning to her capital . . .

Edith. You believe so?

Stanislas. I gathered she would leave Krantz this afternoon.

Edith. It must be wonderful for a young man to follow the Queen to court. You must be delighted.

Stanislas. Her Majesty is not doing me the honor of taking me with her. I shall stay in Krantz. Her Majesty probably intended telling you as soon as she returns. [*He goes to take some other books and carries them to the table.*]

Edith. It's true we are getting quite used to living on the roads and changing residence. Her Majesty rarely stays more than a fortnight in one spot.

Stanislas. But a fortnight in town is bound to appeal to you. . . .

Edith. If we stay a fortnight. I know Her Majesty. After three days, we shall be off to Oberwald or the lakes.

Stanislas. Unfortunately, I don't know Her Majesty well enough to say. [*Silence.* STANISLAS *tidies some books.*]

Edith. Do you know Count von Foehn?

Stanislas. No, Fräulein.

Edith. He is an extraordinarily talented man.

Stanislas. I have no doubt. He must be for that job.

Edith. Of course, I can well see that a police chief could never appear likable to an independent mind like yours. At least, I suppose so.

Stanislas. You are quire right. Naturally, his post does not make him particularly likable.

Edith. He protects the Queen.

Stanislas. I sincerely hope so. [*He bows. Silence.*]

Edith. Listen, young man, you may think it strange, but I have a mission to perform on behalf of the Count.

Stanislas. With me?

Edith. With you.

Stanislas. I thought he had left Krantz.

Edith. He was to have left Krantz at dawn. Probably what is going on has aroused his curiosity. They accuse me of being curious. But the Count's curiosity knows no bounds. He has stayed on in Krantz. I have just met him here. He is looking for you.

Stanislas. It's difficult to see how a man of my class could interest Count von Foehn.

Edith. He did not say why. But he is looking for you. He asked me if I could arrange a little interview with you.

Stanislas. That is a very great honor, Fräulein. Does the Queen know about this?

Edith. Well, you see . . . the Count does not wish to disturb Her Majesty for a simple investigation. He would, in fact, prefer her not to be told.

Stanislas. I am in the service of Her Majesty. I only take orders from her.

Edith. Count von Foehn would be the first to understand your attitude. And he would admire you for it. Only *his* service sometimes forces him to disregard court etiquette. He works behind the scenes and runs everything. As a matter of fact, he guessed what your reaction would be. And he wants me to tell you that, in asking for this interview, he was seeking your help in a matter concerning Her Majesty's peace of mind.

Stanislas. I am not familiar with the court, Fräulein. Is that how a chief of police formulates an order?

Edith [*Smiling*]. Almost.

Stanislas. Then, Fräulein, I have only to obey and to ask you to lead me to Count von Foehn. I suppose he would not like our . . . interview—as you put it—to be discovered by the Queen.

Edith. Oh, if the Queen has gone for a gallop, she gallops far. Pollux goes quite wild. This library is still the quietest and safest place. Tony is with Her Majesty. His Grace the Duke announces himself by ringing three times. Besides, I shall keep watch so that nothing untoward occurs.

Stanislas. I see, Fräulein, that you are devoted to Count von Foehn.

Edith. To the Queen, my dear sir. It's the same thing.

Stanislas [*Bowing*]. I await the orders of the chief of police.

Edith. Of Count von Foehn, please. Why do you say the chief of police! It is the minister, Count von Foehn, who wishes to see you.

Stanislas. I am his humble servant.

FRÄULEIN VON BERG *goes to open the little door, leaves it open, and disappears.* COUNT VON FOEHN *enters by the same little door and shuts it after him. He is in riding boots as in Act Two. He carries his hat in his hand.*

Von Foehn. Please forgive my disturbing you with this surprise visit. In my profession, one can never be sure what one's next move will be. But my profession, strange to say, has a poetic side to it. It depends so largely on imponderables and unforeseeable things. You are a poet, if I am not mistaken, and you should appreciate this better than anyone. [THE COUNT *comes and sits near the table.*] I am right, you are a poet?

Stanislas. I do occasionally write poems.

Von Foehn. One of these poems, if that term is correct when applied to a . . . piece in prose (of course, that is your affair and I do not wish to bother you with questions of syntax) . . . one of these poems, as I was saying, appeared in a little left-wing leaflet. The Queen thought it amusing. She has a somewhat mischievous turn of mind, and had a large number of copies printed and, through her agency, these copies were distributed to the whole court.

Stanislas. I didn't know——

Von Foehn. Don't interrupt. The Queen, of course, is free to do as she likes. She enjoys playing that kind of trick. Only she does not always realize what confusion is created by the forces she unleashes. What may seem to her mere fancies can become a serious matter when it happens in public. You did know that this leaflet was honored by the Queen's kind attention? Answer.

Stanislas. As far as I am concerned, I attach no importance to those few lines I wrote. I was very surprised when I learned from Her Majesty herself that she had read it, and saw no offense in it, and that she had particularly observed in it a more or less novel kind of phrasing.

Von Foehn. That phrasing is so unfortunate, or so felicitous—it all depends on one's point of view—that a subversive piece of writing has resulted which has more scandalous effect than it has merit. You realize, I suppose, how wide-reaching this effect is?

Stanislas. I did not, my lord, and I am sorry about it. And Her Majesty apparently did not consider it necessary to tell me.

Von Foehn. I don't specially want to know now how Her Majesty got in touch with you. I shall learn that on my return. In any case, Her Majesty, as I said, is free to act as she pleases. What is of consequence is for me to know what part you played in Krantz, how you managed to obtain from Her Majesty a change of attitude which none of us could hope to achieve. [*Pause.*] Well?

Stanislas. My lord, you astonish me greatly. What part do you mean? The Queen had the idea of trying as her Reader a poor poet of her town. There is nothing more to it than that. And I could not expect to play any other part.

Von Foehn. Of course. We'll not dwell on that point. But then, since your presence in Krantz has nothing to do with the complete change in the Queen's attitude, perhaps you will not refuse to explain your own?

Stanislas. I am not sure I understand. . . .

Von Foehn. I mean, will you refuse to explain to me by what miracle a violently hostile young writer can be brought in the twinkling of an eye to serve the existing form of government?—in fact, to overleap the whole hierarchy and land squarely in the Queen's library, at the top of a mountain? Such a feat implies uncommon strength and agility.

Stanislas. Sometimes, chance leads young people into circles for which they are not made. A young man's enthusiasm is quickly fired, and as soon dies down. I had reached the stage when we were losing our faith in the ideas in which we had put our trust. There is nothing more saddening in this world, my lord. The Queen is accused of a thousand and one sorts of moral baseness. I decided to accept her offer and judge for myself. A mere glance was sufficient to make me realize that I had been laboring under a misconception. The real tragedy is the distance which separates human beings, and the fact that they do not know each other. If they did, many a sad spectacle and crime would be avoided. Moreover, as you said yourself, my lord, if the Queen were to show herself, the misunderstanding between her and the people would come to an end. [*As soon as he has spoken,* Stanislas *perceives his blunder. He turns his head away.* The Count *pushes his chair nearer.*]

Von Foehn. Where the devil did I say that?

Stanislas. Excuse me, my lord. I got carried away telling my own tale. But I thought . . .

Von Foehn. You thought what? [*He emphasizes the "what" by striking the arm of the chair with his hat.*]

Stanislas [*Very red*]. I thought Her Majesty, when talking to me about you, my lord, quoted that remark.

Von Foehn. It is too kind of Her Majesty to remember the slightest observation made by the humblest of her servants. In point of fact, I do seem to recollect having made some such remark. It is a widely held belief and rather obvious. By the way, let me congratulate you on your being so completely in Her Majesty's confidence. She is not normally communicative. She must hold you in high esteem. [*Pause.*] So, she spoke to you about me!

Stanislas. I was arranging her books. Her Majesty was probably just talking to herself. It was in bad taste on my part, but I listened to her and repeated to you what I heard.

Von Foehn. And it was after I left that you were arranging the books and that Her Majesty talked to herself and that you heard her speak of me?

Stanislas. Yes, my lord.

Von Foehn. How very, very strange. [*He rises and looks at the backs of the books. Then he turns around and stands leaning back against the bookshelves.*] Come toward me. [STANISLAS advances.] That's enough. [STANISLAS *halts*.] An *amazing* likeness. What does the Queen think of it?

Stanislas. I imagine that my likeness to the King, in so far as a man of my class can claim to look like his sovereign, made a profounder appeal to the Queen than my own merits could have done.

Von Foehn. I can understand that. Our country does not often produce so well-built a man as our regretted King Frederick. And it's just as well. Good Lord! If any unscrupulous persons got wind of this remarkable resemblance, they might use it to work upon people's imaginations and start some legend. My dear sir, the country is alive with legends. We are being choked by them. The Queen's legend is playing great havoc. It stirs up people either against or for her. It's a kind of disorder. I instinctively dislike it. That is why I wanted to thank you for the very wise course which the Queen is adopting. I thought you were responsible for it. I was mistaken. No more of that. [*Silence*. COUNT VON FOEHN *seats himself in the chair and thus comes very close to* STANISLAS.] Look, my dear sir. I am going to give you an example of my frankness with you. Take a chair. You look tired. Take it, sit down, you're not in the chief of police's office. We are just chatting together. Besides, amidst all these books of your colleagues, you should feel, in a way, at home. [STANISLAS *takes a chair and seats himself as far as possible away from* VON FOEHN.] Nearer, nearer. [STANISLAS *brings his chair closer*.] I am going to give you an example of my frankness with you and of the great freedom with which I speak in your presence. [*Pause*.] My friend, as a matter of fact, when I called upon the Queen, I fancied—I'm sorry, but I fancied you were present, hidden, and listening to our conversation. [STANISLAS *rises*.] There, there! He's taken it badly. Don't get upset! I did not say you *were* present during our conversation, only that I *fancied* so. A minister of internal security must always be on his guard. We have had so many wiles practiced upon us. [STANISLAS *sits down again*.] Your romantic manner of reaching your post had not aroused my suspicions in the least. You tricked von Foehn. And that's not an easy thing to do! I ought to have realized that this was one of those picturesque pieces of scene-setting at which Her Majesty is so clever. I was completely hood-winked, I must confess. The next day, in her library, thinking of you, I tried an old dodge which usually works. I told Her Majesty that my men had caught you, that I had questioned you, that you had confessed your intention of committing a crime, and that you had sold your accom-plices.

Stanislas [*Rising*]. Sir!

Von Foehn. Calm! Keep calm! I hoped so to infuriate you that you would lose your temper. The Queen was wearing a veil. I could not observe her expression. She is an extremely clever woman, is Her Majesty. As for you, it comes to this. Either you were not hidden in the library, or else you were, in which case, my friend, you showed such self-control I must take my hat off to you.

Stanislas. What do you want of me?

Von Foehn. I'll tell you. [THE COUNT *rises, goes over to* STANISLAS's *chair and leans on it.*] I don't believe a single word of your story, but I like you for trying to make me believe it. It all argues in your favor. The Queen has decided to break with her habits and to resume her posi-tion at court. She has decided this, thanks to your en-thusiasm—I should, at least, like to think so—and I wouldn't mind betting I am right. Let me speak.

But what purpose would this sensational journey serve, if it were a mere flash in the pan? What is the Arch-duchess' dream? To see her daughter-in-law insure the power of the throne, and to die in peace. Instead of which, what is happening? The Queen evades the responsibilities incumbent upon her. She despises them and accuses her mother-in-law of conspiring against her. Conspiring! Where would she find the strength to do so? Not a day passes but she calls me and begs me to try and win over the Queen.

No. It is important that this journey should serve some useful purpose. It is of the utmost importance that the Queen's entry into the capital should not become a fiasco. It is vitally important that she should not revolt against the red tape—the piling-up of a wall of documents between the sovereign and the execution of her will, the winning over of the old ministers and listening to their complainings. Now, the Archduchess has become inured to this. She took upon herself the most thankless tasks, the heaviest burdens, and bears them heroically.

What will happen tomorrow? I ask you. The Queen will be urged to make use of her prerogatives. She will be told that the Archduchess is ruling in her place and has no intention of giving way to her. She will rule. She will get bored, nauseated. She will go.

But what is it we ask of Her Majesty? To be an idol. To mask, beneath her splendor, the sordid realities to which a woman of her stamp could never stoop. With the Queen absent, the people see these sordid realities. There lies the whole problem. We need a man of feeling who is not of the court. A man who will agree to save the Queen. A man who will prove to her that she is not merely being asked to perform a thankless task; that the Archduchess loves her as her own daughter and only seeks to take upon herself the mortal boredom of that obscure labor. Do you begin to see what I am driving at?

Stanislas. You surprise me, my lord. How can a person of your position be deluded for a single moment about the political aptitudes of a poor student like myself?

Von Foehn. You persist in your attitude, then?

Stanislas. It is not an attitude, I assure you. I fear all this must be the outcome of Fräulein von Berg's imaginings.

Von Foehn. Fräulein von Berg has nothing to do with this. Let me tell you that I am accustomed to relying upon my own judgment and acting alone.

Stanislas. She might, at least, have told you that Her Majesty does not consider me as one of her personal staff and is not taking me with her household.

Von Foehn. My dear sir, time is passing and the Queen may discover us here any moment now. Let us put all our cards on the table. You managed, do not deny it, to obtain from Her Majesty in one day what none of us has managed to obtain in ten years. I am not asking you to admit this, nor to reveal the mystery of your methods.

I respect your discretion. I am merely asking you to help us with your occult influence to prevent the Queen from courting disaster. I am asking you to find some reason or other for following her to the capital and preventing the terrible disorder which is bound to arise if the Queen shows open hostility toward the Archduchess, the ministers of state and of the Crown, the Parliament, and the Government. Have I made myself clear?

Stanislas. My lord, I have more and more difficulty in following you. Apart from the fact that I am not bound to accept or refuse, particularly as I do not feel it is in my power to render this service, it seems to me that a cutthroat place like a court would soon begin to consider as extremely scandalous the influence that the humblest of Her Majesty's subjects was exerting upon the Queen. It would moreover provide a further weapon with which to accomplish the downfall of Her Majesty.

Von Foehn. There is nothing to prevent the Queen's attaching to herself a Reader that she fancies. There is nothing to prevent it, provided the Archduchess approves. Your resemblance to the King could make the court react either way. If we disapprove, you are an object of scandal. With the Archduchess' and her ministers' support, you are not, and that resemblance will then charm the court. A Queen's power has limits, that of a chief of police has none.

Stanislas. And if I stay in Krantz?

Von Foehn. Good God! You don't imagine your intervention will remain a secret! The court is a cutthroat place, you are right there. It will interpret this episode in its own way, which is not a pretty one. You cannot make the court vanish with a flick of a fan. We are not living a fairy tale. They will defame the Queen.

Stanislas [*Sitting bolt upright*]. Sir!

Von Foehn. They will defame the Queen and you will be the cause of it. Come, my dear sir, be reasonable. Help us.

Stanislas. And . . . what are you offering me for this?

Von Foehn. The greatest possession on this earth: freedom.

Long silence. STANISLAS *rises and walks up and down in the library.* THE COUNT *remains leaning on the back of his chair.* STANISLAS *comes back to him.*

Stanislas. In clear language, what you are saying to me is this: if my mysterious influence exists, if I use it, and maneuver the Queen into position, if I hand her over to you tied hand and foot, Count von Foehn will undertake to remove my name from the police black list.

Von Foehn. How romantically minded you are! Who is talking of handing over the Queen? And to whom, pray? And why? We are simply asking you to prevent any regrettable outbursts, and to act as liaison officer between two camps which are both fighting for the same cause but imagine they are enemy camps. [*Silence.*]

Stanislas. My lord, I was hidden in the library. I heard everything.

Von Foehn. I never doubted it for a minute.

Stanislas. The Queen wanted the opinion of a common man. It so happened that I had such an opinion. After all, I have nothing to lose. Court etiquette does not exist as far as I am concerned. The Queen asked me what I thought. I told her.

Von Foehn. And may one know what you think?

Stanislas. That the Archduchess fears the far-reaching influence of an invisible Queen; that, not content with spreading infamous rumors about her, commissioning the clandestine leaflets which attack her, inciting organizations against her and urging them on to crime, you are scheming to get her back in her capital, to complete her undoing, to humiliate her, to exasperate her, to provoke her beyond endurance and pass her off as mad—to obtain from both Houses an order of deprivation of her rights, and from the minister of finance the seizure of her property.

Von Foehn. Sir!

Stanislas. And I did not suspect the worst. What a capital piece of scandal it would make, if the Queen were to take back with her to the court a young commoner, a Reader without office, who is moreover the image of the dead King!

Von Foehn. Be quiet!

Stanislas. Take care! The Queen was not reigning. Now she is. She will burn your files. She will sweep away your dust. She will strike you with her thunder. You talk of fairy tales. This is one. A simple wave of the Queen's fan and your whole edifice will crumble. I wouldn't care to be in your shoes!

Von Foehn. You are accused of being party to a criminal act, a projected assault on Her Majesty. I have the warrant in my pocket. I arrest you. You can give your explanations at your trial.

Stanislas. I am under the Queen's protection.

Von Foehn. My duty is to protect the Queen, even against herself and in her own house.

Stanislas. You would dare to arrest me in the Queen's house?

Von Foehn. Why not?

Stanislas. You're a monster!

Von Foehn. And the Queen is a Chimaera. You have flown to her rescue on a Hippogryph. There are charming monsters.

Stanislas. And if I asked one last favor of you?

Von Foehn. Ask away. I am renowned for my patience. I have been trying to save your head from the scaffold for the last quarter of an hour.

Stanislas. The Queen is leaving Krantz at one o'clock. You are anxious for this departure to take place. Never mind for what reasons. They are not mine. But you are intent on it. I would give my very soul, indeed I give it to you, for this journey to succeed. However, it is essential for you and for me that Her Majesty should know nothing of our conversation. Leave me free till one o'clock.

Von Foehn. You speak as a poet.

Stanislas. It is in your interest not to interrupt Her Majesty's preparations with the disturbance that my arrest in the castle would cause.

Von Foehn. That is less ideological. . . . You ask me for two hours' grace. Granted. The castle is surrounded by my men. You could not escape.

Stanislas. Your men can be withdrawn. The Queen will

enter her carriage at one o'clock. At one-ten I shall be at your disposal in front of the stable porch. You have my word for it. You can take me away by the outhouses without my being seen.

Von Foehn. A pity we did not manage to come to an understanding.

Stanislas. For you, perhaps!

The bell rings three times.

Von Foehn [*Starting*]. What is that? . . . Fräulein von Berg?

Stanislas. No. It's Duke von Willenstein's signal.

Von Foehn. How very convenient. [*He goes to the little door on the left.*] I'll be off. So long. [*From the door.*] Don't bother to see me out.

VON FOEHN *leaves. Scarcely has he disappeared when* FELIX VON WILLENSTEIN *opens the door on the right. He enters.* STANISLAS *is standing with his back almost to him, downstage left.*

Felix [*Looking for* THE QUEEN *and seeing* STANISLAS]. I thought Her Majesty was waiting for me in the library. [*He starts and steps back. He utters a stifled cry.*] Oh! . . .

Stanislas. What is it, Your Grace?

Felix. Good God! Yesterday, I was looking at the Queen, it was very dark and I did not see you clearly.

Stanislas. Is my likeness to the King really so great?

Felix. Terrifyingly so. How can there be such a likeness?

Stanislas. Forgive me for having unintentionally caused you such a shock.

Felix. Forgive me for not controlling myself better.

FRÄULEIN VON BERG *appears at the top of the staircase and comes down.*

Edith [*To* STANISLAS]. I congratulate you, sir. Her Majesty has just informed me that I no longer belong to her household. I am going back into the service of the Archduchess.

Stanislas. I cannot see, Fräulein, how these steps Her

Majesty has taken concern me, nor why you should congratulate me on them.

Edith. My dismissal means, I suppose, you have been appointed in my place.

Felix [*Trying to calm her*]. Edith!

Edith. Oh, leave me alone, you! [*To* STANISLAS.] Is that correct?

Stanislas. Alas, Fräulein, Her Majesty can hardly be thinking about me and must have forgotten to tell you that I am not following her to the court.

Edith. You are staying in Krantz?

Stanislas. Neither in Krantz, nor in the court. I am disappearing.

Edith. But then, if no one is supplanting me, can you explain my disgrace?

Felix. Edith, Edith! Please, we have no reason to involve a stranger in our private affairs.

Edith. As if he weren't involved in them already!

Stanislas. Fräulein!

Edith [*Going up to him, beside herself*]. I can see one thing clearly. I was the Queen's Reader. You arrive. I am no longer her Reader.

Stanislas. And how could I have anything to do with that?

Edith. What have you insinuated? What have you said to her?

Stanislas. I have only known Her Majesty since yesterday.

Edith [*Face to face with* STANISLAS]. What have you said to her?

Felix [*In a whisper*]. Her Majesty!

THE QUEEN *appears at the top of the stairs, coming from the left-hand gallery. She begins to come down the stairs. She is in riding habit and has a riding crop in her hand.*

The Queen [*Unveiled*]. Is it you, Fräulein von Berg, who shout so loudly? [*She begins to come down the stairs.*] I don't much care to hear shouting. Are you going to spend all your life quarreling with poor Willenstein? How do you do, Felix? [*Greeting* STANISLAS *with her whip.*] Fräulein von Berg was worried yesterday when your voice reached her in the park. I could hear hers from the other end of the hall. It is true she was not reading. When she reads she is hardly audible.

Edith [*Still bowing*]. Your Majesty. . . .

The Queen. Leave us. You must have so many things to do and to say before our departure. [EDITH *makes a low bow and disappears through the little door on the left.*] Well, Felix, is Edith von Berg still plaguing you? I had asked for you to come to settle finally the details concerning our escort. But it is imperative I first make arrangements about my books. I leave you free to be with your men. I will ring for you in a moment. [FELIX *salutes and retires through the door on the right.*] I could no longer bear anyone else's presence. [*She removes her hat and throws it onto a table. She only keeps her riding crop in her hand.*]

Willenstein looks at me in amazement, and I was rather harsh with Edith von Berg. They must put my nervous state down to this departure. The truth is I could not live another minute unless I were alone with you.

She drops into the armchair near the stove. STANISLAS *kneels beside her as in Act Two.*

Stanislas. As soon as you leave me, I fear that the dreamer who dreams us will awake. But no. He merely turns over in his sleep. I see you, and his dream begins again.

The Queen. My love. . . .

Stanislas. Say it again. . . .

The Queen. My love. . . .

Stanislas. Say it again and again. . . . [*He closes his eyes.*]

The Queen [*Kissing his hair*]. My love, my love, my love, my love.

Stanislas. How marvelous!

The Queen. I rode like the wind, with Pollux madly galloping. We flew toward the glacier, like a skylark flying at a mirror. It drew me. It flashed its white lightning at me. It shone. Tony was following on his Arab. I could feel he wanted to scream, to stop me, but he can only scream with his fingers and he was clinging to his reins. Once, I looked around and he gesticulated. I whipped on Pollux. I rode him straight toward the lake. The lake was gleaming beneath us. Between the lake and the mountain eagles were floating. I was sure Pollux could leap into the air and fly and float like them and set me down on the opposite shore. He was covering me with foam. But his fury abated. He pressed back with his haunches and stopped dead—on the very edge of a sheer drop into space. *He* was reasonable, not like his mistress. Poor Pollux. . . . He is not in love.

Stanislas. Crazy. . . .

The Queen. Meanwhile, you were arranging my books. Do you forgive me? A passion for living, for braving death, impelled me to gallop, to cease to be a Queen or a woman, simply to be a rider at full gallop. And to think that I believed happiness an ugly and obscene thing! I believed that only unhappiness was worth living. To make happiness beautiful is a tremendous feat. Happiness is ugly, Stanislas, if it is merely the absence of unhappiness, but if happiness is as terrible as unhappiness, it is superb! I was deaf, I was blind. Now I discover mountains, glaciers, forests. I discover the world. What use are storms when, with my horse, I am a storm myself?

Stanislas. And I had heard nothing and seen nothing. But in two days I have learned much.

The Queen. Look at my neck. This morning, my locket twisted and turned and leapt here, striking me on the shoulders at the end of its chain. It wanted to strangle me. The death it encloses seemed to cry in my ears: "Do you want to live? This is new indeed!" I took it off in my room. Let it stay there! I will find it there when I am as old as the Archduchess and you no longer love me.

Stanislas. I will throw it into the lake with my poem.

The Queen. It was through that poem that I came to know you, Stanislas.

Stanislas. Was it I who dared to write those lines, and hundreds more like them which I burned in Krantz?

The Queen. So, all the poems you burned in Krantz were meant for me?

Stanislas. Yes, for you.

The Queen. And you burned them because you feared that they might be found during a search?

Stanislas. Yes.

The Queen. That they might be found after my death?

Stanislas. And used after mine. Yes.

The Queen. After my death and after yours, darling, nothing would be of great importance.

Stanislas. I did not want people to use them to vilify my victim, or me. They would have made a heroine of you, darling, but of me a hero.

The Queen. Did they contain such terrible insults?

Stanislas. Yes, my love.

The Queen. Then you were thinking all the time of me, darling.

Stanislas. I was haunted by you. I was obsessed by you. And as I could not approach you, all I could do was to hate you. I strangled you in my dreams. I bought portraits of you and tore them into a thousand pieces and threw them into the fire and watched them curling up in the flames. Their image was printed on my eyes. I could see them on the walls and, in the streets of the town, they defied me from behind windows. One evening, I smashed one with a paving stone. I was pursued and I slipped through an air hole into a cellar. I stayed there two days. I was dying of hunger, cold, and shame. And you? You were shining on your mountains like a candelabra at a ball, and with the cold indifference of the stars. The vilest things which were invented about your life served to embellish my hatred. Nothing seemed abject enough.

The poem you know is an old one. My companions would not have dared to publish the others. But they urged me on to write. And I wrote, I wrote without admitting to myself that this was a way of writing to you. I was not writing, I was writing to you.

The Queen. My poor beloved. . . .

Stanislas. Do you know what it is to amass unanswered

letters, to heap insults on an Indian idol, with its cruel, mocking smile?

The Queen. I sent you letters, too. My father used to make flying kites and let me send messages to them. You pierce a hole in a piece of paper which makes its way along the string to the kite. I would kiss this paper and say: "Find in the sky the one I love." I loved no one but you.

Stanislas. Your kites were princes.

The Queen. Perhaps they were for my father and my mother. They were not for me.

Stanislas. Forgive me if the spirit of revolt still smolders within me. I will turn it against those who wish you ill.

The Queen. Forgive you, Stanislas? I am a brute. Never destroy your spirit of revolt. That is what I adore in you, darling.

Stanislas. Violent natures waste away in an atmosphere of calm. I ought to have killed you in your room that first night and then killed myself. That is undoubtedly a way of making love for good and all.

THE QUEEN *rises, walks away from* STANISLAS, *then returns to him.*

The Queen. Stanislas, are you angry with me for leaving Krantz?

Stanislas. It was I who begged you to go.

The Queen. That is not the same thing. You are angry now that I am going.

Stanislas. If you stayed in Krantz, I would leave you.

The Queen. If I stayed in Krantz for you, to live close to you; if, for you, darling, I gave up all idea of resuming power, would you leave Krantz, would you leave me?

Stanislas. Any tailing off is unbearable. Those are your own words. It did not take me long to see what court intrigues are, and the snares of the ceremonial and etiquette. Behind your back, that abominable spirit spreads its contagion throughout your residences. We should soon be objects of derision there. Let us fly with all speed, my Queen, let us fly, you one way, me another, and let us meet in secret like thieves.

The Queen. Ever since this morning, all manner of woman's follies have entered my head.

Stanislas. And all manner of man's follies mine.

The Queen. I shall be in my capital tomorrow. I shall try to make a clean sweep. May God help me to succeed. I shall make the attempt thanks to you and for you. You know my shooting lodge. That will be our mail post. You wait there for news from me. I will send Willenstein. In a fortnight, I will come up to Krantz. But if I should go up to Wolmar, I will let you know. You will come and join me.

Stanislas. Yes, my love.

The Queen. Pay no heed to anyone else, on any account. I will send you Willenstein.

Stanislas. Yes, my love.

The Queen. The day before yesterday, this task would have seemed repugnant to me and beyond my strength. Today, it amuses me and nothing will deflect me from it. That is *your* work.

Stanislas. Yes, my love.

The Queen. Make me Queen, Stanislas. [*She opens her arms to him.*]

Stanislas. Yes, my love. [*He embraces her and gives her a long kiss.* THE QUEEN, *as if dizzy, leaves him and leans against the stove on the left.*]

The Queen. I still have to give some orders to Felix. Go up to my rooms. You will find Tony there. I will come and see you before I leave. I must learn to drag myself away from you. It is not easy.

Stanislas. What we are undertaking will not be easy. Give me courage, my Queen; I am perhaps less brave than you, darling.

The Queen [*Standing erect*]. A two-headed eagle.

Stanislas. A two-headed eagle.

The Queen [*Rushing to him and taking his head in her hands*]. And if one head is cut off, the eagle dies.

Stanislas [*Holding her in a long embrace*]. I am going up. Give your orders. Don't be too long. In which room shall I wait for you?

The Queen. Henceforth, when in Krantz, I shall never stay in any other than the one where I knew you.

STANISLAS *goes quickly up the stairs and disappears along the left-hand gallery. The* QUEEN *follows him with her eyes. Then she rings three times for* VON WILLENSTEIN *by pulling the cord near the stove. She wanders about the room, looks everywhere, strikes the furniture with her whip. Then she places one foot on the armchair beside which* STANISLAS *had kneeled. The door on the right opens.* FELIX VON WILLENSTEIN *enters and salutes.*

The Queen. Come in, Felix, I am alone.

Felix [*Coming to the center of the room*]. I await Your Majesty's orders.

The Queen. Are we ready? The horses? the carriages? The post chaise?

Felix. At one o'clock, Your Majesty will simply have to enter her carriage and depart.

The Queen [*Pointing to the table with her whip*]. Tony will bring you these books. I am taking them with me. I don't want any servants in the library before my departure.

Felix. Is Your Majesty traveling in her post chaise?

The Queen. I intended to, but I have changed my mind. I shall go on horseback.

Felix. Does Her Majesty mean to enter her capital on horseback?

The Queen. I don't like the post chaise. It reminds me of the King's tragic end. Do you see any objection to my going on horseback? Since I am showing myself, it is best I show myself as much as possible. [FELIX *remains silent.*] Say what is at the back of your mind. Don't be afraid.

Felix. It's just that . . . is Your Majesty aware that Count von Foehn is traveling with us?

The Queen [*Sharply*]. Foehn? I thought he had left Krantz this morning?

Felix. He probably heard of your decision. He is in Krantz. I have seen him. He told me that he wanted to make the security arrangements.

The Queen. Let him make his, Felix. I shall make mine. How many men have you?

Felix. One hundred light cavalrymen and one hundred and fifty Guards.

The Queen. Right. I'll make the journey in the carriage as far as the last halt. I shall dine on the way. See what you can arrange. You will accompany my post chaise with fifty men. For the last stage, I shall mount my horse. The light cavalrymen will form my escort. You . . . How many men are there in von Foehn's detachment?

Felix. Only about twenty.

The Queen. At the last stage you, Felix, will arrest von Foehn. [FELIX *starts.*] You will take with you the fifty Guards from the post chaise. That is an order. You will go before us into the town. Conduct your prisoner to the fortress. I will give you a warrant. You will release all political prisoners from the fortress. They will be free. That will be the first act of my reign. And you will fire a salute of a hundred rounds. Why do you look like that? Were you particularly fond of Foehn?

Felix. No, Your Majesty, but I should like . . . I mean, it would be preferable if . . .

The Queen. Speak . . . speak. . . .

Felix. If Your Majesty would authorize it . . . in such grave circumstances, I should prefer not to leave your side one second.

The Queen. Very good. It is quite natural that you should make this solemn entry into the capital with me. The captain of the light cavalry is your cousin, I believe.

Felix. Yes, Ma'am.

The Queen. Can you be sure of him?

Felix. As of myself.

The Queen. I have seen him jumping. He rides well and has an elegant style. You will hand over to him Count von Foehn and his detachment. As this little surprise is my good-will offering to the Archduchess, I wish him to take the utmost care of them. Of course, you will only tell him what steps are to be taken when we reach the last stage of the journey.

Felix. And I am accompanying the Queen?

The Queen [*Saying "yes" as to an obstinate child*].
Yes! You and the remainder of your men. I must say, I
don't like carriages and footboards. I shall enter my
capital on horseback, unveiled, and in the uniform of a
Colonel in Chief. Is that all understood?

Felix. I shall conform exactly to Your Majesty's orders.

The Queen. Ah, Felix! . . . You won't forget that my
soldiers and their band are to be opposite my window at
noon, the other side of the lake. When your men are in
position in the park, sound two calls on the trumpet.
That will be a signal to me that I can show myself to
my soldiers. [FELIX *bows.*] Fräulein von Berg will travel
in a carriage with the Count. An ideal couple. During the
last stage, Fräulein von Berg will have the whole carriage
to herself. That will give her more room for reflection.

TONY *comes running swiftly along the left-hand gallery
and down the stairs.* THE QUEEN *looks at him in astonish-
ment. He gesticulates.* THE QUEEN *gesticulates in reply.*
FELIX *stands aside near the right-hand door, and he comes
to attention.* TONY *hurries back up the stairs and disappears.* THE QUEEN *hesitates and suddenly rushes up
the staircase. But halfway she stops and looks around.
Her expression has completely altered; it is terrifying. She
is pale.* WILLENSTEIN, *who has retired as far as the door,
gazes at her as he must have done from behind the
Achilles statue.*

The Queen. Willenstein! God alone knows what will
be the end of the journey I am about to undertake. To
be able to undertake it, I must first commit an act so
savage, strange, and against nature, that all women will
think of it with horror. This is the price of the reign to
which I aspire. My destiny is staring me full in the face.
It is hypnotizing me. And see . . . it is sending me to
sleep.

Felix. Ma'am! . . .

The Queen. Not a word! Don't wake me. For, in truth,
to do what I have to do, you must sleep and act as in a
dream. Do not try to understand me better. I had to speak
to someone. You were the King's only friend and I spoke

to you. I ask you never to forget my words, Willenstein. And testify before all men that, whatever happens, I willed it so. [STANISLAS *appears at the top of the staircase. He is wearing the same costume as in Act One.*] You may go. Leave me.

FELIX *goes out.* STANISLAS *slowly comes down the stairs and passes in front of* THE QUEEN, *who is as one who sleeps. When he gets to the middle of the library,* THE QUEEN *follows him. She is harsh, curt, terrifying. During the whole of this scene, she should give the impression of being a fury.*

The Queen [*Savagely*]. What have you done? [STANISLAS *does not speak.*] Answer! Answer at once. [*Silence.*] Tony has just told me an unbelievable thing. Where is that locket? Where is it? Give it to me or I'll strike you with my whip.

Stanislas [*Calmly*]. The locket is in your room.

The Queen. Open?

Stanislas. Open.

The Queen. Swear that's true!

Stanislas. I swear.

The Queen [*In a cry*]. Stanislas!

Stanislas. You explained to me what happens when you swallow that capsule. I have one moment to live. Before you depart, I wanted to admire you once more, darling.

The Queen [*Regaining her self-control*]. Mind how you address me, the police are everywhere.

Stanislas. I know.

The Queen. You know the police have surrounded the castle?

Stanislas. I am a dead man. And I feel I am released from all promises. During your absence this morning, Count von Foehn warned me he was going to arrest me. I managed to persuade him not to do so till after one o'clock. The police are guarding the castle doors so that I cannot escape.

The Queen. You were under the Queen's protection. You had nothing to fear.

Stanislas. I did not act out of fear. In a flash, I realized that nothing was possible between us, that it was far better to free you and disappear while at the height of happiness.

The Queen. Coward!

Stanislas. Maybe.

The Queen. Coward! You counseled me, urged me, forced me out of my retirement.

Stanislas. From where I am going, I shall protect you a hundred times better, darling.

The Queen. I didn't ask for protection!

Stanislas [*In a sudden movement*]. My beloved. . . . [*He starts to go toward her. She recoils.*]

The Queen. Don't come near me!

Stanislas. Is that my beloved speaking?

The Queen. Don't come near me! [*She is pale, erect, terrifying.*] You are dead and you horrify me!

Stanislas. It *is* my beloved. It is you, darling, who are speaking.

The Queen. You are before your Queen. Don't ever forget it again.

Stanislas. That poison must have acted at lightning speed. Is this death?—to think you are alive and living in hell? [*He walks like a madman around the library.*] I am in hell! I am in hell!

The Queen. You are still alive. You are in Krantz. And you have betrayed me.

Stanislas. We are in Krantz. Here is the armchair, the table, here are the books. [*He touches them.*]

The Queen. You were to kill me and you did not.

Stanislas. If I have offended you, forgive me. Speak to me, darling, as you spoke to me this morning. Do you love me, darling?

The Queen. Love you? You are losing your wits. I order you, I repeat, not to be so familiar in your speech when you address me.

Stanislas [*Bewildered*]. You don't love me, then?

The Queen. My feelings can change as quickly as yours. You have robbed me . . . robbed! Don't grimace so. Don't writhe. Stay still. I am going to tell you something I did not wish to tell you and which you deserve to be told. What do you suppose? What do you imagine? I tell you Count von Foehn would not dare to act without my orders. Everything here is intrigue. I thought you had noticed that. It embarrassed me to drag you along after me. It embarrassed me to see you indiscreetly interfering in the affairs of the realm. If the police are surrounding the castle, if Count von Foehn is waiting for you at my doors, it is by my order. Just by my order. It is my royal pleasure.

Stanislas. You lie!

The Queen. Sir! You forget where you are, what you are and who I am.

Stanislas. You lie!

The Queen. Must I call Count von Foehn's men?

Stanislas. Here, right here [*he thumps the armchair*], did you not tell me you loved me?

The Queen. It was then that I lied. Did you not know that queens lie? Remember your poems. In them you described queens as they are.

Stanislas. My God! . . .

The Queen. I will reveal their secrets and mine, since I am speaking to a dead person. I decided—for I decide —I decided to charm you, to put you under a spell, to conquer you. Strangely enough, it all worked to perfection. I acted well. You believed everything.

Stanislas. You! . . . You! . . .

The Queen. Me. And other queens showed me the way. I merely had to follow suit. Queens have not changed much since Cleopatra's day. If they are threatened, they cajole. If they choose a slave, they make use of him. If they have a lover, they kill him. [STANISLAS *lurches as in Act One. He puts his hands to his chest. He looks as if he is going to fall.* THE QUEEN *cannot restrain an impulse.*] Stanislas! [*She was about to dash toward him. She restrains herself. Instead, she thrashes a piece of furniture with her whip.*]

STANISLAS *slowly straightens up.*

Stanislas. You are lying, I feel that. It is written all over you, from top to toe. I was going to faint, you could not

restrain a cry. You love me. You are trying on me I don't
know what horrible experiment. You were seeking to know
perhaps if my love was not a young man's passing fancy,
if it was true. . . .

The Queen. Why should it interest me to know if
your love was a passing fancy? Or you, to know whether
my kindness for you was just a caprice? You have more
urgent problems before you.

Stanislas. What? I steal a poison which you carried
upon you like a constant threat of death. I make it disappear. I commit suicide with it. I prevent a trial which
your enemies would not fail to exploit so that the scandal
would fall upon you. I pray heaven that this will not take
effect in your presence. I give you gladly my honor, my
candor, my work, my love, my life. I——[*He suddenly
stops.*] But, now I think of it . . . How horrible! Was
it not you who explained to me how this delayed suicide
works? Was it not you who boasted its advantages? Was
it not you who told me you had removed the locket from
your neck and that it was in your room? Answer me!

The Queen. I am not in the habit of being interrogated,
nor of replying to interrogations. I am not answerable to
you. I have made use of you. And don't imagine I mean
in affairs of state. I merely made you think so. You had
nothing to do with the steps I am taking. I flattered your
vanity as an author. It was a fine play! Act One: plotting
to kill the Queen. Act Two: persuading the Queen to
reascend her throne. Act Three: getting rid of an indis-
creet hero!

How could you possibly not understand that your likeness to the King was the worst of insults?—that I should
avenge myself for having been momentarily taken in by
it? You are simple! I did whatever I liked with you. But
I did not foresee that you would anticipate my order and
take upon yourself to decree your own death. I was going
to hand you over to Count von Foehn. You have decided
otherwise. You have taken poison. You are free. Good
luck! Die, then. Before keeping that capsule about me,
I tried its effect upon my dogs. They were taken out of
my sight. And the same thing will happen to you.

STANISLAS *has thrown himself on his knees in the arm-chair beside which he had listened to* THE QUEEN *talking of love in Act Two.*

Stanislas. O God! O God! Stop this torture!

The Queen. God does not like cowards either. You should not have betrayed your companions. They trusted you. You were their strong right arm. And not only did you betray their trust, but through you they have been caught. For Foehn spoke to me of your organization. He knows it. When I hid you in the library, I was afraid you might notice his knowing looks and signs of secret understanding. You must have thought us very foolish. How could I have had the slightest confidence, I ask you, in a person I did not know, one who betrays and flaunts before me an example of his treachery? On what did you base your assumption that I was sincere, when you showed yourself to me as a turncoat? [STANISLAS *has slowly risen from the armchair, where he could be seen only from the back. Now he turns toward the audience, unrecognizable, disheveled, with unseeing eyes.*] You might never have guessed the things I have just told you. I could have deceived you till the very last. You would have seen my escort leave. Foehn would have arrested you, taken you away. You would have been judged, and executed. You would have died glorifying yourself as the savior of your country. You are escaping from my justice. You prefer your own. That is your affair. But I must first try you. [*She goes up to him.*] What have you to answer? Nothing. You bow your head. I was right to call you a coward. I despise you. [*She raises her whip.*] And I hit you. [*She strikes him. At this moment, the trumpets sound in the park.* STANISLAS *has not moved.*]

That is my signal. I shall probably not have the joy of seeing you die.

THE QUEEN *turns her back and goes to the foot of the staircase. She stops there with one foot on the first step.* STANISLAS *watches her. He grasps his hunting knife, un-sheathes it. The second trumpet call sounds.* STANISLAS *rushes towards* THE QUEEN *and stabs her between the shoulders.* THE QUEEN *staggers, straightens up and mounts three steps with the dagger planted in her back—like the Empress Elizabeth of Austria.* STANISLAS *has stepped back to the front of the stage.* THE QUEEN *turns around and speaks to him with infinite tenderness.*

The Queen. Forgive me, my little hero. I had to make you mad. You had to strike me. Thank you for having made me live. Thank you for having made me die. [*She mounts four more steps, then turns around again.*] I loved you.

The band strikes up the Royal March. STANISLAS *is rooted to the spot, stupefied.* THE QUEEN *mounts the stairs like an automaton. She reaches the landing. She seizes hold of the curtains to steady herself and to present herself at the window.*

The Queen [*Looking back toward the library and holding out one hand to* STANISLAS]. Stanislas. . . .

He rushes forward, leaps up the stairs, but is struck down by the poison just as he is about to touch THE QUEEN'S *hand.* STANISLAS *falls backwards, rolls down the stairs and dies at the bottom, separated from* THE QUEEN *by the whole length of the staircase.* THE QUEEN *collapses, pulling down one of the curtains. The Royal March continues.*